HOWARD SENZEL

BASEBALL
AND THE
COLD WAR

BEING A SOLILOQUY
ON THE
NECESSITY OF BASEBALL

HBJ

Harcourt Brace Jovanovich
New York and London

Printed in the United States of America

Library of Congress Cataloging in Publication Data

Senzel, Howard.
    Baseball and the cold war.

    1. Baseball—Miscellanea.   2. World politics—
1945–   I. Title.
GV867.3.S46   796.357   76–27427
IBSN 0–15–110693–2

First Edition
B C D E

BASEBALL
AND THE
COLD WAR

A baseball team decided not to play in Havana.

—Hugh Thomas, *Cuba: The Pursuit of Freedom*

PART

1

Being unemployed, both economically and psychologically, and at the will of whatever wind happened to be blowing, I found myself, one afternoon, sitting in the left-field stands in Pittsburgh, watching a game between the home-town Pirates and the Los Angeles Dodgers.

Mike Marshall won the game for Los Angeles. I think the score was 5–0, but I honestly don't remember. I had been a very serious and devoted fan as a child, but that was long ago, half my lifetime in the past, and I wasn't a baseball fan any more.

I saw the game as a quaint American folk ritual, and nothing else. This was, after all, the proverbial heartland of Pittsburgh, where they erected bronze statues to baseball players, but I was an adult now, no longer interested in baseball. The afternoon was neither memorable nor important.

Just one year later, in the eleventh inning of the sixth game of the World Series, Joe Morgan, of the Cincinnati Reds, hit a fastball off the Boston pitcher Dick Drago, and it looked like a home run. But just before the ball crossed over the fence, Dwight Evans, the Boston right fielder, somehow jumped and fell and somehow caught the ball. Morgan was out. The game was still alive.

In the twelfth inning, Boston's catcher, Carlton Fisk,

hit a home run, and Boston won the game. The Series would go to a seventh game, and we—that is, Boston and I—were still in it. At the time, it was the most important thing in the world, and that moment remains something I will never forget. I was still an adult, but now I was a baseball fan.

Something happened to me in the course of that year. Or, more accurately, something happened to me in the course of one baseball season. It wasn't that I converted, but rather that I returned to baseball. Because of how it was then, and the temper of the times now, my return to baseball was also a return to my childhood. And I discovered that my childhood, its baseball, the cold war, and various other historical realities were available within my own memory.

I went through a series of realizations so profound that even now they are still both significant and impossible—and slightly peculiar. I had a small idea, no more than a daydream. It was a baseball story, pondered in innocence, but it grew into an obsession. Without my will, or my desire, or determination, or perseverance, this small idea took me over, and I became strictly devoted to memory, then to history, then to baseball, and finally to the articulation of my identity.

I chased baseball through politics, and through the styles of thought that produce the changing realities of history. I chased baseball through my memory, and into the historical identities that I have lived. And as my motives shifted between political intent, curiosity, investigation, and baseball, I discovered my own identity, the function of history in its formation, and the necessity of baseball to it, even in the face of political and psychological adversity. And really, there is no way to explain what happened to me, except to tell the story.

In advance of what seemed to be a coming detente with Cuba, I began to examine one small baseball event from my childhood memory. Frank Verdi, the third baseman from my old team, the Rochester Red Wings, was shot during a regulation game in Havana at the time of the Cuban revolution, and soon after, American baseball left Cuba. Why I remembered it, and how I remembered it, and why I pursued it, is the story of my single search for meaning, history, and baseball.

It was a successful search, but it all began in ambiguity just as the baseball season was getting under way. Circumstances conspired against my indecision, and I got in my car and drove up to Rochester, New York, which is my home town. Riding with me was my childhood friend Sammy. We had often made this trip together, but not in many years. Still, it did not seem special.

Then we stopped for coffee at Homer and Annie's Diner, in Roscoe, New York, and I began to notice that I held what can only be called a historical attitude. Twenty-five years ago it would have been an ordinary roadside diner; now it was strange. The predominance of fast food has taught America that places like Homer and Annie's no longer exist, but Homer and Annie don't know it yet, and continue un-self-consciously to make the past available.

I couldn't help noticing that what had once been a familiar landmark was now a monument to a bygone era. Homer and Annie's is a Quonset hut, that cheap, fast, and temporary solution to the housing emergency of the World War II effort. It is no more than half a cylinder of corrugated steel with holes cut out for doors and windows. Though temporary, quonset huts were durable enough to linger on throughout the postwar era, and only disappeared from the landscape when corporate prosperity replaced them with golden arches.

Annie made bad hamburgers out of real meat, and mediocre homemade pies. Weak coffee was served in thick cups. Truck drivers, loaded up on pills, discussed the evolution of the thirty-five-cent soda, as they sipped on glasses of water. Homer himself was in tears over his inability to get a starter motor for his 1963 International

[5]

truck, but he was able to transcend his sorrow for a moment, and remember that the nickel soda had gone up to ten cents when he came out of the service.

When the jukebox played Hank Williams' "I'll Never Get Out of the World Alive" and Hank Snow's "I'm Movin' On," I began to realize that I was experiencing a slice of the living past. What was Homer and Annie's Diner doing in the present, when the economic and social institutions that shape our lives have relegated it to the past? How was it possible for history to layer itself in such a way, so that the now ended postwar era was able to coexist with the new mentality and organization that replaced it? Homer and Annie were not only alive and capable, they were in business. The past was not only available, it was achievable.

Our conversation drifted. There was no talk of the function of memory, or the uses of history, or the nature of truth. We never tried to keep the conversation serious, but it was nevertheless clear that in the everyday world of American culture, and in my own mind, something was taking its course.

The tropical-fish trade, Sammy explained, is a nasty matter of teen-aged Samoans, Micronesians, and various other exotic nationals scooping up great numbers of rare and valuable fish, and then selling them to a series of smugglers and middlemen. The fish mortality rate is about ninety percent for each transaction. In the end, a handful of sturdy survivors wind up in the fish tank at the local Woolworth's. Except, as I told Sammy, Woolworth's doesn't sell tropical fish any more, which is exactly the kind of phenomenon that forces us to accept the fact that we no longer know what is going on. Instead of knowledge suggesting problem-solving activity, we are left with the knowledge that even such an apparent innocent as my goldfish was brought to my life by activities steeped in evil, greed, and corruption.

As this arranged itself in my mind, I felt pushed toward the realization that, Homer and Annie notwithstanding, life in this society was undergoing a drastic change. It was time to examine where I had come from, and how I fit into the newly wrinkled social fabric.

And then the conversation shifted to baseball. As a child, I had thought and talked about baseball every day; as an adult, I had never done so. But these were special days, and old things were frequently happening in new times.

After eighteen years of bad press for its revolution, Cuba was back in the news as a potential ally and trading partner for the United States. And Cuba, if I traced it back in my memory, as the times suggested I do, meant baseball.

"Remember the time the Red Wings' third baseman got shot in the head in Havana, in a game against the Sugar Kings?"

"Yes," I said, astonishing myself as well as Sammy. "His name was Frank Verdi. The game was called in extra innings with the score tied, and American baseball left Cuba, never to return."

My facts were all wrong, unfortunately, and I was quite unaware of the importance of the process that was beginning.

The conversation remained light. An idea formed in my mind and came out as a joke. "The time has come to finish that last Rochester Red Wings–Havana Sugar Kings game. What a theater for baseball. What a shtick for detente."

I was unemployed. I had promised my mother that I would drive upstate and spend a few days painting the house. And I departed with only that and my reluctance to travel in mind. But as the road conversation had already revealed, the ante was changing.

The past was revealing itself so easily that it felt like I was going home. And it seemed like I could effortlessly pry open my own life, and see the forces that made me who I am and brought me to the life I live.

You see, I was a baseball fan, but I was a mere child,

[7]

struggling and suffering in Jewish suburban Rochester, New York. It was fifteen, or seventeen, or twenty-two years ago. How could I distinguish between the sense and the nonsense, when my entire adult life has continually proved to me that the suffocating atmosphere of my childhood was all nonsense? That there was nothing to choose between.

Yet here I was all these years later, thoroughly unhinged from my childhood, and floating through American time and space with neither culture nor identity. And it's not that I successfully escaped the confines of the world that I was raised in. That world died, a victim of the aggressive and relentless energy which makes progress, but in the process destroys tradition, identity, and rationale.

I survived and, without glory, entered the next phase of the social organization. Like every American, all that I had left of roots and home was a yearning and the dream. And this was enough to send me back to where I came from to tamper with my own past. I had no choice. History became reality knocking twice, and I could not resist.

Rochester is a medium-sized city, just south of Lake Ontario in western New York. When I was growing up, it was the twenty-eighth largest city in America. Even as a child, I thought that awfully high on the list for what seemed to be going on around me. My father once explained to me, with great civic pride, that Rochester was the world's biggest village.

Rochester is part of what upstate New Yorkers call the Snow Belt. The average yearly snowfall often exceeds one hundred fifty inches. I can always remember a few days every winter when we wouldn't have to go to school because forty inches of snow had fallen the night before.

In summer, it is hot and muggy. Though I lived in Rochester for the first twenty-two years of my life, I was never able to see any connection between the character of the city and its climate. The climate is one of extremes.

The city grew up around the flour mills that were water-powered by the Genesee River. The Genesee flows into Lake Ontario, just outside of town.

The beaches of Lake Ontario are more beautiful than any in Europe. They consist of very fine, very white sand. Before my family prospered and moved to the suburbs, we went to the beach nearly every summer day. As the pollution of Lake Ontario intensified, the beach itself began to fill up with dead fish. Then people began to get headaches and vomit if they went swimming. Finally, the beautiful beaches were permanently closed.

The city of Rochester has always been dominated by the Eastman Kodak Company. My uncles have told me that this is no longer true, and that there are many large industries where there used to be only Kodak, but I still think of Rochester as Eastman Kodak's company town. When you ask someone where they work, they never answer Kodak. Instead, they name the specific Kodak plant they work in. Kodak Park, Hawkeye, State Street, and so on.

Eastman Kodak has always been an extremely paternalistic company. They pay good wages, allow time off for civic or church work, and in every way cultivate the stability and security of their workers' lives. In many ways, Kodak workers represent the realization of the American Dream. They are factory workers, but they live in nice houses, drive nice cars, and see as modest and normal a standard of living that would be envied by most of the country.

All other industry in Rochester has emulated the Kodak model. Employees are well cared for, long term, stable, reliable, white, and pacific.

Consequently, Rochester is a very conservative place. In fact, the city became famous for its conservatism. New brands of cigarettes and soap powders were often test-marketed there. The local theory was that if they

[9]

bought it in Rochester, they would buy it anywhere, because no place was more resistant to the new than Rochester.

Broadway plays were sometimes previewed in Rochester, too. Bette Davis came to Rochester to star in Tennessee Williams' *Night of the Iguana*. She broke her arm the afternoon before opening night, but still, she was supposed to play Rochester.

And Constance Bennett was in my Uncle Hymie's taxi. That is, Constance Bennett was almost in my Uncle Hymie's taxi. What happened was that Constance Bennett actually got into my Uncle Hymie's taxi and told him that it was too filthy for her to ride in. My Uncle Hymie, who, despite other shortcomings, always had an excellent sense of occasion, looked her up and down and said, "What do you want it, lady, wrapped in a silver sock?"

Then Constance Bennett, with nothing on the meter, got out. Not exactly the French Riviera, but it is worth pointing out that Rochester did have its little touches of elegance and color. And by way of contrast, these showed what a dreary little village it really was.

And there were other, deeper, conservatisms about Rochester. Government in Rochester was always conservative and it was always Republican. Rochester always considered its own districts to be the safest Republican seats in Congress. Rochester was ruled by open paternalism rather than ideological rhetoric. Its streets were the cleanest, its signs the brightest. Rochester's lilacs were "the largest free exhibition of flowers in the world." The city fathers decided what should be done and how it should be done. With their substantial industrial wealth, they decided that what Rochester should be was the little bijou of New York State, and it was. Every bench in Rochester's renowned park system had a coat of paint every year, and everyone in town knew just how lucky they were to be raising their family in such a wonderful place. No federal or state funds were ever allowed in;

Rochester needed no public housing projects that it could not provide itself. It was believed that there were no poor people in Rochester, only Kodak workers.

The smug self-satisfaction that pervaded the place hid a multitude of other local realities. Until the riots of 1964, there was no reason to believe that Rochester wasn't everything that the city fathers said it was— unless you happened to be black or poor or having a hard time. But these segments of the population were not upwardly visible before the 1964 riots.

This was partly true because Rochester was a one-newspaper town, and later a one-newspaper and one-television-station town, and both were owned by Frank Gannett. And Frank Gannett was one of the city fathers. In 1937, a deal was made with the Hearst chain. Frank Gannett got out of Albany, and Hearst got out of Rochester. Ever since, it has been a Gannett morning paper, a Gannett evening paper, and never a liquor or cigarette advertisement between the two. And given the character of the time and place, it would have been unthinkable for things to have been otherwise.

Jewish Rochester, though not visible to the naked eye, was a separate and distinct village. The rumor was that there were ten thousand Jewish families in Rochester (Jewish populations always being counted in families rather than individuals), but I never believed that. It always seemed that everyone knew everyone, and that there couldn't possibly be more than a few hundred of us. The important demographic statistic was that if you ever did something wrong in public, someone who knew your mother would see you.

This wasn't as important for adults as it was for children. Adults could drive to a bungalow in Buffalo if they wanted to sleep with shiksas, or whatever, but even adults had reputations. At every wedding and bar mitzvah, hundreds would gather and give testimony about each other. No matter how prominent or obscure, no matter how well or poorly you were doing, if you were Jewish and lived in Rochester, you had a reputation. And you knew about it.

There were no railroad tracks dividing Rochester. The slums and the exclusive sections were both east of the river. West of the river there were only Italians and other sorts of goyim. Those who were able to secure a larger mortgage and move to the suburbs often spoke of "the other side," but it was never so much a geographic as it was a financial and spiritual category. I was a reasonably adequate young lad, living on the other side, but I didn't hear the term until after my bar mitzvah, when we moved to the suburbs. The suburbs confused me for years. When we were poor we lived closer to the lake and enjoyed cool breezes on summer evenings. In the suburbs it was hot and muggy.

When we were too poor to move, we lived in a neighborhood of Kodak workers, mailmen, barbers, and other symbols of stability in a highly mobile society. They sat out on the streets in the evening and talked to one another. One Kodak worker repaired bicycles for children at children's prices. One mailman used to lend me his World War II helmet and canteen when we played war. My cousins lived around the block. There were buses that stopped one street away from my house. I had adult friends, I had cousins around the corner, and I had mobility. I had a reasonable identity and an independent life.

In the suburbs it was very different. The neighbors never came out of their houses on foot, there were no sidewalks. When I cut the lawn they would drive their big cars up to me, push a button that lowered their electric windows, and ask me which gardener I worked for. I would tell them that I lived there. Then they would push the button up, their electric window would close, and they would drive away.

The buses in the suburbs ran once every two hours, from nowhere to nowhere. I was forced to beg my parents

[12]

for a ride whenever I wanted to leave the house. This led to having to say where I was going and why—an informal trial. Even a favorable verdict often saddened me. I didn't want to go where my parents were willing to take me.

I did hold out against dancing lessons. On one occasion, I attended a class given by Gar Lester, who was a butcher and a bond salesman but who also gave dancing lessons on Sunday at the local Jewish Y. His feet were not only talented, but about size sixteen, so you always had a good view. But I refused to go. My parents offered to starve me unless I went. I offered to starve. I never had my second lesson and I never missed a meal.

No one had explained to me that, early in the twentieth century, George Eastman had built his mansion east and south of downtown, and that, since then, to arrive meant to move east and south of those outskirts of town. Never mind that the lake with its cool breezes and swimming was north of the city. George Eastman, founder of the Eastman Kodak Company and great creator and employer of Rochester and all its inhabitants, had moved east and south, and what was good enough for the prime mover was the decent thing to do.

I didn't know anything about any of this before we moved to the suburbs. What I did know was that we lived in a neighborhood where it was unquestionably safe for an eight-year-old to walk the streets after dark. And that we lived within walking distance of Red Wing Stadium, where on evenings and weekends the Rochester Red Wings played baseball seventy-seven times a summer.

Now, I wasn't very good at school, I was terrible at Hebrew lessons, and on the baseball diamond itself, I had my problems. I mean, I was okay as a neighborhood baseball player, but slightly to the mediocre side of okay. I knew how to judge a fly ball. I knew what to do with the ball when I finally got hold of it, but I wasn't brilliant. And those guys in their snappy Red Wing uniforms were positively brilliant.

[13]

In my neighborhood it was believed that you had to be seventeen to try out for professional baseball, but one day Richard Fleischer found out that you could try out for the Detroit Tigers at the age of sixteen. And who could question the erudition of Richard Fleischer? Not only had his own father listened to every Red Wing game on the radio and remembered it, but Richard himself had been the only one of us to get home in time to turn on the television, have it warmed up, and actually see Bobby Thomson hit that home run off Ralph Branca and win the pennant for the Giants. And that happened when we were very little kids. I mean, I didn't even have a television yet.

And so I participated in the secret pact we all made to run away from home and try out for the Detroit Tigers, if I ever grew enough and lived long enough to reach my sixteenth birthday. But even as I was making that pact, I somehow felt my participation in the collective handshake was dishonest. I knew that I would never be able to play the game as well as even Pete Whisenant, who was the worst ballplayer ever to wear the Red Wing uniform. (Although there was this catcher, John McArdle, who batted .062 and was the regular catcher for an entire season because the original catcher, whose name is blotted out of my mind by that of Wes Westrum, which I'm sure is wrong, had a heart attack and had to become a coach.)

I made the pact, and I worked on my baseball fundamentals, but somehow it was never in me. What really interested me, even from my earliest memories, was the world of baseball. What the papers in our minor-league town used to call O.B.: Organized Baseball. There were the major leagues, but they never really held my attention. Everybody in the majors did everything perfectly. Occasionally I would watch the big leagues on television, and all the players looked like machines. No wild pitches, no errors, no dumb plays. Big-league baseball just didn't have the emotion. I always thought of big-league baseball players as no more than highly paid prima donnas. They

[14]

just lay around all winter, and ran through the motions with ease all summer. Those guys were tough as nails, and they appeared to have no hearts. Big-league baseball never allowed for grand tragedy or outrageous comedy.

I know that I cannot make a truthful case for the superiority of minor-league baseball. All the minor-league teams were either owned outright by, or had working agreements with, the major-league teams. If a player seemed ready, he would go up to the majors, even if it were the day before the crucial game. Part of the drama of being a minor-league baseball fan was the worry over which of your big stars would be yanked up in the middle of the pennant race. There was always the confusion of hoping that whoever it was kept hitting home runs, but didn't hit too many home runs. If he did, he would be gone.

And there was something else. Something beyond the awe of a little child watching grown men skillfully playing his own game, something that has nothing to do with the recent changes America has undergone. All this was taking place a long time ago, when it was possible for Americans to worship and identify with things that had no chance of being nationally famous, of being undisputably the best. The Red Wings were not the best team in baseball. They would never be heard of outside of Rochester. None of the Red Wings who ever went on to achieve fame and fortune would ever have their identities linked with that team. Players who played for the Red Wings would, by definition, always be minor. Red Wing stars would frequently remain unknown even in Rochester.

But, back in those days, which now seem part of another century, there was the game itself. Aside from the glory, the fame, the money, the groupies, or the status, was the internal drama and tension of the game. In the minor leagues, the game was played mostly by grown men who would never be famous and who would never be rich, men who would always travel by rented school bus and always stay in fleabag hotels. These were grown

[15]

men playing baseball who had to sacrifice money and comfort in order to play. And that is a kind of heroism that is larger and more noble than any superhuman athletic dexterity. That is a kind of heroism that is as foreign to our times as it was common in those middle years of the postwar era.

You know, I have watched some modern baseball. And it has its Victorian quaintness–the mustaches and sideburns, the white shoes, the return of the open stance, which faded out in the thirties. But this Victorian veneer is superficial. Modern baseball is played by corporate-minded executives, who have been physically and mentally perfected with one goal in mind. They are as serious as bankers. They are playing for big money. They are shrewd, calculating men. And they are superb athletes, which the baseball players of my Rochester childhood were not.

And in the end, the nobility and capacity for making grand human gestures rests with my old minor-league memories. It may be just because they weren't so goddamn serious. Minor-league ballplayers were not getting money, status, or fame. They could play the game with a bit more daring and spontaneity. They could allow themselves to be seen to be having fun. And it turned out that watching serious baseball played by people who were enjoying themselves was far more inspiring than watching baseball played by superb, but nonetheless cold and professional, athletes.

The evidence is that minor-league baseball was a much more widespread phenomenon then than nationally televised baseball is today. There were hundreds of minor-league teams even as late as the middle nineteen-fifties: The Texas League, the Sally League, the Three I League, the Florida League, the NY-P League, the Southeastern League, the Western League. There were scores and scores of leagues. And there were lots of little towns that could turn out twenty-five percent of their population nearly every night, and thus maintain a professional baseball team. The Wellsville Braves, a Class D team from Wellsville, New York, was the most famous small population–large attendance town that I knew.

Leagues ranged from Class D to Class AAA. At the top of the pyramid was the International League, although the Pacific Coast League was also AAA. The International League was the oldest continuously running minor baseball league in America. Since 1844, and from the very beginning, home of the Rochester team.

Seldom in my life have I ever been impressed by anything the way I was impressed by the Rochester Red Wings. Red Wing games were one of the great joyous events of a childhood filled more with fear and struggle than with great joyous events. Jewish children, at least in my neighborhood, were as fascinated by suffering and fear as Jewish adults were. Wondering and worrying were as much part of my child's play as they would become of my adult life. But when the sun went down, I could step out of my life and head for Red Wing Stadium. Without permission, without interference, almost without explanation, I was going to the ballgame.

Whatever suffering and pain my older cousins might have brought to my life during the day I could endure, because I knew that however difficult and ugly the present seemed, I was, at some higher level of consciousness, on my way to a Red Wing game. I knew that whatever seemed to be an irrefutable case of apparent reality —whoever I seemed to be—as soon as I had finished eating and singing the interminable grace after meals in as loud a voice as I could (which was usually down in the whisper category) I was magically transformed into a little adult, on his way to Red Wing Stadium.

Alone and proud and often swift enough to catch batting practice, I went down Seneca Avenue to Norton Street. I was going to watch my heroes display their dexterity. I was going to watch my team undergo a massive public confrontation with a bunch of well-known strangers. My life inside Red Wing Stadium was the highest reality I experienced. I felt that I had to be there. The proof that there was some greater force at work was that even my parents recognized the necessity of my journey. That I would usually go to the Red Wing game was assumed. That I deserved to go was obvious: I had suffered the vagaries of living all day on God's own gentile earth, hadn't I? That I was going to the ballgame was understood.

Red Wing Stadium has no bleachers, except a few crummy ones alongside right field, but they were the same price as the general unreserved seats. I always sat in section R1 of the unreserved seats, right behind first base. All of my friends sat there. For the Junior World Series one year, I watched from the third-base side in section L3 as pitcher Al Worthington of the Minneapolis Millers won four games against the Red Wings. I enjoyed the view from L3, but R1 was where I was from, where I knew people and where people knew me, and that was where I sat.

Most years I saw fifty to sixty games. In my neighborhood, everyone kept careful record of how many games they saw. Status went with consistent attendance. One year I saw seventy-five out of seventy-seven games. All I missed were opening day, and the no-hitter by Duke Markell. My cousin saw both of these games and no others that year and judged that he had seen all the important baseball. But he was from Avenue D, and what could you expect from that neighborhood? In my neighborhood, it was strictly a matter of how many games you saw (except if you saw Bobby Thomson hit that homer). We went for breadth and depth of experience.

All adults in my neighborhood hated baseball, with the exception of Richard Fleischer's father, who was a very antisocial man and could, therefore, afford that indulgence. Richard Fleischer's father had never in his whole life attended a Red Wing game because he didn't like crowds or spending money, which also explains how he was able to listen to every single game on the radio.

[18]

I consider myself fortunate to have come from a place where no one but me and my peers was interested in baseball. It allowed us to take adult models for our baseball-fan behavior. I cheered and booed, alternately, at certain precise times and for certain precise reasons— and only after a reasoned judgment, tempered on the one hand by my desires and on the other by what was possible. I may have had my difficulties with everyday life, but when it came to Red Wing Stadium, I was a citizen of impeccable comportment and style. I was classy. In fact, I was every bit as classy a fan as the Red Wings were a baseball team.

I always bought my own program and kept score. As the years went by, I got into a more and more elaborate scoring notation. A strikeout was a K, but if he went down swinging, I wrote the K backwards. And I began to add a little wavy line if the fly ball was deep, and a little straight line if it was shallow. If anything unusual came up and I couldn't fit it into my expanded hieroglyphs, I put an asterisk and wrote out what happened at the bottom of the page.

By the time I was twelve years old, I had become a seasoned fan with a certain air of saltiness about me. After all, I had seen Eddie Merkowitz make that incredible diving catch which caused him to hit the left-field wall head-on and suffer a brain concussion. (I later saw him receiving a brand-new car, courtesy of the fans, on Eddie Merkowitz Night.) I had seen Allie Clark hit the longest home run hit out of Red Wing Stadium. (It was rumored to have landed on the roof of the Packard dealer next door.) I had been given a genuine Red Wing uniform sock by Gene Green, whom I had seen turn from an outfielder to a catcher in the middle of the second game of a double-header. He went on to the majors as a catcher. I don't know why he gave me his sock, but it didn't seem odd at the time.

Joey Cunningham was always one of my favorite Red Wings. I remember going up to him and asking him where he was from. I listened carefully while he said, "Saddle River Township, New Jersey." I watched Tony Jacobs, so small that he wore the batboy's uniform when he first came to the Red Wings, win eleven straight games through lousy pitching and incredible circumstances. He was once brought in with the Red Wings leading seven to nothing going into the ninth. He gave up seven runs in that inning and became the winning pitcher when the Wings scored a run in the bottom of the ninth.

I saw Bob Blaylock, a pitcher and the worst hitter in baseball, served up a home-run ball by a Montreal pitcher after Montreal had cinched the pennant. In the same game, I saw catcher Nels Burbrink play shortstop with his catcher's mitt.

Between games of a Sunday double-header, I saw the local saxophone sensation, Chuck Alaimo, punched in the face in the middle of a song by an irate fan who pleaded with the police that a wailing saxophone drove him crazy.

I had heard Pete Whisenant, who wore number one, call me a dirty little son of a bitch when I asked him if his number was his batting average.

I saw Ruben Amaro's unassisted triple play. Playing shortstop, he caught an incredible line drive, and then, not moving an inch, tagged both the runner heading for third, who had hesitated, and the runner rounding second, who had run.

I saw Chuck Connors play first base for the Red Wings before he went on to make cowboy movies. I saw Satchel Paige, the grand old man of baseball, supposedly in his fifties at the time, pitch for both the Columbus Jets and the Miami Marlins. He took so long to walk from the bullpen to the pitcher's mound that his beard grew during the trip, which I read in *Baseball Digest*.

I remember that famous Red Wing lineup of power hitters, Allie Clark, Gene Green, Stan Jok, and Tommy Burgess, who were better known as the Boomer, the Bomber, the Basher, and the Belter.

I saw Tom Poholsky pitch twenty-two innings to

[20]

beat Reading when I was seven years old. It was a Saturday afternoon knothole game, which meant that if you were under twelve, you got in for next to nothing. The place was packed with little kids. It takes a long time to play twenty-two innings of baseball. None of those little kids got home until way after dark.

On many occasions, I watched Rocky Nelson play baseball. He was the International League's Most Valuable Player three times. Greatly gifted for the game of baseball, Rocky had a psychological problem with big-league pitching. Every year he would go through spring training with a big-league team. He even spent one entire season on the Pittsburgh bench. He played a dozen-odd seasons with Montreal and the Toronto Maple Leafs, and I will always remember him as the greatest baseball player who ever lived.

I had seen a number of the reigning major-league stars when they were young punks, still learning the game. Billy Virdon, Jackie Brandt, and Gary Geiger were all former Red Wings. And I watched older players return to the International League for what the papers referred to as the "twilight" of their careers. And what I hadn't seen, I heard about from Richard Fleischer's father. He filled me in on the Red Wing careers of the big stars of the St. Louis Cardinals—"Rip" Repulski, Ray "Jabbo" Jablonski, Red Schoendienst, and the great Stan Musial. And Mr. Fleischer never hesitated to name-drop former Red Wings like Preacher Roe and Johnny Mize.

And the time came when I could even drop my own names. Gene Oliver, Bob Gibson, Boog Powell, Leon Wagner, Ray Sadecki, Bob Miller, Vern Benson, and Billy DeMars. All of them Rochester Red Wings who went on to other places and fortunes.

I remembered Dave Ricketts pitching for the Red Wings in the summer and playing NBA basketball for the Rochester Royals in the winter. I remember Stan Jok's torn-off sleeves and bulging shoulders and, even on the coldest September evening, never an undershirt. I remember seeing Eddie Kasko ordering a Seven-Up float with vanilla ice cream in the neighborhood diner.

I had a not-inaccurate sense of having seen it all.

All of these Rochester and baseball memories and God knows what else are down firmly in my memory as irrefutable recollection, drawn from actual true-life experience, faithfully and accurately recounted. And whether actually accurate or not, all these connected details form the basis for my notion of culture and a kind of residual datum by which I specifically define my unique place in history and the social structure.

In the sense that the self is the sum total of all experience, these little baseball memories have the same weight in determining who I am as, say, the answers to: Where were you when the lights went out in New York City? When John Kennedy was shot? During the Cuban Missile Crisis? Yuri Gagarin's space flight? Or any of what the papers call "the happenings and events that made today history"?

So, however misplaced and inaccurate my memory may be, it is in all innocence that I can recall being a little boy, lying in bed listening to the Red Wing game over the radio. Tom Decker, the Voice of the Red Wings, is doing the re-created play-by-play. Re-created because it saves the travel and transmission expenses of sending an announcer on the road. And re-creation is, in fact, a very clever way to broadcast a baseball game. According to Richard Fleischer's father, the technique of re-creating baseball games in the radio studio was invented in Rochester by Gunner Wiig, the Voice of the Red Wings in the early days of radio. In fact, re-creating baseball games goes back to pre-radio days, when the telegraph ticker was the only electronic medium available. The now-famous system works like this: the play-by-play comes into the studio over a ticker tape. The announcer has a tape recording of crowd sounds, providing a constant background murmur. The announcer also has a little

[22]

wooden hammer, and other pieces of sound-effects para-
phernalia. As the information comes over the ticker tape,
the announcer pretends that he is actually at the game,
reporting what he sees. "Here's the windup and the pitch
... swung on ..." Tom Decker deftly bangs his little
wooden hammer on the table and turns up the volume on
the crowd noises. "And it's a long drive going deep ...
deeper ... deeper ..." By now the volume of the crowd
noise has been turned up to a fever pitch. And from my
bed at home it sounds exactly like a live broadcast with a
bat hitting the ball and the crowd going wild in response.
Except for the background clickety-click of the ticker
tape, it is impossible to tell the difference between a live
broadcast and its simulation.

And I am lying there, the young innocent in the
process of making his self, collecting sensory impressions
to be experienced, noted, judged, and filed away in the
unconscious. The game I am listening to is between the
Rochester Red Wings and the Havana Sugar Kings. It is
taking place in Gran Stadium in Havana, but coming directly to me from the studios of WROC in downtown
Rochester.

It is in extra innings and the score is still tied. The
crowd is enormous, festive, and unruly. And suddenly
gunshots go off and the Red Wing third baseman, Frank
Verdi, is shot in the head. Because he is wearing a metal
helmet liner, the bullet only grazes his scalp, and in fact
he never loses consciousness. Chaos ensues, the players
leave the field and fly back to Rochester, and Americans
never play baseball in Havana again. And I remember
feeling what a pity it was, because the Cubans were such
a slick and speedy ball club, and so colorful. They used
to bunt a lot, hit and run a lot, try to steal home, and
execute other daring feats, but I guessed they were just a
little too hot-blooded, as a people, to play in the International League. And very much, O those crazy Cubans! I'll
bet they know how to have fun!

I vividly remember the picture in the papers the next

morning of Frank Verdi holding up his baseball hat and poking his finger through the bullet hole.

The real truth is that it never bothered me; I totally failed to grasp the significance of what happened that day in Havana. Even later, my memory's reaction was no more than, After all, it was the fifties. Nothing memorable from the fifties was ever newsworthy and nothing newsworthy from the fifties was memorable, so what possible fuss could there be? I always accepted as fact that, after the McCarthy era and the Korean war, nothing happened until the assassination of John Kennedy. And that period in between, which is now called the Fifties, is about other things. The invention of rock and roll; juvenile delinquents with grand ambitions but only neighborhood fame; abstract expressionist hairdos; a few beatniks swallowing bennies; Howdy Doody; Tom Corbett, Space Cadet; the Cisco Kid; and—appearing in person at the RKO Palace Theater in Rochester, New York —Jock Mahoney as the Range Rider. I remember waiting in a line that circled the block to see Range Rider up on the stage, sitting on a split-rail fence with a long strand of grass between his teeth, and shouting into the microphone, "Hey, liddle pardners." *That*'s how the fifties are supposed to be remembered.

Our elders, post-teen-age friends and relatives, were children of the McCarthy era, the Silent Generation. They taught us nothing. They told us nothing. Our elders wanted their own childhood years forgotten as swiftly and completely as possible.

Years later, my friends and I would boast of our ability to remember anything at all about what we proudly identified as the most boring years in the history of mankind. Any little detail from *Leave It to Beaver*, or of Big Bob Mitchum in *Thunder Road*, was sanctified first as trivia and later as nostalgia. So scarce were memorable events that even the recollection of the matching fender skirts and sun visor on my father's 1953 two-tone Chevrolet was good enough.

[24]

The tendency of my generation, steeped in historical ignorance, was to continually abandon what came before and seek identity in the present. After all, my generation was big stuff! There had been nothing like us since the Thirties. We invented the civil-rights movement. We invented the peace movement, which later became the antiwar movement. We recognized black music and invented for it the notion of the big time for the music business. We invented hair styles and clothing styles. We invented our own newspapers. And we went further. We invented the notion of taking drugs to make you feel more good, rather than less ill.

All those cultural attributes that were traditionally handed down, we invented for ourselves. Born in a cultural vacuum, we were ignorant and disrespectful of the culture of our elders, and we invented our own. As adolescents, we took history, always the sacred property of the elders, and made it our own. We took a world of calcified and inflexible institutions developed to deal with the Great Depression and World War II, and ended them by decree. And we were astonished when these enormously powerful institutions did not lie down at our feet.

We taught America to remember that disaffection and unrest were always available options in any social situation, and that outrage and protest were always reasonable responses. Where our immediate predecessors were timid, afraid, and therefore silent, we were visible, arrogant, and aggressive. We dressed up like Jesus Christ, fucked on the Boston Common, and punched policemen in the face. We did not make a revolution, but we did make the once-frightening notion of insurrection tolerable, if not socially acceptable. Whatever it was that came before us, it couldn't possibly have been as hot-shit as we were. Besides, if anything ever did happen before us, how come nobody ever mentioned it?

Of course, in the process we denied our own heritage, and even our own childhood. We cut off all ties and traditions. We cut out the very concept of home. We

[25]

called mobility freedom, and overlooked the compulsion behind it. We championed happy wanderers, but we ourselves were driven to wandering.

We couldn't deny that we had been children. And so we trivialized our childhood, remembering only little bits of baseball stories, television shows, and old records. Yes, we could remember, but the organization of our memories guaranteed us that there was nothing serious to remember.

And throughout this entire process, we insisted that what we had really invented was a new life style. A serious life style to replace the grim tinsel and materialism of our insignificant childhood.

The values handed down by our parents formed a particular notion of progress. That is, more wealth, more leisure time, and more possessions. As war babies, we had no alternative but to reject this notion of progress. We were raised in material opulence and total leisure. We could not strive for what was given, and so we fought against it.

And all this made us particularly naïve about our own growth and development. And consequently naïve about our personal identities. We always thought, and we still think, that anything desirable is possible, and you can't get more naïve than that.

I have always seen my own development as nothing more than a process of increasing alienation from the accepted norms of moral behavior. Growing up, for me, was primarily an exercise in deciding how to act. The criteria for action were moral rather than economic, and social rather than personal. My first adult notions of how to behave became synonymous with struggling against the conventional values of American society.

In the process of forming my grand and gestural moral attitudes, baseball got closed out. The kinds of functions that baseball served in my life were taken over by another drama—politics. Racism, Imperialism, Anticapitalism, Revolution, Drugs, and Rock and Roll Music replaced baseball as the arenas where I could define myself as an insider.

My loss of interest in baseball began shortly after my bar mitzvah, when we moved to the suburbs. Our new house was correctly south and east of Rochester proper, and a long way from Red Wing Stadium. It was nearly two hours' journey by bus. Night games were out. I made the tortuous bus journey, involving three changes, for a handful of Sunday double-headers, but each time the distance seemed longer and the changes more a pain in the ass.

I listened to the radio and scored the games from my bedroom, but it was never the same again. My interests began to spread to the front sections of the newspaper, which I hadn't realized existed. My fantasies shifted from baseball player to beatnik, and I began to see black turtleneck sweaters and wrinkled corduroy jackets, not baseball uniforms, as proper costume for heroes.

Out in the suburbs, where evenings were spent sitting in your father's car with your friends, shifting the gears and waiting around for the time when you would be old enough to drive, baseball became a child's game. Baseball fans began to look like textbook cases of arrested development. I came to disdain the sport, though I still kept my finger on it. I would never have admitted to it, but I always knew how the Red Wings were doing. My great wealth of baseball history and personal experience, once the center of my pride, was now a source of shame.

Without sentiment or sadness, I turned my back on baseball. Invigorated by that great American energy of progress and self-development, I was moving on to more important things. Baseball was dying inside of me, but at the time, I saw it only as an awakening out of childhood and into the wonderful world of serious things. I was growing up.

I was still a devoted and knowledgeable amateur practitioner and fanatic, but my choice of game changed.

This new one offered me more of the same. I was still able to define myself historically, analyze past performance, and make my own judgments and predictions. I felt, both as a baseball fanchild and as a New Left Radical, a sense of pride and self-esteem, because I knew what was going on. I had a deeper sense of experience and understanding than "ordinary" people.

Just as I had once learned to study the box scores of baseball games, I now learned to read the footnotes, and with the same results. I would never forgive Luke Easter for repeatedly striking out with men on base; I would never forgive Maurice Chevalier for collaborating with the Nazis. For the moral judgments that create a political position, I had, as I had for baseball as a child, a memory like an elephant.

Of course, there were lots of other things going on, and I don't mean to draw the parallels too closely. Red Wing baseball was ritual, whereas politics was all of life. But I didn't approach them as differently as I might have hoped.

The papers knew more about baseball than anyone. It was the newspapers that compiled the charts and statistics that were the very substance of baseball history. When it came to politics, the papers were both ignorant and given to telling lies. They deliberately contorted themselves to see every event through the eyes of the richest people in town. The papers were quite open and honest about the whole thing, taking pride in the professionalism of the newspaper business. They not only sucked up to the wealthy city fathers, they were, themselves, wealthy city fathers. Nowadays, metamorphosis has made them corporation executives, and this does represent a change in attitude, but not in activity or status. These people were, as they are today, making money, not information. Accuracy in the sports pages was always essential; elsewhere in the paper it was not.

The newspapers caught me when I was young, and

through their baseball coverage instilled in my mind their own odd framework for the understanding of reality. I still read them. Despite the change in the kind of information I encountered when I moved off the sports pages, and despite my changes in attitude, I have always read newspapers with the same devotion. As a child, I sat on the porch steps on summer afternoons and waited for the paper boy to bring me the news of baseball. I never abandoned the habit, merely shifted from studying the behavior of heroes, in baseball, to studying the behavior of bums in politics. I shifted from analysis in order to better revere, to analysis in order to deny legitimacy. But all along, I stuck with the newspapers.

Although it was of critical importance to most of the left, Cuba was never an area of particular interest to me, though I had my Cuban position. Everyone seemed to be a Cuba expert in the Sixties. I was surrounded by people who had either been to Cuba, or who subscribed to *Gramma* in Spanish. I never felt quite qualified to study Cuba. The Cuban revolution never drew me in or aroused me, compared with, say, Vietnam, the Military-Industrial Complex, or the structure of capitalism. I was a member of the know-your-enemy school, and Cuba was an ally.

So it never occurred to me to examine the question of what happens to the baseball team in time of revolution. And this turns out to be a very interesting question. Also a question that I should have been particularly capable of asking. After all, I came out of Rochester, I knew about the International League, the Havana Sugar Kings as well as the Red Wings. I knew, in one sense, about the Frank Verdi shooting incident. And I knew, in quite a different sense, about the meaning of the Cuban revolution. Still, I never saw the connection; I suffered from a personal inability to carry my history with me. Baseball, even Cuban baseball, even revolutionary baseball, was a part of my life that had been rejected. Baseball was necessarily insignificant. I might have romanticized cutting sugar cane, but never baseball. Professional sport was part of the Death Culture and I stood for life.

Not only did I fail to tie my bits of Cuban baseball knowledge to my bit of Cuban political knowledge, I never even considered the possibility. The process of becoming political was, in part, a process of learning that capitalist culture had deluded me about almost everything. Yet it never occurred to me to take my newly raised consciousness and apply it to the events of my past. It never occurred to me to examine the Frank Verdi shooting incident in the light of what I had learned about the working of the world. My own past was rejected automatically and instantaneously. It could not be examined. And this was a serious failure. And a specific kind of failure that is a strong cultural characteristic of American society.

The American model for self-improvement has always been a process of death and rebirth, rather than an accumulation of knowledge. Americans have always been obsessed by leaps in and out of various faiths. We reject religion for politics, politics for drugs, drugs for religion, and so on. And after a time, it becomes quite ordinary to find yourself surrounded by people finding and losing themselves through leaps: the leap from the aluminum-siding business to the motorcycle gang. Dentistry rejected for astrology. From middle-class professionalism to the rural commune and naked babies. It came to seem quite normal to be transported to unbelievable places and careers, literally overnight, and all in the admirable everyday process of growth and improvement.

Somehow the traditional American obsession with raising your own consciousness, which older people called self-improvement, took a turn. Self-improvement was no longer a matter of attending a lecture series at the YMCA. Now it required nothing less than the total and utter renunciation of whatever came before. The possibility of a better future meant that the past had to be denied. Consciousness is never retroactive.

Very rapidly, my generation began to establish a collective identity, based on a widespread agreement about values. The materialistic dreams and aspirations of our parents were the realities that we were born into. In the poverty of the Depression, these might have been beautiful dreams, but as realities twenty years later, they were nightmares.

So we rebelled. But in our rebellion, we failed to examine what came before. We failed to see the dangers inherent in the notion of progress. We failed to see that progress would do exactly the same damage to us internally as it did to our parents materialistically. This was a major failure.

Our parents threw out their beautiful old furniture and bought pretentious, badly made, ugly new furniture. We laughed at them as we gathered in the beautiful old furniture. But we were abandoning our childhood and our identity as fast as they were abandoning their old cars, furniture, and black-and-white television sets. And for very much the same reasons. It was old, it no longer worked. Why bother to reconsider when the new model is so much better?

And so the antiwar movement died of old age, nearly five years before the Vietnam war ended. And so, too, the civil-rights movement was split asunder. Political movements began to spread in too many different directions to allow very many people to continue to identify with them for very long. There were too many frustrations, too many inner struggles, and too much moral exhaustion. The only alternative was to go on to the new.

As their numbers grew, young radical activists received increasing attention from the society and its media. A once docile public now polarized and identified itself as both friend and enemy. Tensions mounted with each confrontation, and then, at a point where the social

[31]

structure began to crack, it subsided. Government adjusted to the reality of a hostile citizenry. Insurrections became acceptable as part of everyday life. The revolt of the young no longer felt threatening. Moral outrage no longer caused even guilt. Even the hard-core troublemakers and criminals could no longer provoke, frighten, or fascinate. The revolution began to be ignored, even by its enemies.

Eventually, the whole business of politics became too difficult to identify with, or be defined by, and the generation moved inward. To food and health obsessions, bicycling, pottery, and whatever, so long as it was inward, so long as it was subject to personal control. The world was still impossible, as a place, but there were other, newer things to be done. Interests always shifted to the new, and the new always seemed to reveal an even greater understanding of the true nature of life.

And so my generation moved, never stained by the failure of our abandoned dreams.

We continued, perpetually struck by a cataclysmic perception of the perfect life, always at the ready to junk yesterday's understanding of the ultimate truth. Even the restlessness became incorporated into the search. Now that we are adult wanderers, and have reached, as a generation, a collective longing for roots and home, and a condemnation of wanderlust, we continue to wander forward. Baking bread and canning vegetables are not a return to tradition if you've never done them before. Practicing handicrafts in the machine age is not a return. Any attempt at tradition rings empty in a culture that denies the very notion of tradition.

American society has never allowed for links between the past and the present. The homes and roots we left no longer exist. I can eat white hot dogs at a Red Wing baseball game and be titillated, but I can never draw from that titillation a sense of identity. And though little bits of the life that I lived as a child still remain, I can no more understand myself through them than a tourist can understand the glory of nineteenth-century technology by visiting the Eiffel Tower. The sentiments are just too foreign.

By the time I defined myself as political, I had no active memory of ever having been a baseball fan. I could certainly recall baseball if I had to, but it no longer had anything to do with my identity. I was political. I was a moralist. And by necessity, baseball fans were archetypes of the opiated masses.

And so it was and seemed it would always be. And then, when everyone was looking in the other direction, the postwar era ended. Reality would no longer respond to political myth. Economic remedies, after decades of success, failed to cure. Relevance no longer seemed necessary. Spiritual enlightenment no longer seemed urgent. Political visions, whether moral or opportune, sophisticated or crude, now bored the country they once held spellbound. In the hearts of the young, as on the factory floors, growth had stopped.

Eras do not end clearly. But when the Vietnam war, the oldest established permanent floating radicalizing phenomenon of my lifetime, ended, times had clearly changed. All that remained was illustration. My own personal preference, for the moment when structural social changes altered the American mind is this historical pinpoint: It ended on the day you waited in line for gasoline with two hundred other cars. Simplistic but precise. And there were also Watergate, Arab sheiks, and plain physical and emotional exhaustion. And for each of us, hundreds of personal experiences that will forever seem unique and isolated, but nevertheless causal.

The search for the perfectability of life ended. Self-improvement stopped spiraling and became cyclical, which is no improvement at all. For the first time, a set of tires, a muffler, and an overhaul became an acceptable alternative to a new car. Junk became antique, the cult of the old replaced the cult of the new, and the frenzied search for roots began. I was finally able to go to sleep as a responsible adult and awake as a little suburban Jewish boy, aware of the transformation, and exclaim, "Who am I?"

The problem with mind, that seat of consciousness, volition, and thought, is that it moves according to habit rather than design. Changing habit is a slow and ponderous process, so that even the most obvious realizations are often a long time in coming to mind. And so it was, while visiting my family in Rochester, seventeen years after I saw my last Red Wing baseball game, sixteen years after the Cuban revolution, that my mind began to see that there was a significance to these events.

The threads of the story weave together much further on. The pattern has only begun to emerge. It reveals an increasingly quaint and surrealistic stylization in the actions and political fantasies of the American government. It reveals an authority structure so remote from the lives of its people that its activities no longer seem real. And it reveals a method, style, and way of thinking that, having served well in the past, works less and less.

The presentation of the first human being to land on the moon abandoned science and became a television show. The plot involved the placing of the plaque with Richard Nixon's autograph, and the fluttering of the American flag in a place with no atmosphere. Though the ratings never equaled those of the Super Bowl, it was presented as a success.

The process of placing the unbelievable before the American public as a television melodrama was established. When the time came for reconciliation with China, the surrealistic touch was once again applied, and the public was warmed up with a ping-pong tournament. That too was treated as a success.

As detente with Cuba began to develop, it became a short jump in my mind to the next great television special. The replay of the last Rochester Red Wings–Havana

Sugar Kings baseball game. And who would be a more suitable organizer?

I knew that the State Department would be a hurdle. I knew in my heart that it was virtually impossible for me to organize this event. But I was in Rochester to search through my beginnings anyway, and Red Wing–Cuban baseball seemed the perfect medium.

You cannot establish a conspiracy without a coconspirator, so I sought out my friend Sammy. He was the only person in town I really knew, and besides, we were coconspirators already, whether I knew it or not. Years ago, we had both seen Saul Landau's film of Fidel Castro playing baseball. And last autumn, while I was visiting Sammy at his home in Maine, we watched a television documentary showing American senators visiting Havana. As Claiborne Pell and Jacob Javits complained about the plumbing in the Havana Hilton, the same seed was planted in both our minds.

I accepted this conspiracy as a fantasy from the very beginning, but I wanted the earliest and most timid stages of plotting to be real. I wanted to pretend that we might, just possibly, spring from a sense of humor into direct action.

But I have no record for taking on the real world, and Sammy wasn't the slightest bit interested. There were no telephone calls to Washington, not even letters to the editor. Instead Sammy and I decided on the most dangerous and terrifying approach: a direct confrontation with the Rochester Red Wings. We would march into the head office with straw hats, dark glasses, big cigars, machetes, phony names, chickens, maracas, and bongo drums. And then, between the whoops and hollers, we would make outrageous demands in pretend Spanish as I rhumbaed and mamboed around the room. If no one else, at least the CIA and the FBI would take our gesture seriously, and we would never have to tell our grandchildren that we were Good Germans.

In politics, even fantasy requires theory. And for this, research was necessary. My days were taken up with painting my parents' house, so Sammy got to go to the Rochester public library and spend twenty minutes going through the old newspapers and getting the facts.

Meanwhile, with an intensity that can only be achieved in situations of active guilt, I threw myself into my housepainting. As I labored, the work mushroomed. First the dry rot, then the damp patches, and then the wet rot. Aspects of the job began to work against me. On my way out to get a piece of sandpaper, I ran directly into a drawer labeled "sandpaper," filled with tiny pieces of worn-out sandpaper. My anguish and disbelief were met by my family with the smug satisfaction that accompanies thrift.

And all that I had for relief in this difficult time were my meetings with Sammy. He would pull out his tiny piece of paper, with three or four words of notes he took in the library, and from that he would spin out a thread of the newspaper history of Frank Verdi and the cold war.

"And then, Eisenhower removed the sugar quota," Sammy would say, snapping his fingers in my face and drawing them back, as if he were Eisenhower, maliciously pulling the sugar quota out of my nose—*tweak*. Sammy supplied his own sound effects, and for an instant I was Cuba, and my nose hurt.

As the days passed, the work went worse, and my envy grew. How come Sammy got to go to the library? Why was I doing this paint job? While I prepared the walls, my family mixed and remixed and finally concocted the perfect off-white color. I finished painting one room, and with a sense of accomplishment and relief, went out to plot a baseball detente.

The next morning, I was informed that the color had dried, sadly enough, too blue. I would have to begin painting again, with a new color. It was clear that this sort of thing happened often. Everyone took the news calmly, and carried off a sporting manner. My own hysterical objections and doubts seemed out of place.

I repainted the room. It was time to begin the next room and the hallways, but the repainting arose as a metaphor for all the frustrations of my childhood, and I escaped.

By this time, I suspected Sammy's research as revisionist. Sammy wanted only fantasy, but I had history on my mind. I had an emotional feeling about a historical event, about Frank Verdi and the Rochester Red Wings and guns in a baseball stadium. I was only a child during the Cuban revolution, but through baseball, I was actually there at the time. And when I put that together with what I later learned about the nature of political realities, I begin to understand what had happened in Cuba. And this aroused my anger for what had happened in Cuba, and for the laziness of my own memory.

Look: the loss of Cuba was a far more serious error of American foreign policy than loss in Asia. The primary evil of the American Imperial age might have been Vietnam, but the primary mistake was Cuba. Cuba was not a foreign culture halfway around the world, but a familiar, willing, next-door neighbor. It was only the inflexible rigidity of American relations with Cuba that drove the Cubans away. Cubans, unlike the heroic Vietnamese, considered themselves, culturally, part of North America.

And yet, the way in which the story was told, and accepted and remembered and forgotten, reveals a kind of democratically determined stupidity running through the American consciousness. Cuba was a missile crisis, us against the Russians, right? Baseball had nothing to do with it.

For America, detente with Cuba should be a time of confession and catharsis, a time when America comes to understand the self-destructive delusions of the Imperial mentality.

But instead of self-understanding, America is anxious merely to resume trade and forget the whole thing. A few weeks of the media wheels grinding the Cubans back into reasonable fellows, the resumption of sugar imports, case closed, and on to the next crisis.

With this anger, I resolved to enter the library myself. As much as I needed to leave the painting, I wanted to read the old newspapers, the old sports pages, and see what really happened. Now I needed to know not just for myself, but for history. Cuba was about to be back in American business; history would be forgotten. And I could have, as my mission, to remember it.

Unless something was done, the day of reckoning would come in the form of a television program. Some gray president of the great republic, standing on a podium in front of the camera, his smiling powdered face just above the great seal of his office, having practiced his pronunciation in the bathroom for half a day. *"Bienvenidos, amigos.* Welcome back, Cuba." At the very least, I would be there to say it ain't so. Politicians distort history, that ain't the way it happened in Cuba.

During the nineteen-twenties, a blueblood out of Groton and Harvard named Richard Whitney rose swiftly through the institutional hierarchies of Wall Street to become president of the New York Stock Exchange in 1930.

Some years later, on June 25, 1938, after his arrest for misappropriation of funds and his sentencing to Sing Sing, he was reported to have lined two solid base hits in three times at bat, and fielded flawlessly, while playing on the prison school team.

When visited by his old teacher from Groton, who turned out to be his last loyal friend, Whitney was asked if there was any way to help. "Yes," he said, "I need a left-handed first baseman's mitt."

It was possible for Richard Whitney to learn this lesson way back then. Would it be possible now to unseat cold war memories and modern-day political realities?

So I entered the library and ordered the microfilms of the local newspaper. All along I had known it would come to this, because I wasn't interested in mere information. I wanted a re-creation of the times that were, after all, my times. I had lived through the radicalism of the sixties, and I knew that the simple newspaper version of the facts is never what is significant. But if I could slip back between the lines and into my childhood self, I could transpose the present and the past.

The problem is that once you start looking through old newspapers, it becomes harder and harder to stay with the story that got you interested in the first place. Perhaps it is a problem that colors all of life, but it is particularly poignant in the reading of newspapers. Which is a very unprofessional approach and, believe me, I was at every moment aware of it. Unprofessional attitude was only the beginning of the problem.

I had intended to absolve both Cuba and myself, as victims of the mentality that dominated America as it conducted its cold war. But as I read through the newspapers, I could not interpret this strictly. From the very beginning, the context was more interesting than the facts it contained. In a very medieval and religious way, I began to copy down selections from the text, verbatum.

May 3, 1954. Hanoi, Indochina. (AP) The red-led masses of the Vietminh unleashed a new assault on Dien Bien Phu, overran three strong points and occupied part of a fourth today in their attempt to wipe out France's Gibraltar of the Jungle. . . .

May 3, 1954. Rochester's high-school youth will play an important part in the civil defense of the city in the event of an emergency attack by serving as stretcher bearers for the Emergency Medical Services of Civil Defense. . . .

May 3, 1954. WINGS BOW TO HAVANA 3–1
(Dugout Diggins) . . . "This is really a beautiful ballpark," said Coco Bacallao, collar-ad model road secretary of the Cubans. "It's the greenest grass I've seen in any stadium."

[39]

This was just a day like any other, where history could be pursued in any direction. Involvement in Southeast Asia, cold-war fears of enemy attack, baseball. But it was also a special day. This was the day of the first game played on American soil by the Havana Sugar Kings, also called the Cubans. I saw it. I remember someone trying to steal home, unsuccessfully. I remember the oldest and loudest of the regular fans who sat in my section. None of us knew his real name. He was called "Red Smith" after the famous New York sportswriter. Red Smith was reading from this little bit of paper and shouting at the top of his, the most powerful of all lungs, *"Napoleon, a qui Napoleon, a qui!"* He was attempting to call the Havana manager, "Nap" Reyes, in his native tongue. It was not an incident. I remember nothing else about the game.

As a media event, the game marked the twenty-fifth anniversary of the opening of Red Wing Stadium. The newspaper story, on May 3, was filled with mentions and pictures of old Red Wings who were brought out of the woodwork to celebrate the anniversary. Havana's entry was not noticed except subliminally by "Dugout Diggins." That was the name of a sort of gossip column tacked on to the end of every Red Wing story. And Dugout Diggins' only hint that this was the first-ever United States of America game for Havana was that Coco Bacallao, the collar-ad model road secretary, was commenting on the beauty of the ballpark because he had never seen it before, because Havana had never played in the United States before. It's not that Cuba's entrance into American baseball was overlooked. Havana was not yet a foreign country in the minds of Americans. It was still regarded as one of the more colorful outposts of that all-American place where rich people from New York went in winter, and poor people from New York went in seasons they would rather not discuss. In 1954, Havana was an extension of Florida.

According to the papers, Congress had begun a debate on racial segregation, it was thirty-eight degrees at the Red Wing night game, and an unfortunate named Cpl. Edward S. Dickerson was being sentenced to ten years of hard labor for "currying favor" .with his Red Chinese captors while a prisoner of war in Korea. In Pine Bluff, Arkansas, the local baseball team was trying unsuccessfully to integrate the Class C Cotton States League, while in Hollywood, Robert Mitchum was suing *Confidential* magazine for one million dollars because of a story which said that he showed up at a party nude, covered himself with catsup, and posed as a hamburger.

These were the notable things happening on the day Cuba began playing American baseball. I would have been a very different twelve-year-old, and a very different adult, if I remembered them. But these were the times when my realities and values were being structured. I remember when they closed the lunchroom at Number Eight School, due to overcrowding. After that, a school bus brought my sister and me home for lunch.

I discovered that my mother was always watching television when we arrived. The television program was always the same. Politicians sitting down, behind tables, talking into microphones. My mother told me that it was a tragedy, because some of the people on this program were Jewish. Ten years later, I found out that these programs were the Army-McCarthy hearings. If not for the civil-rights movement, I might never have heard about it.

I was eleven years old, I didn't know about eras, or politics, or nonbaseball institutions. In many ways I was naïve, but I was not idle. One day I wrote a letter to Mr. Paul Pinkney, sports editor of the evening paper. I told him that I wanted to be a baseball writer. He took me to see the coach of the local university football team, bought me a hot dog, and said I should learn how to type by the touch system. I thought the football coach a strange and disappointing choice; I had no interest in meeting him. But by the end of the summer I was typing thirty-eight words per minute, by the touch system.

As I cranked the microfilm-reading machine in the Rochester public library, the years rolled by, presenting a picture very different from the softness of my memories. Intercontinental ballistic missiles were being perfected and launched, rebels were kidnaping officers of the United Fruit Company in Cuba, terrorists were tossing grenades into French barracks in Saigon. Jack Anderson was apprehended for planting a microphone in the hotel room of Bernard Goldfine's right-hand man. Caryl Chessman was pleading for his life. National Boy Scout leaders were chastising America's youth for being sissies. And of course, federal grand juries were continuing to demoralize the civil service by hunting and finding communists wherever they looked.

Diligently, I worked and skipped my way through enough newspapers to arrive at the middle of the 1958 baseball season. By this time, Rochester area men were hitting the beaches in Lebanon and I was wondering what I was doing.

The Sugar Kings would go on to finish 1958 in last place, twenty-five games behind. I knew that there was nothing much to be learned from this season, but something drove me to read through the entire summer. On the same day, July 1, 1958, Alaska entered the Union as the forty-ninth state, Nelson Rockefeller announced that he would seek the Republican nomination for governor of New York, two more Americans were kidnaped by Castro's forces in Cuba, the Buffalo Bisons beat the Havana Sugar Kings 5–2, and Communist China announced that it had successfully exploded its first nuclear bomb.

On the one hand, oh my God! Could this possibly be the staid and sober fifties when nothing was happening? The papers seem bursting with historical significance. And on the other hand, I can rush through this day's newspaper as if I were the teen-ager I was then! Just a lotta garbage, nothing important today. Then I look at the box score of the Bisons–Sugar Kings game and feel shivers run down my spine as familiar names spring unexpected memories to my mind. Davalillo, who I remember was called Yo-Yo. Escalera. Chacon at shortstop. Quintana at second base. Isquierdo, the catcher. Cuellar, the pitcher. The same Mike Cuellar who is still pitching in the majors for Baltimore. How can I possibly know from memory that Escalera's first name is Nino? How could such information possibly be locked inside my mind without my knowledge, consent, or understanding? And consider what I left out! Imagine the wisdom I might have held if my memory had been as selective as it was retentive! And yet, there it is. The Havana lineup has lingered beneath the surface of my consciousness, in a way that the mainstream of history has not. It should be no surprise; I was not a historical child.

But now, all these years later, when the newsprint has turned to microfilm, I find my relationship to its contents to be very different. My motives have become irrelevant, and my will has been arrested. A lust for memory has taken over and no matter how I try, I am powerless. I am just reading the papers, unable to focus or direct myself. I cannot research the subject. I am no more than an audience for my own memory, constantly astounded at its capacity, and disappointed by its content.

Surrounding me on three sides, the microfilm-reading machine became my cubicle. I sat on the hard wood chair, hunched over, consciously monkish. My feet began to feel excessively warm, but I dared not even untie my shoelaces, for fear that comfort might lessen the sacrifice I was making. Meanwhile, Ike and Mr. K (RED BOSS OF RUSS) were blasting, denouncing, demanding, and hurling epithets at each other through the headlines. And the world was busy trying to keep Orval Faubus away from the schoolyards of Little Rock, Arkansas, and Red China away from the islands of Formosa, Quemoy, and

Matsu. And every once in a while, some startling piece of information bearing no possibility of context would appear, and without hesitation, be copied into my notebook. On July 30, 1958, Arthur Payne, deputy sheriff of Dade County, Florida, who resided at 3673 S.W. 24th Street in Miami, was killed, along with thirteen other men, when he attempted to lead a revolt in Haiti.

And once in a great while, there would be something vaguely resembling a clue.

> August 18, 1958. (Dugout Diggins) ... Cuban attendance for the season will more than double last season's rebel-scared total of 82,000. ...

And the part of my mind still keenly searching for the true history of the Havana Sugar Kings was awakened, and subsequently horrified. I had read through the entire 1957 season and there was never any mention of rebel scares affecting the attendance at the baseball game. My newspaper did not want me to know about the rebels. I should have known that it was a little late in the day to preserve my naïveté, but I didn't. Because without that naïveté, I could no longer blame myself for not having seen beyond the baseball game. And without that naïveté, I was reduced to merely learning, over and over again, about the highly subjective business notion of objective journalism, rather than the facts of the story.

Either that, or I was losing my grip. My original allocation of a few hours stretched into day after day, and no matter what I decided in my brief moments of sane reflection, I could not stop going all over the place. Not only did I fail to locate my story and follow up on the leads it suggested, I got sidetracked and residetracked until I was looning all over seventeen years of newspapers. I spent days reading through years that had no relevance to the Cuban baseball story. Every day I went through sixty or seventy newspapers and could only relate to them as if they were today's paper. I checked

out what would be on television that night, in years
where the radio program listings were given five times
as much space as the television listings. I don't know
why I did it. I always noticed what movies were playing,
particularly in my old neighborhood. And I compulsively
copied into my notebook everything that struck me
deeply, sometimes at the expense of what I was looking
for.

The 1958 baseball season ended. Not only a literary
confusion, but some colossal and unwieldy object I picked
up cheaply at a junk shop, now made expensive merely
by the labor it took to get it home. And I can't bear to
part with it. Nothing more significant than a few obscure
hints in the sports pages. I spent days straining my eye-
balls in the reading room of Rochester's Rundel Memorial
Library. It turned me into a demented machine. My
fingers were sore from gripping my ball-point pen. The
fruits of my labor left me torn between admiration for
my effort and inability to instantly recognize its value
or beauty.

I recorded pages full of attendance figures at Gran
Stadium in Havana, but without any notation as to date
or significance. Attendance: 7,134; attendance: 847; attendance: 2,200; attendance: 4,250; attendance: 1,648;
attendance: 1,737; attendance: 1,842; attendance: 2,491;
attendance: 1,937; attendance: 2,200 (est.) ; attendance:
4,250 (est.). Each of these figures represents my finding
the box score of a game played in Havana, and then
carefully copying it down from those tiny blurred numerals on the constantly shifting focus of the microfilm-
reading machine. All that I have achieved in the collection
of these figures is some illusion of my capacity for concentrated effort, and a parody of high-school term-paper
research.

What do these attendance figures reveal? Where is
the indication of budding political consciousness in a
restless population straining to throw off the yoke of
imperialist colonization? Where is the graph that will

metaphorically reveal the panorama of revolution? And where is the genius that will locate the origins of revolution, even in such an out-of-the-way place?

Is it possible that all these hot Cuban statistics lay buried because they reveal nothing? Is it possible that my particular personal history of having been a Rochester Red Wing fan in the fifties, and a left-wing radical in the sixties, remains unique but strikes no universal chord? Is it possible that history and circumstance have put me on this path but refuse to reveal any plot? I know that it is not part of human rights for life to reveal thematic structure, but that's suddenly what it means to be backing this long shot. This is, without attempting to be melodramatic, my life. These are my roots laid bare. And the correlation of events remains no greater than random. There is no escape except to cut off my past, and that has already been done. There is no possible reconciliation between my conscious identity and my roots. Home is not available.

I had traveled to Rochester to experience that peculiar modern ritual of the home-town visit, the home town being that place where everything is strangely familiar. It is an environment that makes you feel comfortable until you try to move in it and find that everything has changed. And then you find that certain things haven't changed, and you still know about them, but you didn't realize that you knew. And eventually you relate to all the changes that have taken place with theatrical grumpiness and a mock astonishment that hides a total bewilderment as to what time zone you have found yourself in. The streets have all been rerouted, the neighborhoods have all been transplanted and scattered, but there remains a familiar understanding of North, South, East, and West in what is otherwise an alien place. The place that you can find your way around no longer exists, but on the other hand, you don't get lost. The old stores are still intact, but their names have changed. Noah's Ark, the hardware and auto parts dynasty, is now just another dozen links in the Western Auto chain. Harry's Hots and a hundred places like it have been replaced by McDonald's, Kentucky Fried Chicken, and Jack in the Box. The 25 Club's best hamburgers in town have been out of business for ten years, they say. The Towpath Inn has been replaced by a parking garage that bears a startling resemblance to the Guggenheim Museum in New York City. But those white hot dogs have survived. The pork-flavored frankfurters, found only in Rochester, New York, are still available, still delicious, and still evil. They are a rare combination, being at the same time tasty, juicy, and not kosher. I mean, not merely not kosher, but flesh of the swine, the most evil of all possible evil, and still easily obtainable.

Though most of the geographic landmarks are gone, I was still able to find the mood of my adolescence in Rochester. The mood of the home-town visit is always ritualized adolescence. To return and revert to youth, so as to see how far you've come. To return briefly to provincialism always bolsters and inflates feelings of sophistication. That's why we dutifully return. That distance you've come since leaving home, however small a step it might be, becomes, for a while, glorious and dramatic.

But this time, all ritual behavior was sacrificed so that I could sit in the microfilm-reading room of the public library and fill my notebook with mementos. And these mementos evoke, more powerfully than real-life reruns, the mystery and wonder of the home-town visit. Here in the pages of the *Rochester Democrat and Chronicle* are my formative years. Here are the refutations to all the plastic memories of the benign fifties that this mischievous and constraining American society has put into my identity over the years. And here are the crude realities which I never noticed as a boy. Never mind that the facts are rhetorical and not historical, that they are in style and not content. Never mind that I will know

[47]

the truth only through its mood and never through the accounts of deeds. It is making me a home-town visit with a power of reality that the past was never intended to convey.

I fended off my old friends and relatives who sought me out in good faith. I explained to them that I had the key to my own past, the character of Fidel Castro, the meaning of the Cuban revolution, definite proof of CIA intervention in Red Wing baseball—I had the hottest story of the century locked up in the box scores of the baseball games of my childhood. It was all sitting in the library and it would not wait twice.

My old friends and relatives thought I was crazy. They couldn't begin to respond to my ravings about the Havana Sugar Kings and changed the subject as quickly as possible. "I don't know nothing about that crap," one told me. "I just read the sports pages. Ha ha." What could I say?

I had abandoned my task of painting the house as completely as I abandoned friends and family. And from this withdrawal I drew determination and commitment. I would get the whole story. Every twist and turn. Every subtle rhetorical change in the sports-page clichés. I would continue to record attendance figures, because some pattern would have to emerge as the Cuban revolution built toward crescendo.

I became committed to running my interests all through the paper. I became confident that the sidetracks were more fascinating than the mainstream. I accepted the seemingly inconsequential events of 1958 as relevant to my story. I was hypnotized by the microfilm. I knew that I was basically crazed, but I felt driven by a power greater than sanity. My index finger began to tremble, and finally did blister. My eyes began to tear, since every passing car altered the machine's focus and there was a constant stream of traffic. The old viaduct that used to run behind the library is now a superhighway.

There was no smoking allowed in the public library.

And each day that I was there I allowed myself two cigarette breaks, midmorning and midafternoon. And during each of these breaks, I realized that I was ruining my eyesight and my penmanship and I had really lost track of why I was doing it. Then I would take a long last drag on my cigarette, stub it out, and go back into the library, leaving my serious reflections behind.

I frantically searched through paper after paper, no longer aware of hunting for anything specific. Sometimes concentrating on just the baseball scores, which were always boxed on the front page; then, with great guilt, going back to the front page to properly check out the major news, and then on to the sports section.

I was seized with moods, which often lasted hours, when I was certain that all the important documentation on cultural change could be found on the movie page. Brigitte Bardot in *The Girl in the Bikini*: "BB as the lighthouse keeper's daughter who believes in dressing light" (*Democrat and Chronicle*, July 21, 1959, p. 29).

Then Frank Horton. The arch insect-demon of my political years. My own local congressman. The third from last member of Congress to publicly repudiate Richard Nixon over Watergate. But worse than that, my own congressman was a low-profile moderate and the least colorful of all federal employees, including the mailman. During all my loyal years as a Red Wing fan, and without my knowledge of it, Frank Horton was the president of the Rochester Red Wings Baseball Club, and the chief legal counsel to the International League. And so, I had to copy into my notebook any mention of Frank Horton.

So what if he's just another dull Republican party hack? He has personally disappointed me for the last decade, and prior to that he had his dull, sober, conservative hands on the baseball team I loved. If there was any justice in this world, there would have to be some dirt on the sports pages that would expose Frank Horton as an avant-garde minor version of Nixonism and conveniently

[49]

turn me into the Woodward and Bernstein of Rochester, New York, who uncovered it all while visiting his home town.

Yes, what my relatives failed to understand was that circumstance was throwing me into the limelight of investigative journalism, as I sat there in the public library. For the last five years, I have been able to open the newspaper and read a piece exposing a major politician as a cheap crook. And over these years, I learned that the extent of the scandal was limited only by the imagination of the investigative reporter. Misused funds, rigged elections, illegal contributions, money-washing, call girls. All you had to do was dream it up, search through a few old telephone bills, make a few phone calls, and the hard evidence would turn up. I sat through all those years watching various mediocre journalists come up with evidence proving the pervasive corruption and total moral bankruptcy of the American political system.

I, who said "Fuck you" to the entire capitalist system when Walter O'Malley moved the Dodgers out of Brooklyn in 1957, had to sit on the sidelines. At the time of the move, the Brooklyn Dodgers were the most profitable operation in baseball. The hearts of literally millions of fans were broken, only because the move to Los Angeles would yield even greater profits. I was one of the few fourteen-year-olds in the nation who realized what was going on, and I wasn't even a Dodger fan. This enormous potential had remained dormant for the last eighteen years. Meanwhile, a bunch of alcoholic liberals who were earning good money as journalists were rising to fame, fortune, and affairs with beautiful lovers, simply by saying what I had always said and by proving what I had always known.

The Nixon government, which had personally insulted and frightened me, was destroyed by a bunch of reporters who were more comfortable embracing the system than they were pulling it down. It was my dirty work that they did to build their careers. I was robbed.

Here in the microfilm-reading room of the Rochester public library was, at long last, my salvation. Through the quirks of fate, history, and complex social forces, here was the raw material of a history that I, and I alone, could recognize. The unique political, cultural, historical, and geographic experiences that had shaped the process of my socialization left me with the perfect identity to accomplish this one task.

The headlines, the sports pages, the movie advertisements, and the bridal pictures seemed to reveal no theoretical whole. This period of history didn't even suggest a name for itself, not to mention a theme. But I could sweep all this anxiety, doubt, and confusion out of my head as I stubbed out my cigarette and went back to my microfilm newspapers. I had been a Red Wing fan. I had seen the CIA and various other lackeys meddling in Latin America in every other issue of *New Left Notes*, the *North American Committee on Latin America Reports*, and the *Monthly Review*. I had a point of view derived from such perfectly coincidental experiences that I could not fail. However I went about it, I could round up all these seemingly unrelated newspaper articles and tie them together in such a brilliant way that the meaning of the postwar era, or whatever it would finally be called, would be clear. I would fit together these random, hokey stories about Formosa, the U-2 Affair, Orval Faubus at Little Rock, the first intercontinental ballistic missile, Brigitte Bardot, red-baiting, Trujillo dating film starlets, the withdrawal of the Cuban sugar quota, and lots more. I would weave a complicated collage of all these threads and it would stand as wisdom. I could even pick out exactly the right sentence from the *Democrat and Chronicle*'s Teen Scene page and have it stand as metaphor for some deep insight into how American culture evolved.

I wouldn't have to be reasoned or judicious as I read through the newspapers. I had only to listen to my heart, and when it quivered hardest, write down whatever it was that made me tingle. I knew that what made me tingle was the memory of something so obscure and so remote that it was surely impossible to remember. And I knew that what was going on in the microfilm-reading room was so intensely personal that it could not fail to have universal significance.

This was no ordinary work of library research. My heart and my entire apparatus of emotional sensitivity were organizing this research. Any old research would show scandal and unsportsmanlike behavior on the part of the low-profile, but nevertheless imperialistic, Eisenhower era. But this was to be more than an exposition of information. This story was from my heart. This would be literature, drama, and nothing less than high art.

Who cares if nobody ever heard of Abby Pose or ever cared that she was the valedictorian of my school, Brighton High? By the time I had analyzed it as a news story, examined my emotions, and revealed my sentiments, the mere reprinting of the Abby Pose valedictory would be enough to bring tears to the eyes of every man, woman, and child on the face of the earth.

This, then, was the spirit in which I labored in the library. These were the delusions that pushed my concentration beyond its limits. Each night as I left the library, all of reality seemed to waver in and out of focus to the same rhythm that the traffic beat out on my microfilm reader. But the next morning, I was out on the steps ten minutes before the library opened, impatiently puffing my cigarette, waiting to get back to my mission. I was on the road to salvation, and not even intelligent doubt could stop me.

Leaving the library has somehow damaged the romance. Now that both the hysteria and the magic are gone, it has dawned on me that I might be the only person on the face of the earth who could possibly appreciate what I am doing. And if I don't understand it myself, it won't be legitimate. It won't be real. The eyestrain, the sore finger, the offense to the relatives may all be petty considerations, but at least they contain a reality.

September 10, 1958. CITY COUNCILMAN FRANK
HORTON WITHDRAWS FROM HOUSE RACE
"It was my own decision," Horton said. He is
president of the Rochester Red Wings Baseball
Club. . . .

Somehow no dull-witted party hack leaps out of this and makes clear the meaning of a legacy of tapes, bugging, and nursing-home scandals. Not a kernel of evidence here, but the odor of scandal is always available to the sensitive nose, isn't it? How did the head of a minor-league baseball club get to be a Congressman right after his league ditched Cuba? The truth is that I don't know. I don't even have a hypothesis or a misconstruction.

And oh, if I had the faith or the patience to wait. If only I had known what was coming, I would certainly have been able to bide my time cheerfully until the 26th of July, 1976. On that day, the eighteenth anniversary of the Cuban revolution, the local papers carried an AP story that covered my vengeance.

Representative Frank Horton was arrested, one week previous, in the middle of the night on the New York State Thruway. It seems that he had been speeding, reckless driving, and driving while intoxicated, until the state police caught up with him after a six-mile chase at speeds of up to 105 miles per hour. With the congressman were two attractive ladies, one of whom was identified as a suburban divorcee, and the other as someone whose name Horton couldn't recall. Horton is married.

It took a week for the papers to find out, but as soon as they did, Horton called a press conference and revised his position from secrecy to gallantry. He admitted that he made what he called a mistake, and criticized the police for roughing him up and calling him a "drunken son of a bitch" after they found out who he was. He also remembered the second lady. "You can put a gun to my heart, but I still won't tell you her name."

A month after the incident, life granted me the extraordinary experience of sitting in the stands at Red Wing Stadium, and watching Frank Horton being introduced as a big-shot in the pre-game ceremonies marking Pizza Night. Horton waved and smiled like a genuine celebrity, but his few words were inaudible, as 6,000 partisan Red Wing fans booed, hissed and stomped their feet.

Horton quickly escaped into the dugout, and I had, with neither patience nor action, a taste of revenge sweeter than anything that would ever be my own doing.

In terms of current events, it was small scandal indeed, but it appeared in the papers, and that says something. We live in a time when authority has lost face. We are fascinated, but reluctant to face that fact. So our newspapers are filled with the scandalous sex lives of current congressmen and past presidents. And filled with reexaminations of assassination, Army drug tests, and old CIA plots. We are no longer interested in how government is acting, so long as it is purged of its bad apples. The cleansing process requires that every evil act must be exposed. American consciousness must find out where it turned off the road to good.

And in these times of shock and revelation, moral judgment has been revived; not for the political struggle to deny or establish legitimacy, but for its own sake, as a purgative. This time, moral judgment is in the newspapers. This time it poses no threat, not even to reelection.

But while the present enlightens me, it also kept me trapped, back in the microfilm reading room. Present consciousness notwithstanding, there will be no Frank Horton scandals in the postwar Rochester newspapers. Not even hints. It was a different time, when newspapers served a different function. I am the victim of temporal relapse.

The future will expose me, but meanwhile, here in

the sanctuary of the public library, I am neither a coward nor a quitter. I remain courageously trapped in the melancholy Hollywood romance of a besotted old journalist. In shirtsleeves, snap-brim hat pushed back on his head, rimless spectacles up on his forehead, pinching the bridge of his nose and heroically struggling against the story he is too drunk and too burned out to write, even though he won prizes as a war correspondent years ago. How I wish that I were he, engaged in a failure so heroic that it would carry him to the very pinnacle of wisdom in the struggle for life. But I am not he. *Oi vey.*

The central emotional, as well as historical and political, fact in the life of the community in which I was raised was The Nazis. Most of my mother's side of the family had personal experience of Nazis. My cousin Aaron Blum had seen Adolph Eichmann from the inside of a concentration camp. Eichmann, touring the camp, asked my cousin Aaron Blum if he liked the food. Aaron says that he didn't answer.

By the time the postwar era had gained momentum, the horrors of the Nazis were deeply buried in the past, but the lesson was still very much alive. And the lesson was that moral judgment was not an abstract decoration, but the very center of human survival. My relatives had all judged badly, and paid that price. In terms of a community of shared knowledge, all of the people I knew as a child had lived, either personally or vicariously, through the most terrifying and dangerous of all hostile environments. And they never recognized its dangers until it was too late. Right up until the last minute, they felt safe, secure and okay enough to be able to live exclusively private lives. They felt so at ease with what was public that it became invisible. There was no need even to acknowledge it. And then, suddenly, everything they had ever known as stable turned on them, exposing their political apathy as a series of fatal misjudgments. The survivors fled to Rochester.

[55]

As fully mature and reasonably well-adjusted American citizens, they were able to control the fear of all others. They were able to hold jobs, make friends, and participate in the great carnival of production and consumption that was the postwar era. They accepted, at least for the sake of appearance, that America was a good place. But there was still that essential understanding that had to be passed on to the next generation. There was that recent lesson of the possible extreme and excessive consequences to bad judgments. Outsiders had to be carefully judged. You had to be able to spot the difference between good and evil. And if you could not or would not make that distinction, you might not survive.

I was raised on a culture of Jews and Nazis, evil aggressors and innocent victims. Good and bad were always of heroic dimensions. And choosing between the two was always one of life's most serious activities. And in the midst of this cultural bias, I was surrounded by behavior that I simply couldn't judge. However necessary clarity might be to the strength of human feelings, I always seemed to feel vaguely. Bad people were always doing good things, and nearly everybody seemed to be both good and bad, often at the same time.

I remember the day my sister went swimming at the Seneca Park pool without a bathing cap. This caused her carefully straightened and definitely gentile hair to frizz beyond wildest expectation. When she got home, my mother picked up the lamp, which was the second most valuable article in our house, and threw it at her. My sister ducked. The lamp went through the leaded stained-glass door, which was the most expensive article in the house. This was my mother, whom I dearly love, and this was bad behavior.

I couldn't understand the necessity of my sister and me having straight hair. My own curly hair was safely camouflaged by a crew cut, so I didn't have to actively concern myself with the problem. But here were the two most valuable articles in the house, destroyed over curly hair.

My mother's side of the family had straight hair, and my father's side, curly. My sister and I had somehow betrayed our maternal genes. And I knew that it was American to look as Nordic as possible. My upbringing had taught me to fear the Nazis, but I accepted the Nazis only as real, and couldn't understand their metaphorical importance, years after their defeat. I knew that in the American suburbs, it was safe to let the curls grow.

That my mother threw the lamp at my sister was crazy behavior, plain and obvious, and I saw it as such. But what I couldn't come to terms with was the enormous emotional impact that resulted in so much property damage. I saw, for the first time in my life, just how important crazy behavior could be.

And herein lay the necessity of baseball. Baseball was outside of life, and it was able to provide and control emotions. Baseball had its own particular hold on the heart. However temporarily, personal feelings could always be replaced by the formal feelings of the baseball fan. I had to learn how to be a baseball fan; I had to learn how to feel in a ballpark. But the safety and comfort in what I learned was that everything had a reason. Within the internal logic of the game there were no feelings that could not be understood, and articulated, and explained.

The psychological mysteries that made my team play well or ill went no deeper than the score. The hitting slumps and streaks of individual players, the momentum or disarray of the team—all the psychological imponderables were eventually resolved in the statistics. The events on the baseball diamond are capable of moving fans to both joy and sorrow. They dance and shout, and sometimes they even cry.

But there is a difference. Nothing ever happens in

[57]

baseball that is not foreseeable. At any point in the game, and at any point in the season, what can happen next is always a matter of known alternatives. The uneasy bewilderment that comes with the reality of the unexpected has no place in baseball. Baseball is played by the rules.

As I grow closer and closer to the core of my childhood alienation a shiver begins to run up my neck. Everyone needs to feel, and I was no different. But when the feelings got too strong, too crazy, too morally ambiguous, or just too much to take, I had an alternative. And as a child, I preferred the formalized, rule-book feelings of baseball to those of my own life—something I was not interested in discovering.

There is a bias in memory to preserve essential delusion. Any threat is countered with an amusing vignette which, given the structure of the human ego, is distracting. And as I slipped back into baseball and floated to greater profundity, I was powerless or, as they say, carried away.

I remember my Uncle Hymie as one of the great noble and comic figures of my life. I remember his 1957 powder-blue Dodge convertible and his 1949 Cadillac. I remember his red-and-white striped shirt that had "Lucky Strike Means Fine Tobacco," inside-out, bleeding through the stripes.

I will never forget the argument that took place in my kitchen between my Uncle Hymie and his sister. My Aunt Harriet and her seven-year-old son had been trapped in an elevator in the Midtown Plaza for an hour and twenty minutes. Hymie wanted to hire a lawyer and sue. Harriet was certain that you couldn't collect on something like that. Hymie was even more certain that in America, you can collect on anything. The argument soon got out of hand and sprawled into general criticism of character. Harriet repeatedly accused Hymie of being mean and rotten. Hymie's temper was rapidly rising, as he desperately tried to invent the deepest possible insult, without using dirty words. He told Harriet that she was no better than a broken spring. Then, as his anger surged, he edged over the limits of decency and told Harriet that he wouldn't piss on her if she were on fire.

Instead of crushing Harriet, Hymie's remark only confused her. She didn't get it. To put it out, Hymie explained, but the dramatic advantage had been lost and the argument was over.

One evening, my father's boss came to dinner and Hymie just happened to arrive in his taxi. The mere fact that Hymie drove a taxi for his living was a source of shame to my parents. The humiliation of a family littered with contradictions to the American dream of upward mobility was being nakedly displayed before my father's boss. To my parents, Hymie's arrival was seen as a clear cause of unnecessary suffering. Hymie cut through the contradiction by showing my father's boss the complicated circuitry of his two-way radio. This was not merely a taxi, it was a radio taxi, and the radio had more wires than Grand Central Station's got tracks.

Despite the sisterly glares and veiled hints from my mother, Hymie took the liberty of joining us for dinner. He had had a fare out to the race track that morning and had decided to stay for the day. The theme of our dinner with my father's boss was an accurate report of what had happened that afternoon at the horse race. With knives, forks, and spoons, Hymie diagramed each race on the table and explained the pattern. In race after race, just as Hymie's horse approached the finish line, he slowed down and some other mule won. This was an event that my parents never forgot, although they did, I think, eventually forgive.

In 1950, Hymie went to Israel, which in our family was, and still is, called Palestine. To the disgrace and disgust of the family, he left for the land of Israel on a brand-new Indian motorcycle which he later sold to the Water Board of the city of Haifa for more than it cost. Perhaps my fondest image of my uncle is his leaving the disgruntled relatives in a cloud of smoke, as he sped toward Israel, wearing a purple silk jacket with "Flying Spyder" written across the back in yellow letters. Everyone in the family had been so proud that one of us was going to the promised land. And then Hymie, in some ways the most deserving of the trip, spoiled everything by going off like a juvenile delinquent.

Hymie came to my bar mitzvah in a starched white shirt and his prewar toupee. Though he had, in his bedroom, an entire shelf of hair creams, my Uncle Hymie was bald. He used the hair creams on his sideburns, but special occasions called for the wig. The toupee, wavy hair parted in the middle, was specially made for him in New York City, and he put it on only for weddings, bar mitzvahs, and appearances in court. The only other time I had seen him wear it was for the arrival of my cousin Aaron from the DP camp in Poland.

It was a bar mitzvah party and Hymie was throwing back double shots of whisky. A bald friend of my father's, attempting to tease Hymie, told him that his hair was mussed up and that he should go in the bathroom and comb it. Hymie pompously, but quite seriously, inquired if the bald man were jealous and carried on with the double shots. Cutting through social pretension was his genius.

My break with my uncle came when I went away to college. Hymie knew that a college degree was a ticket to the top. And he was overjoyed that one of his nephews was going there. He insisted that I study law. He knew that law was the easiest way to make money and he assumed that everyone knew this. It tried his patience greatly, but he condescended and explained the law to me when he realized that I was not on the path to becoming the family lawyer. His proof was that when he called his lawyers, they were never there. He was always told that they were in court. Now, two lawyers can't be in court at the same time. So it was obvious that one or both of them were either playing golf, at the race track, or shtupping a shiksa in Buffalo.

I knew in my heart that I would never be a lawyer. And I also knew that I could never explain that to my uncle. He persisted. A lawyer comes to work in a clean white shirt, with clean fingernails and a shoeshine. Nice. He sits behind the desk and only does what he wants to do. He doesn't have to do anything. If he wants to write something down, he doesn't even have to do that, he just calls in a broad and she writes it down for him.

Hymie was hurt by my refusal to study law. There was a rift between us. Nothing particularly serious, but before it closed, the tumultuous sixties had flowered. I began to drift to the political left and Hymie began to drift farther and faster in the opposite direction. He was no longer the doting uncle playing with his sister's children. He was no longer the young man searching for adventure. The total of countless failed schemes to make big, fast money had dampened his spirit. The upward mobility that surrounded Hymie's life remained forever unattainable and depressed his pride even further. My Uncle Hymie was never broken by his circumstances, but he was substantially distorted.

Hymie began to buy and carry guns. He practiced target shooting. The word "nigger" crept into his vocabulary. Our meetings became confrontations. He assured me that half of the dirty hippies couldn't sign their own name, and I assured him that people who wore neckties and shaved every day didn't know joy.

Uncle Hymie became a patriotic, racist nut case. I never became a lawyer, or anything else, for that matter. I had an education, and I had opportunity. And it was clear to Hymie that, whatever else I was, I was a deluded bum who didn't understand what was going on in the country. Quite understandably, I lost touch with my uncle.

So, between the housepainting and the compulsive

behavior in the microfilm-reading room, I did look up my uncle. He was no longer the lunatic racist, and I was neither a potential candidate for the law nor a hippie. But too many things had happened, and there was too much distance between us. He wasn't amusing or irritating, and neither was I. All our conversation was directed to various third parties in the room. We simply had nothing to say to each other.

When I examine my relationship with my uncle, all of my historical insights and generalizations begin to lose their focus. I don't really know much of my uncle's life. I know of the social circumstances he was caught in, and I know of some that he transcended and some that squashed him. And I can explain the distance that arose between us. But where are the feelings that hold people together through such divisive difficulties as the postwar boom? I know these feelings from the dream of roots and home, but I do not know them from my own life.

Nothing destroys love like insult. And nothing is more painful than to feel undesirable in the presence of someone you love. When a relationship becomes a meeting ground for mutual inability to tolerate a presence that was once desirable, then that relationship dissolves. People move away from each other and the love is forgotten, whatever the institutional or genetic ties.

This worked very well for postwar America. The destruction of the family was seen not as a casualty, but as a solution. People moved away from their families, their neighbors, and their institutions when they could no longer stand them. And though this process eventually tore apart the social fabric, it was, throughout the postwar era, the only possible solution to the problem of everyday life. And it was quite successful.

Having identified that feeling of being in the wrong place when my Uncle Hymie walked in the door, I began to remember it. It was a feeling so familiar to my adolescence. I was trying to grow out of the personality my environment had selected for me by tentatively asserting a self I preferred. I didn't want to risk rejection, but neither did I want to be the person that the authorities wanted me to be. That feeling of being in the wrong place became familiar as I found myself frequently facing that delicate moment of decision between presenting myself as socially acceptable, the very role in the suburban pantomime I found most disgusting, or presenting myself as straightforwardly as possible, thus incurring the criticism, for no particular reason, of those I would have preferred to think of with fondness. It was a bad choice in either direction, and I became determined not to make it.

And so I was lost to my family, baseball, and Rochester. They were all sorry to lose me. But the loss was that I had changed, not that I was leaving. They weren't prepared for the drugged, bearded communist hippie, and I, having found my feelings for the first time, was not prepared to relinquish them.

The more I search for the sources of my alienation, the more I am struck by the stark contrast between the comforts of my identity as a political moralist and the discomforts of my identity as a baseball fan. In direct contradiction to the way things appeared, this was simply true. My generation was raised in the silence that followed the McCarthy era. Those of us who became political moralists in isolation were pleased to find out that other political moralists existed. Our moral stance had developed in reaction to the only community we had ever known. We saw ourselves as marginal figures, but being the only one in town was always a desirable part of the identity. Then, as the postwar boom continued to extend itself, lines of polarization appeared. At some critical point in the process, people found themselves in a community of like minds.

For the political moralists, building that new community, outside of roots and home, became just as important a task as organizing the workers or creating the revolution, if such a division of purpose can be made. Now that the psychological force of that movement has ended, it appears quite possible that the community it created was the most important product of those radical politics, even though the community turned out to be largely temporary. But it did teach all of us that it was possible to share feelings, and that there was an alternative to the social organization of the postwar suburbs. There was a sense of unity and loyalty. And there was an understanding of shared feeling, and a shared concept of knowledge, that was unprecedented in all of our lives. Anyone with these feelings was acceptable, and once you were accepted, any behavior was tolerated. It was how you felt that mattered. Outrageous behavior was not only tolerated, but became a symbol of closeness in its forgiving.

Outrageous behavior eventually went over the top, and the community did not last socially any more than it did politically, but it did happen. And it changed my life forever by giving me a sense of relief that I have never lost. Becoming political was also a social process of learning that life can change. It was a process of realizing that in all those places where I didn't fit, it was a matter of being out of place rather than being the wrong person.

I had spent so much of my childhood in the wrong places. I could never understand synagogue, or school, or even trombone lessons as anything other than arbitrary discipline. And I feared any authority that would be cruel enough to impose that discipline. And at the same time, I presented myself as pleased to obey, because authority seemed to demand it. I was locked into obedience and I looked down on myself for being powerless and fearful enough to obey. The praise that my obedience brought humiliated me further. It was all part of the same authority, and behind it stood the ultimate specter of the Nazis.

To spring from this to the warmth and comfort of radical politics was to find a home. Radical politics never offered the shelter or sustenance of the hearth, but it provided a much more important emotional shelter, the legitimization of feelings. Feelings were no longer hidden or disguised or presented to gain favor with the authorities. Feelings became the most valuable currency available. They were trusted and acted upon. They became the basis not only for political action, but for the whole of one's relationship to reality. Feelings were no longer a source of inadequacy; they became instead the very basis for pride and self-esteem. To constantly remind ourselves that we would not be good Germans served a variety of purposes, but it also reminded us that, whatever, we would follow our feelings.

Being true to oneself is only simple and obvious in situations where it is not possible. It requires a level of self-knowledge that seems possible only in times of delusion. It is, in one sense, an impossible approach to life, and yet to be forced to deny a personal sense of truth is the worst of all possible approaches to life.

I learned all this in the transformation that left me a political moralist. And it caused me to look back at my childhood with horror. Where was my own truth as a baseball fan? Where were the feelings that drew me to the game, its statistics, and its particular sense of history? Where was the emotional content that would allow me to stand behind my own truth?

As I float back to my childhood, I find all evidence contrary. The emotional content of baseball was wrapped up in my denial of feelings. Baseball was the escape from feelings. Baseball was my relief from the tension between how I felt and how my environment demanded that I act. There is no place more important in life than your hideout, and baseball was my hideout.

Then my life changed, and I no longer needed a hideout, and that was the end of my interest in baseball. Now the postwar era has ended, and with it the communities of shared feelings and concept of knowledge. The radical movement evolved, and the demands on identity were as strict as they had been in the suburbs. They became more and more difficult to accept. And finally, in feeling true to your own feelings, you no longer felt a member of that community. And it all happened too fast for you to be able to simply shrug and move on one more time. And the past, even before it disappeared, became exciting.

And there I was, up in Rochester, desperate to unlock the secrets of my past, but going about it in a way that my Aunt Ruthie would call "another story, altogether." I can't help thinking that I knew, at some level, what was at stake. And so, rather than seeking out the authentic candidates for evaluation, I hid out in the microfilm-reading room. And even there, I hid out in baseball. Once again, my feelings had become dangerous. Both the attractions and repulsions of my childhood posed their own threats. And those threats expressed themselves as a rekindling of my passion for baseball.

It is all very nice, to keep to the lofty levels of mind and explain away the motives and intentions that move us through everyday life. As an educated and philosophical snob, I have no difficulty in dismissing baseball. But the postwar era is ended, and with it the dream of a duty to perfect life. It is getting more and more difficult to live by moral paradigm alone, now that all available versions of the good life have come into question. In times like these we forgive ourselves and others for flaws and tendencies to weakness. The postwar era was a time for building character. And in the process, the sense of good character was lost, and the building stopped. Nowadays we indulge our passions. It is no longer the postwar era, and now a passion is a passion, whatever the guardians of mental health may say about it. Whether it be sex, crime, television, or baseball, we do it in ways that we never would have allowed before. It is a time of indulgence, and baseball is the passion.

During the winter between the baseball seasons of 1956 and 1957, the St. Louis Cardinals, who had owned and operated the Rochester Red Wing Baseball Club for twenty-nine years, decided that the operation was neither lucrative nor interesting enough to continue. They put the business up for sale and left town.

The citizens of Rochester were shocked and outraged at the possible loss of their baseball team. Led by a band of city fathers, they formed a public corporation, Rochester Community Baseball, Inc. The Gannett Newspapers gave publicity and subscription forms. Legal services were provided by Frank Horton. In bars and grocery stores all over town, shares of stock in the baseball team were sold for ten dollars each. It became the civic duty of every citizen to buy at least one share.

In the end, 8,222 shares were sold and the team was saved. The word "community" was added to its name, a little patch showing baseball stitches and the number 8,222 was added to the sleeve of the uniform, and it was "play ball" as usual.

Throughout the first few seasons, there was what seemed to me to be an undue amount of self-congratulation and breast-beating about the baseball team around Rochester. Although there was no drastic increase in attendance, the citizens of Rochester became baseball fans overnight.

I never asked my father, or anyone else, to buy a share of the community's Red Wing Baseball. I skipped the annual Shareholders' Night game. My suspicion was always that it was those old city fathers, rather than the real fans, who had saved the Red Wings. Even though I was in some sense grateful, I did not like the business of being beholden to them. However noble their gesture, the community of Rochester failed to arouse my enthusiasm, or even much of my interest. And I am forced to admit that, in some profound way, I never liked Rochester, in its civic aspects, one bit. If it was the respectable citizens who saved my beloved Red Wings, I didn't want to know about it.

Of course, in my search through the microfilm, I was

practically unable to pass over anything as irrelevant. My interest was continually aroused. But the story of community baseball was something I wouldn't go near. As a child, I saw noble behavior as something that happened only on the baseball field of Red Wing Stadium. As an adult, I think of nobility as something that necessarily and by definition takes place outside of Rochester. And though this attitude may be a bit crazy, it is one of the few inclinations I hold that has not been contradicted by experience.

May 12, 1959. Poplarville, Miss. (AP) Two suicide attempts and an American flag stunned Poplarville today as officials denied any threats against the family of Mac Parker, twenty-three-year-old Negro taken from Pearl River County jail and lynched last month. . . .

May 12, 1959. VEES DEFEAT HAVANA 5–1.
PITCHING DUAL BETWEEN CUELLAR AND
FLOWERS (attendance: 1,900)

May 13, 1959. EDDIE FINALLY MARRIES LIZ
(sigh) AFTER DIVORCING DEBBIE (sob)

May 16, 1959. DULLES WORSE, STILL PLAGUED
BY PNEUMONIA

May 22, 1959. HORTON TO FIGHT I.L. PLAYERS'
SUIT

The baseball season has started, but all I can feel is the gothic quaintness in every story. Dulles, having structured an empire and held it together with string and airplane tickets, is finally dying. Five full years after the historic Supreme Court ruling that separate is not necessarily racial equality, and all that that implied, it is now news, but still reasonable news, and not quite as important as Eddie Fisher fooling around with shiksas, for a black man to be dragged out of jail and lynched.

And the refrigerated Satan himself, Frank Horton, is going into court to defend ruling-class ideology against two valiant ballplayers who, having failed to get a pension plan out of the cheap and stingy International League, are bringing a civil action for antitrust violation. "The league told the player's attorneys that it has no funds with which to finance a pension plan" (same story). Not that you would expect subtlety or eloquence from Frank Horton, but still, and this could be said for the entire era, how did they dare to peddle such an unlikely story in such a naked and blatant way?

Memorial Day weekend, 1959. I spent the entire time at home, reading the book assigned by my English teacher. It was an old classic, *The Deerslayer*. I thought it was awful and forgot it as quickly as I read it, but I didn't have the nerve to stop reading.

Meanwhile, in Dallas, a drunken bricklayer had killed somebody and was holding four hostages, in chains, as he failed in his fantastic plot to kill the governor of Texas. And in Toronto, Clayton Johnson, age fifteen, was crossing the border to appear on a local Buffalo television show called "Dance Party." During the spotlight dance, viewers all over Buffalo saw Clayton dancing with his schoolmate Patty Banks, who happened to be a white girl. Clayton, who happened to be black, was asked to stop dancing and leave. And before the incident was over, it had been put on the Associated Press wire service.

In Florida, segregationists were trying to get *The Three Little Pigs* removed from the public library. Presumably a cheerful, but not naïve, dig at the campaign against the racist storybook *Little Black Sambo*. These were calm times, but they were definitely not cool.

June 1, 1959. RED CHINA KILLS 30 MILLION, MISSIONERS TELL U.S. PROBE. HUAC TESTI-MONY OF CHRISTIAN MISSIONARIES CITES ATROCITIES RIVALING THOSE OF THE BLACK DAYS OF BUCHENWALD

June 1, 1959. HAVANA OVER BUFFALO 5–4 ... The Sugar Kings, who only a month ago were destined to transfer to Jersey City because of public apathy, drew more than 15,000 fans tonight.

The huge turnout for the homecoming was attributed partly to a triumphant road trip but mainly to a publicly inspired drive called Operation Fan.

The crowd didn't cause a proportionate jingle in the cash register, however. Many Havana fans bought season tickets for six dollars apiece when the Sugar Kings were scraping up funds to get the season started.

In my search for historical absolution and the Boy Scout merit badge that search might represent, preparedness, as any tenderfoot could tell you, is all. Havana beat Buffalo, 5–4, as reported in the newspaper of June 1, but the real story is how a budding revolutionary government attempted to make baseball available to its people.

Batista had fled the country six months before. By now Castro had consolidated his position and was still the darling of his patron and provider, the United States of America. He is a baseball fan, and Cuba is a nation of baseball fans. And Castro has made baseball available to the people in a way that it has never been available before.

Cuban baseball had realized naïve democracy—a government was actually acting out the collective will of its people. But this story could not be fit into the cold-war conceptual framework as anything but an unrepresentatively large crowd, padded by Castro with cheap tickets. Never mind the joy of baseball fans, there was no "proportionate jingle in the cash register." The lesson is to notice what is possible if you have a good many years and conclusions between the publication and reading of a particular newspaper. Which is another item in the dossier for absolution.

June 4, 1959. BISONS NIP CUBANS 1–0
(attendance: 5,700 [est.])

June 4, 1959. FOUR MORE ROCKETS BLAST
OFF, MISSED ORBIT SCIENTISTS FEAR

[70]

June 7, 1959. CUBANS BOMB RICKETTS
WITH HOME RUNS (attendance: 5,084)

June 8, 1959. CUBANS CLIP WINGS 2–1 IN
FIRST, CURFEW HALTS SECOND (attendance:
6,159 plus 19,000 children admitted free as part of
Cuba's National Children's Day observance)

June 18, 1959. Color televisions's best friend,
outside of General Sarnoff, is unquestionably the
United States of America. While home color set sales
have yet to be commensurate with wishes of the
makers, government agencies nurture such great interest in the tinted medium that they've urged and
sponsored its appearance in every major country in
the world but Communist China.

June 20, 1959. LAST CIVIL WAR VET, 116,
RALLIES FROM ILLNESS

June 23, 1959. FIRING SUCCESS, BUT VAN-
GUARD FAILS TO ORBIT

July 20, 1959. AMERICAN EXHIBIT NEARLY
READY IN MOSCOW. VICE-PRESIDENT NIXON
TO OPEN SHOW. TOP-QUALITY CONSUMER
GOODS TO SHOW AMERICAN WAY OF LIFE

July 21, 1959. VIRTUAL PRISONER QUITS
BEAUTY REIGN

A shapely redhead from Albuquerque, who de-
fied her Catholic archbishop to enter the Miss Universe contest, abruptly quit today.

Sue Simmons Ingersoll, 22, whose dispute was
over whether it is proper for a Catholic girl to wear
a bathing suit in a public contest, indicated ...

July 22, 1959. ADDITIONAL NEGROES REG-
ISTERED FOR LITTLE ROCK HIGH SCHOOL

And so the summer went. Neither the best of times
nor the worst of times, but setting the stage for a tale of
two cities. It is the eve of the big series between the
Rochester Red Wings and the Havana Sugar Kings. It is
the eve of the first celebration of Cuban Independence
Day. Both events will coincide and interact on the 26th
of July.

[71]

It is one week since Fidel Castro resigned the Cuban premiership to "devote himself to redeveloping Cuban agriculture." A man named Osvaldo Dorticos Torrado is running the government for a week while Castro, as they say in the papers, makes up his mind. The resignation was a ploy which successfully forced out a man called Manual Urrutia, who as president was paying himself the same salary as Batista, $10,000 per month. Castro, still in the process of consolidating his power, will use the impending celebration to announce his official return on July 26.

It is now three weeks since the *Democrat and Chronicle* ran their first anti-Castro editorial, accusing him of condoning communist infiltration. It is one week since they published their own personal finger-wagging warning to Castro, in an editorial titled "Castro Cracking."

July 20, 1959.... Small wonder tourists are staying away in droves, American businessmen are clutching their pocketbooks, and investors are downgrading their Cuban stocks.... Castro must understand the unwritten rule. Don't kick your best customer....

Okay. We know that there is building tension on the eve of the big Independence Day celebration and baseball series. Castro was still pro-American, but American opinion had already begun to drive him to the left, or to allow him to reveal that he always was a leftist, or something. I think that I have learned that I have no idea whatsoever about what's really going on in Havana at this point, since all our information comes from the Rochester newspaper. I realize that it is, in a sense, farcical to attempt to learn history from the local papers, and yet the very structure of my memory is bound by the ludicrous categories of current events created by that specific postwar newspaper mentality. Memory being the central focus, I must stick between these blinders.

[72]

Meanwhile, there is a separate drama unfolding at precisely the same time. On the same Sunday that Fidel Castro resigned, exactly one week before the big series is due to open, Bobby Maduro, owner of the Sugar Kings, tells the press that he is planning to sell his baseball club. He is losing money because nobody is coming to watch a last-place team play. He is Cuban and wouldn't dream of moving the club out of Havana, and therefore will be forced to sell the club at the end of the season (*Democrat and Chronicle*, July 19, 1955).

Two days later, Maduro is summoned by Castro to talk about the future of the club. According to the *Democrat and Chronicle* of July 21, 1959,

> Castro reportedly told Maduro his regime is prepared to carry out his promise of last April to give the Cuban ball team any assistance it needed.

Ever so slowly, the papers are revealing that Fidel Castro is a baseball fan, and that baseball is, in fact, very important in Cuba. This is something that the sports pages have been reluctant to admit, given the mood of the editorial pages and the nature of the feelings growing in the American government.

But some guy named Jerry Burns, of Miami, writing in *The Sporting News* ("Baseball Paper of the World"), was either more ignorant of the emerging official line or more liberal with what he was prepared to leak. The issue is July 29, 1959.

MADURA READY TO SELL: CASTRO OFFERS NEW AID

Fidel Castro has gone to bat for organized baseball in Cuba. Within 48 hours after owner Roberto Maduro of the Cuban Sugar Kings had announced he would quit after this season if he loses money on the club, Castro offered assurance of aid. . . .

"The Sugar Kings are a part of the Cuban people," Castro declared. "It is important for us to have

[73]

a connection with Triple-A ball," the Cuban leader continued. . . .

Two months ago, Maduro was on the verge of giving up. Castro at the time pledged to make certain the Sugar Kings remained in Havana, "even if I have to PEETCH."

The Cuban Tourist Commission provided some funds. The Chief of the Army, Camillo Cienfuegos, bought $10,000 worth of tickets for soldiers, and the Sugar Institute bought time on the radio to help promote the team.

"The Sugar Kings are a part of the Cuban people," Castro said, "even if I have to PEETCH." These are the words of a dedicated baseball fan. Saving the team is a traditional matter of baseball, not of anticapitalism. And yet the American government and its sportswriters couldn't see the need for sympathy in this situation. American baseball fans couldn't be told. What would have been a logical rallying point for pro-Cuban sympathies was simply ignored. A cultural ally was being driven away only for political and economic reasons. This is a cultural blindness, an inflexibility of thought, and a complete misunderstanding of the nature of human relationships, which is what politics is supposed to be about.

Where were my all-knowing objective sportswriters? Where were the professional journalists who made their living by singing the praises of the game they loved? Where was anybody who loved baseball more than his adherence to cold-war ideology? I was just a boy. I kept myself as well-informed as possible, under the circumstances. And fifteen years later, I find out that I was not informed at all. What no one would tell me was that baseball, as well as being America's National Pastime, was a Cuban game. A Cuban obsession, even.

The lack of insight in American foreign policy is legendary. Foreign policy is always made by businessmen, who always see the world primarily as a place to do business. Organized sport, in America, is always business. And business is never sporting. In fact, it is a particular point of pride among the business community to be unsportsmanlike, and in a sense much of America's power has been gained through the inability to recognize sportsmanlike behavior. I mean, if you have no concept of fair play, you don't have to play fair.

In Cuba, baseball was not seen as a business. The bills had to be paid, but, however inconceivable the notion was to American government and sportswriting, the rationale for the Havana team was not the accumulation of profits. Fidel Castro, in terms of his relationship to baseball, was no different from millions of regular Americans. He was a fan. However great the distance between the politics of Fidel Castro and the politics of the regular American baseball fan, they did share one political notion, and that was that baseball was a special case. But the businessmen, politicians, and sportswriters of America insisted, as had Walter O'Malley, that baseball was ordinary business and not a special case. The facts were scattered around, but the story was never put before the people, and the interaction between politics and baseball, in Cuba, remained invisible.

Two items from *The Sporting News* of August 5, 1959, reveal a model for the sportsmanlike interaction between baseball and politics.

Gran Stadium attendance during the week that ended July 10 averaged only around 1,500. Maduro revealed that the gate for July 16 amounted to a mere $690. The following night only about 500 fans turned out as most fans remained at home to hear Premier Fidel Castro's resignation speech on television.

* * *

Premier Fidel Castro has announced that the Cuban government will pay off all debts incurred by the Sugar Kings this season. Owner Bobby Maduro received further good news with the disclosure that the razor-blade company which pulled out as sponsor

[75]

of the Cubans' telecast in 1957 plans to resume sponsorship in 1960.

The government of Cuba had undergone change and upheaval. An unintended consequence of that upheaval was that no one attended the baseball games. Recognizing the baseball team as a special case, and as an innocent victim of political activities, the government, in accordance with fair play, repairs the damage by covering the losses of the baseball team. A simple act of sportsmanship, but of course, one that could never be presented to the American people, and certainly not on the sports pages, God forbid.

That Cuba's government might be sporting, or even just crazy about baseball, was never admitted to, but there was one little ray of theoretical insight. The analysis proved to be so sophisticated that it might just as well have been planted by the CIA, but there was someone with a real sense of what was going on. Sports reporter George Beahon, who covered Red Wing baseball for, of all things, the *Rochester Democrat and Chronicle*, was about to leave Rochester with the team for Havana. A week before the big game, George began his Sunday-morning column with a little item that revealed him as either an incredibly good guesser, an astute analyst, or someone with access to a genuine oracle. The date was July 21, 1959. The item was called "What's New in Havana."

In Havana, the problems are economic with the ball club and with all of Cuba. As for the Red Wings, who spend the coming weekend there, the Sunday, July 26, anniversary date of the revolution's conception promises to be exciting if not hazardous.

Bossman Castro has asked 50,000 citizens to invade Havana from the interior, and to travel with machetes. General feeling of Cubanos toward Americans, whom they consider hypercritical of revolutionary government, is such that a few rum-filled machete wielders could create a serious international incident, and we don't mean the International League.

How George Beahon could possibly know this is grounds for endless speculation. It smells extremely fishy, but it is an incredibly accurate preparation for what was about to happen. In a larger sense, George Beahon missed the boat, but as a sportswriter, he was sitting on a royal flush.

And so the table was set. Without compassion or diplomacy, but with sensitivity, an island of intelligence, played by Cuba, was created in a sea of ignorance. And even the poor little baseball fan, educated into ignorance by his local newspaper, is, at the last minute, provided a shrewdly accurate sense of dramatic expectation. The rekindled desire for understanding linked to baseball, after fifteen years of avoidance and ignorance, is finally on the verge of illumination. The sports pages have begun to yield. Such is the genuine wonder of American Democracy, for whatever that's worth.

The series opened with a game on Friday. The Cubans won 4–3, on two home runs in the eighth inning. The game itself was of secondary importance. The major event was the celebration. Those jubilant, fun-loving Cubans, carrying on as they do, to the fulfillment of North American stereotypical preconceptions, celebrating their revolution. *The Sporting News* (August 5, 1959) presented it as a light program.

26,532 CROWD AT HAVANA, CASTRO PITCHES IN EXHIBITION

The International League's biggest crowd of the season, 26,532, jammed Gran Stadium here, July 24, but the Rochester–Cubans game was strictly a secondary feature.

The banner turnout was attracted by the appearance of Fidel Castro as a pitcher for the "Barbudos" in a special preliminary exhibition game. Trading his political trouble for a uniform of the

Army team, Castro pitched the "Bearded Rebels" to a moral victory over the Military Police in a two-inning match.

Castro, who played some baseball with the University of Havana, fifteen years ago, pitched one inning, striking out two—one with the aid of the umpire. When the arbiter called the batter out on a high, inside pitch, Castro dashed to the plate and shook hands with the ump. In his own turn at bat, Castro bounced out to the shortstop.

Proceeds from the big crowd, less expenses, went to the Cuban agrarian reform movement.

The warm-up proceeded not as a cause for alarm, but rather as a party. The big game took place Saturday night. My unverified memories of listening to the re-created play-by-play on the radio are behind me. The reality I am forced to deal with is Sunday morning's newspaper. In my memories, I am a twelve-year-old baseball fanatic, but the truth turns out to be that I am actually fifteen years old at the time, and hostile to the vestiges of my passion for baseball. I am nine days away from my sixteenth birthday, which in my real world meant that I was nine days away from signing up for my New York State Motor Vehicle Bureau Learner's Permit, one road test away from that all-American rite of passage, my driver's license. I was also nine days away from becoming technically qualified to try out for the Detroit Tigers, but the child who had actively waited for his chance to work out with the Tigers and show them his stuff was nowhere in my mind.

And I know for certain that I was searching out the Sunday-morning paper not for the current events, and not for the sports section, but to check out the classified advertisements to see if there were any clean 1952 Oldsmobiles going cheap.

I had fallen in love with the '52 Oldsmobile as I had previously fallen in love with the Rochester Red Wings.

History was playing another of its practical jokes on my identity. After years and years of preparation, I was about to be taught, by history itself, the universal truth of collective human behavior through baseball. And on that very day I kept my intelligence available only for automobiles, which I could neither drive nor afford. Who could care about baseball or self-understanding when there might be a clean '52 Oldsmobile going cheap? There was no finer deal in the universe of concepts than that Oldsmobile. At the center of the dashboard, where you would expect to find a clock, the five-two Olds had a compass. The notion of compass as standard equipment was as tasty as it was unique. And, eccentrically mounted in the steering wheel, was a wind-up clock. Even before I had my learner's permit, I could see myself behind the wheel of an ethereal, cherry-red, five-two Oldsmobile. With the heel of my right hand around the neck of my sweetheart and the heel of my left hand resting on the ticking clock, I would corner at high speeds. Centrifugal force would throw my sweetheart's body up against mine as we sped along.

I knew, as I approached this particular microfilm reel, that if there was any single newspaper that might explain it all, this was the edition. If it was possible for a newspaper to be lifted from its context, and then reveal itself as art, this was the moment for it to happen.

As I picked up that Sunday-morning newspaper, sixteen years later in the microfilm-reading room, the two moments became one. History was knocking, and I was getting another chance. There were no thoughts of Oldsmobiles and sweethearts, only politics and baseball. This is the day of the hottest sports story of my life, I thought as I cranked my reading machine up to page one. It might have been the hottest sports story of the century if history were reasonable in any view other than the long one, I thought as I adjusted the focus. And here is the morning paper:

[79]

MARINES STORM ONTARIO BEACH
IN WINDUP OF LAKES OPERATION

The lead story is of how 25,000 Rochesterians watched the Marines go through a simulated amphibious atomic attack staged at the beach, which would otherwise have been crowded with bathers. Not nearly as sportsmanlike a gesture as Fidel Castro playing baseball, but in some sense, a compliment to the celebration in Cuba. Cubans celebrating their freedom from the imperialist yoke, and Rochesterians being assured that the army of the empire is demonstrably well-oiled and at the ready.

Beneath this assurance of America's military preparedness:

HE ADMIRES IKE, KHRUSHCHEV SAYS
AT NIXON DINNER. MRS. NIXON GIVES
SICK CHILDREN LOLLIPOPS, GUM, AT
MOSCOW HOSPITAL

And at the top of the page, in the right-hand corner, and obviously a bit late in arriving:

BULLET HITS VERDI
IN CUBAN BALLGAME

Frank Verdi, coaching at third base for the Rochester Red Wings, was grazed by a "July 26 Celebration" stray bullet early today. The Wings immediately walked off the field with the score tied 4–4 after eleven innings.

Havana shortstop Leo Cardenas was also hit by another stray bullet. Neither player was injured seriously, the bullet not breaking the skin.

An outbreak of stray firing in Gran Stadium began shortly after midnight, the beginning of the anniversay of the July 26 Movement. Many troops were in the stand, some carrying tommy guns and side arms.

And that is the entire story. The Red Wings refused to play the double-header scheduled for Sunday and left the country as soon as they could. Umpire Frank Guzetta refused to work the double-header, even if it cost him his job. He left the country as well.

Much was made of the fact that Verdi was wearing a plastic helmet liner which saved his life. Red Wing manager Cot Deal, who was ejected from the game shortly before the shooting, went so far as to claim that, since he did not wear a helmet liner and would have been coaching at third base if he had not been thrown out, his life was saved by his loss of temper.

In the aftermath of the game, umpires revealed that they wanted to call the game when the crowd went out of control in the top of the eleventh inning. But with the home team two runs behind, they feared the consequences of postponement, and play proceeded. When the Sugar Kings tied the game in the bottom of the eleventh, civil disobedience broke loose.

The Red Wing management was clearly frightened, but they didn't know what to do. Frank Horton, still president of the club, was away on vacation in Old Forge, New York, but he managed to abandon his rocking chair and insect repellent long enough to telephone Havana and tell his team to leave. And they did.

The Cubans, characteristically sporting, saw the whole thing as a baseball game. More angry than conciliatory, they felt the incident had been greatly exaggerated. Maduro said, in Monday morning's paper,

> If the umpires and [Red Wing General Manager] George Sisler did not exaggerate their reports to Frank Horton, this would not have happened.
>
> All these years nothing has ever happened to any team in Cuba. How can Sisler or anybody else so misconstrue a show like we are having here; it's like the Fourth of July in the States. You can't control things like this.
>
> Rochester's refusal to play today will damage baseball in Cuba, in our league, and baseball everywhere.

Prophetic words, maybe. But at the time, the most pessimistic interpretation available was merely that seeds of fear and mistrust of foreign behavior had been planted in the far from influential interest group of minor-league baseball. And that is the very worst. Within twenty-four hours, the incident was being revised in tones bordering on frivolity. The *Democrat and Chronicle* of Monday morning was careful to point out that "Verdi wobbled, but he did not fall."

Columnist George Beahon, whose insights seem trustworthy for the moment, was considerably cooled out in his on-the-spot dispatch, also appearing in Monday's paper (July 27, 1959).

> ...Was the danger that prompted the Red Wings to refuse to finish the series today and pull out of Cuba several hours ahead of schedule real, or imagined, or exaggerated? The answer to that question is not easy. ...

He goes on to say that the hotheaded Cubans may not have been dangerous, and certainly there was no intent to do harm.

By the end of the week, *The Sporting News* was taking the line of business-as-usual. The box score of the game had a tiny "x" next to the eleventh inning and, at the very bottom, the legend "called on account of gunfire from the stands" (August 5, 1959).

The official story gave the event as low a profile as possible. The business-as-usual line required the judgment that it was correct for the Red Wings to leave, as it would be correct for future teams to play out their scheduled games in Havana.

INT'L WILL PLAY OUT HAVANA SKED
DESPITE SHOOTING, SHAG DECIDES.
"NO OFFICIAL PROTEST" SAYS LOOP
PREXY AFTER RULING, WINGS SHAKEN
BY GUNFIRE

According to the story, the president of the International League, Frank "Shag" Shaughnessy, with a suitably pompous and courtly manner, ruled that "Ballplayers should not be exposed to any more danger than the natural hazards of the sport."

Therefore, the Rochester team had done right. A few days later he decided, in far less ceremonial tones, that the Havana schedule would have to be completed: "I have had no official protest from any of our other clubs, and I am not planning to call a special meeting of the board of directors because no one has asked me for one."

As the sense of crisis passed, the tone of the newspapers changed from light programing to outright comedy. My father had taught me, at a very young age, that nobody likes a wiseass. And now the newspapers were making fun of my wisdom. This gave me doubts, but it did not put me off. I knew that an almost unbelievable story was being told in a completely unbelievable way. I knew, with my sense of history, that the function of humor in the news from Cuba was to demonstrate the archetypical behavior of an un-self-conscious imperialist mentality. Classic insecurity, classic paternalism, and a classic example of institutionally supported bias overcoming the reality of events, in the testimony of eyewitnesses.

I shifted to the *New York Times*, and in the special dispatch from Tad Szulc on July 27, 1959, I found an even deeper commitment to the lightness of it all.

GAY CUBANS HAIL CASTRO'S TRIUMPH

HAVANA. Cuba's bedraggled but proud rebel army paraded today in happy confusion before its idolized leader, Dr. Fidel Castro.

It was as gay and casual a military event as has ever been witnessed here. . . .

There was little attempt to keep in step, although the bands, one playing "Stars and Stripes Forever," and the other breaking briefly into "Jingle Bells," helped pace the soldiers. . . .

Yesterday, baseball was part of the celebration. Frank Verdi, who was coaching at third base for the Rochester Red Wings in a game against the Cuban Sugar Kings at the Gran Stadium, was struck by a spent bullet. . . .

Tragedy would have to wait until next year to be a current event. The shooting of Frank Verdi was strictly comic. Even Frank himself got into the act: "If that bullet had been two inches to the left, the boys on the ball club would have had to chip in five dollars apiece for flowers."

George Beahon said: "The chariot scenes from *Ben Hur* would have suffered in comparison to the sight of players from both dugouts and bullpens exercising the grand old military maneuver of 'getting the hell out of there.' "

A local hotelier said: "This will set the tourist trade back another six months."

The media had decided on gentle judgments. Yes, the Cuban army lacked training and discipline. Yes, the crowd was excessively emotional, but no evil of any consequence resulted. No such happening should ever take place again, but at the same time, this was a first-ever independence-day celebration, and strictly a one-of-a-kind. The final decision was that there were no future dangers threatening this ongoing business enterprise, and therefore no new safeguards needed to be installed.

One week later the Red Wings received a cable from Captain Felipe Guerra Matos, director of sports for Cuba.

REGRET UNFORTUNATE INCIDENT DUE EXCLU-
SIVELY TO DEMONSTRATION OF JOY AND FEELING OF
FREEDOM STAGED BY OUR PEOPLE SIMILAR TO FOURTH
OF JULY IN U.S. CAN ASSURE YOU YOUR TEAM WILL BE

GRANTED IN FUTURE ALL COURTESIES AND SAFETY
MEASURES AS HERETOFORE.

Formal apology was extended and accepted. The
incident was closing, and no grudges were retained, according to the reality that the newspapers had chosen to
present. George Beahon, who earned his living by writing
about the Rochester Red Wings for a partisan audience,
certainly had to be the most loyal of Red Wing fans.
Within two weeks of the shooting, he had bent his column
far enough backward to have swung his objectivity almost behind the Cubans. On August 6, he said,

HAVANA, OKAY

Immediately after the recent Red Wing escapade
in Havana, there arose a gosh-awful howl from exactly six International League points. In Montreal,
Toronto, Miami, Richmond, Columbus, and Buffalo,
field managers and/or general managers were loud
in not wanting any more part of Havana. Several
were quoted flatly as saying they would not return
to Havana.

Not until Tuesday, that is, when Montreal,
Toronto, etc. will roll back into Gran Stadium on
schedule. Some of the loudest squawkers following
the July 26 shoot-em-up have claimed misquote.
Others have simply changed their minds.

George Sisler, Jr., Frank Horton, Cot Deal, and
Frank Verdi have chosen not to hang up Cuban
clubowner Bobby Maduro, who might be under ter-
rific pressure from Fidel Castro. The Rochester people tabbed it a "spontaneous one-day incident that
should never happen again providing the league does
not schedule in Cuba again on July 26." Even Verdi,
the near-victim, now says, "If we play in Havana,
I'll be with my ball club."

Judging from cables received by International
League clubs from Cuban government officials, the
Cubans are still blushing over the gunfire incident.

... Not just incidentally, those International League officials who hollered the loudest after the Rochester incident are amongst the same league directors who six years ago begged Havana to join the International League. These same directors later insisted on having their travel costs paid to Cuba; even later, they demanded and received an $800 per diem guarantee in Havana while they hand the Sugar Kings a $200 per diem guarantee here.

No one can say for sure, but it appears here that the Rochester group, which could have fronted a movement to ruin Maduro in the eyes of his new government, and could have pressured Havana right out of the league, instead has kept Havana in the International League. It would have been a simple thing for the Rochester entry to lead a stampede movement.

Now it is up to the Cuban government officials, whose recent cables indicate extreme concern, to execute both preventative and corrective measures. They were thoughtless and stubborn last July 25–26.

How neat and clean it all is, if you trust the newspapers. And how close to the brink of self-abnegation my self-understanding of my memory has been driven. I must remind myself to go about these things more slowly, and to remember that the newspapers are not to be judged, but to be analyzed as vehicles of a historic mentality. And I must remember to save my anger for the present, which out of context will probably feel worse.

There remained, however, one small piece of the puzzle that didn't fit. On the first of August, the same day that the Red Wings received the apologetic cable from Captain Matos, Cot Deal resigned as manager of the Red Wings.

They had been playing badly, and attendance at Red Wing Stadium had been slipping commensurately. The Red Wings lost to the Columbus Jets and fell to last place in the league standings on the night that Cot Deal's resignation was accepted. Buried in the *Democrat and*

Chronicle's story of the game was a one-sentence statement from Deal saying that he had offered his resignation five days earlier, but it had been rejected. Five days earlier was the morning after the night before, when Frank Verdi was shaken by gunfire. Now it seems rather strange that after three years of being Rochester Community Baseball's first and only manager, Cot Deal would both have his resignation accepted and be mentioned, by name, in George Beahon's column for his exemplary gesture of forgiveness to the Cubans. And it seems even more strange that he would offer his resignation because the team was losing, on the very day after his substitute was shot. It is very much as if someone were refusing to obey future orders to return to Havana, even if it meant banishment forever from Red Wing Stadium.

The offices of the International League and the Rochester Red Wings were filled with self-congratulations. Havana had just moved into second place and was closing in on the pennant. And somewhere hearts were gay, but there was no joy in cellar-dwelling Rochester on the day Cot Deal resigned. The gloom is, however, open to all kinds of theoretical speculation.

Organized Baseball, as the papers call it, appears to have acted quite admirably thus far. They have added glory to themselves and dashed my fantasies of crusade. But before getting carried away with praise, it is important to go back and remember that Organized Baseball is a business, and that none of the teams in the International League was prosperous enough to write off even a small part of the season, since the whole show runs on customers parting with their money. In those days, minor-league teams traveled primarily by bus. The season was divided between long road trips and long home stands. The northern swing was Rochester–Buffalo or Syracuse–Toronto–Montreal and back, all cozy motor-vehicle distances. The southern swing was Columbus–Richmond–Miami–Havana. Financially, it was not so

[87]

simple to miss a beat. Business-as-usual was at stake. And money was far more important than a spent bullet grazing a temple and bruising an ear.

It is also important to remember that in acting from a position of power, you never take drastic action at a time of crisis. And you never have to, because your own existence is never in question; that is what it means to be dealing from a position of power. The pose of the powerful is never hysteria, but rather a calm scheming for a return to the status quo. A position of power desires only more of the same.

Besides, Fidel Castro still appealed to the American sensibility at this point. Something of a frontiersman, but with a Ph.D. in law. He was a popular hero figure at home, without embarrassing the democratic and libertarian fantasies of the rulers of the American empire. Compared with Batista, Castro looked like a piece of apple pie, and he was certainly a man you could do business with. Of course, anybody could be forced to do business with the United States, or so it seemed, but Castro was also a rare and special breed of Latin American potentate. He could give brilliant lectures at fancy East Coast American universities. And that was a rare potentate in those days.

It would have been very unusual for the baseball business to have acted differently. My faded and shoddy memory is as naïve as it is inaccurate. But Cot Deal wasn't ever going back to Havana. Maybe he knew something. And maybe, in between my transfixing dreams of Oldsmobiles and sweethearts, I did too. Something happened in Havana that demoralized my once beloved baseball team. Insults were forming in my subconscious that would not surface until years of forgetfulness cleared the coast. Passions were subduing intellect in the deepest hollows of my mind, and a lie was being formed in all innocence.

August 13, 1959. LITTLE ROCK INTEGRATES
5, POLICE QUELL JEERING MOBS

[88]

August 14, 1959. GIANT TITAN BLOWS UP;
THREE MISSILES LAUNCHED

August 20, 1959. COWBOY GENE AUTRY EN-
TERTAINS THOUSANDS AT MONROE COUNTY
FAIR
. . . riding his horse of equal renown, Champion.

August 21, 1959. KENNEDY FRONT RUN-
NER IN POLLS, SET TO TOSS HAT IN RING
FORMALLY

August 22, 1959. . . . advancing in years, now
she's 25, Brigitte Bardot would now like to trade her
"sex kitten" motion picture roles for more difficult
parts. . . .

September 3, 1959. THREE CHICAGO DE-
TECTIVES ACCUSED IN NARCOTICS RING
INDICTMENTS

September 5, 1959. RED WINGS SPLIT WITH
CUBANS AS THEY END THEIR '59 HOME
SEASON

And so the baseball season ended. The Havana Sugar
Kings, having survived business failure and unruly be-
havior in the stadium, went on to win the Governor's
Cup Playoffs and the Junior World Series. The Red
Wings finished fifth, fifteen and a half games behind.

The Frank Verdi shooting was remembered, but
dormant. Baseball was able to deal with the incident
easily. A swift, orderly, disciplined series of judgments
and statements left all concerned shaking hands, smiling,
and feeling proud of themselves.

In my mind, the Frank Verdi shooting incident took
a different course. It disappeared from active memory
almost immediately, whereupon it fell prey to the crafting
of my fantasies.

A generation raised on Hollywood and television
melodramas becomes quite skilled at swapping plots and
characters to suit personal preferences. An average
evening's viewing requires that this be done several

[89]

times. And I, a genuine war baby, had fallen into the habit of unconsciously swapping plots.

And far away from reason, judgment, or even consciousness, the memory was reworked. Frank Verdi and the Red Wings became Rochester and all it stood for. Dour, serious, staid, religious, hard-working, hardhearted, honorable, but emotionally bankrupt Rochester. And the Havana Sugar Kings and their unruly fans became the passionate guardians of revolution. And the courageous soldiers of liberty, who knew neither emotional nor political restraint, chased the repressed, serious, tightwad businessmen off the field. Like the Lone Ranger chasing away the rustlers, or the moralism of Marxist ideology chasing away a fascination for the daily events of the baseball season, or the political travesties portrayed on the front page chasing away the sports section in newspaper reading.

Always morality chasing evil in the name of truth. At the same time that I cannot stop this, the newspapers are teaching me that the truth is something that shifts and changes with the pressures of the moving present. The truth, unlike judgment, is not decisive. Moral judgment is self-assurance, the truth is part of life's insecurities.

Time passes, no matter what psychological preferences demand. Planets change position, obscure species of insects appear and disappear, icecaps melt, and human beings grow old. However subtle the daily changes, these things do happen, undeniably. And I am left behind, stuck in the library. The microfilm-reading machine has paralyzed my body and caused balloons filled with light bulbs to bubble from my brain. This particular baseball has become an obsession.

What could possibly be happening to me? I wondered, and in response, I looked for the patterns of effects. Even a pretentious desire to know reality must admit to effects as the only common reality. Eyewitnesses

[90]

quarrel endlessly, but they agree that what really matters is the facts.

And the facts are that I arrived in Rochester, and thanks to the particular curve of the nose dive of the postwar era, found myself mentally awake, morally straight, and emotionally prepared to make contact with the past and force it to yield its meaning. Ignorant of any notion of method, but driven by intention, I closeted myself in the library, not unlike the patients in the dentist's waiting room who read medical magazines in an attempt both to prepare for and be distracted from the unknown events soon to follow.

There I was, in the library. Safe from imperialism, capitalism, and life. Warm, cozy, and separate. Institutionalized, but nothing like a total institution. Prisons and mental hospitals remind you that you have been removed from the possibility of genuine social interaction. Confinement symbolizes not only punishment for having broken the rules, but also not being allowed to play any more.

And while there is no comfort in isolation, there is no place more comfortable than the public library. The library removes the possibility of social interaction, but it provides instead a parody of its most serious aspects, namely, the celebration of material consumption. The public library, of course, is capitalism without fangs. They never send the bills and you never keep the books, and so the ceremony can be endlessly repeated. And in its repetition, any derelict can instill in himself a sense of work, duty, and accomplishment. And there I found myself, in the company of other ambitious vagrants whose wounded identities needed meaning, working feverishly. Investigating.

I was investigating my memories, the newspapers, baseball, and any distinction I could make among them. But my memories were within me, not on the microfilm. And the newspapers were business, not historical record. That left baseball.

And what does baseball know of love, or realization, or power, or longing? Where is the emotional content in baseball? Where is the heart? Sitting all those days in the library, instilled with a sense of urgency by baseball. And baseball, in matters of the heart, knows neither pleasure nor pain. The obsession with baseball is an obsession for information without emotional content. Abstracted, historical, folksy, and sentimental information, but always reducible to matters of fact. Where everyday life would produce feelings, baseball produces only loyalties. And even those are the particular aestheticized loyalties of the interested outsider, who plays no part in determining the outcome of the activity.

Americans could accept black baseball players before they could accept black people. In the early postwar era, when racism ran high in white America, it became reasonable to allow a black man to become a major-league baseball player, and even a star. As long as he could obey the rules, perform the feats, and be available for statistical analysis, he could play. Baseball fans didn't mind that Jackie Robinson was black. Baseball fans worship the players, but they never make contact. All fans are partisan, some extremely so, but they can never help or hinder their team. Not that anyone would choose to have it otherwise, but in the world of baseball, unrequited love is the only kind there is. Baseball is always the pornographic fantasy of love without consequence.

And there I was tracking Frank Verdi and the Havana Sugar Kings attendance figures, and avoiding the real question of what I am doing here.

On my way home from the library, I would stop at Sammy's. We had traveled to Rochester together, he for his father's retirement, I for my housepainting. But we both know that behind those transparent justifications lay our own embarrassed desires for an old-fashioned home-town visit, which we knew was no longer possible. Somehow, the dilemmas of who we were and what we were doing in Rochester got swept aside and funneled

[92]

into our own dreams and hopes and plans for the final
solutions to the problems posed by the shooting of Frank
Verdi.

Sammy and I would sit in his back yard and plan
the great rapprochement between Red Wings and Sugar
Kings. The conversation wavered between serious discussions of the sugar quota and planning the cigar attack on Red Wing Stadium.

"Some things are too important to be taken seriously." Sammy had borrowed that line from a singer,
but he was prepared to live by it. I, on the other hand,
leaned increasingly toward seriousness. After an exhausting and astounding day at the library, I would
measure the growth of my writing blister and the inability of my eyes to stop compensating for the movements in the focus of the microfilm machine. And by
then, I wanted my sacrifice to be for history and for
identity, not for fun.

The fantasy between us was dividing along emerging lines. I wanted to understand the meaning that my
life, thus far, demonstrated; Sammy wanted the best
possible conversation. Not necessarily contradictory goals,
but that was no matter since whatever I resolved, Sammy
would dangle his elegant fantasies in front of my weary
eyes, and I would indulge both him and them.

"How much could a last-place team cost?" Sammy
would ask rhetorically. "The Pawtucket Red Sox are in
last place. We could buy them up."

"With what?" I asked, and Sammy's face lit up.

"We establish our contacts and fly down to Cuba.
We'll talk to Castro himself. We can arrange that. And
then, with some carefully laundered Cuban money, we
can quietly buy up the Pawtucket Red Sox.

"And then" (Sammy has a habit of pausing for
excruciating lengths of time) "and then, when the State
Department makes its move, and offers Cuba a combination weenie roast and baseball detente rematch, Castro
could smile coldly and announce that he was already in

possession of his franchise, and ready to play. Uniforms, sewn up in the underworld and hidden beneath left field, would be dug up. Cuban players would be flown in. And overnight, the Havana Sugar Kings would be reborn."

I could never dismiss these evenings of political baseball dreaming as mere recreation, but neither could I sustain the dream. Each evening, I would lie in bed awaiting sleep and basking in the glory of the proposed surreal and highly imaginative political activity. And each morning I would awake, having returned to my serious mode. As time passed, it seemed more and more like morning, whatever the time of day.

And so I plodded on. There weren't that many newspapers left to read. My familiarity with the *Democrat and Chronicle*'s sports section was dampening my faith in my ability to find poetry, but my accumulation of past commitment wouldn't let me go home. That single sentence of such absolute beauty, clarity, and power that it would spring me to consciousness and understanding hadn't been in any of the previous reels. It was getting harder and harder to believe that it might be somewhere in next season's sports pages but I kept searching.

From the beginning to the end, I remained dedicated, obsessed, and compulsive. I never developed the courage to reflect and decide, but a growing fear coexisted with my desire. Perhaps the *Democrat and Chronicle* wasn't that kind of place. Perhaps it had no song to sing me.

Besides, I had my own Cuban detente fantasies. They were my own and seemed to come from inside of me. But the Cuban detente fantasy industry was expanding faster than the marketplace. There was about to be a glut. Interviews with Fidel Castro were lining up for network television. United States Congressmen were taking junkets to Havana. Even baseball was no longer my own fantastic province.

In 1961, young Luis Tiant left his home in Cuba to seek his fortune as a baseball player in the United States.

Luis was talented and fortunate. All the years that I spent ignoring baseball, Luis Tiant spent rising through the ranks in baseball, and suffering the cruel whims of consequence in politics. Now he is a star pitcher for the Boston Red Sox. Now he is a professional athlete and a famous American. Commensurate with that position, Luis Tiant is entitled to have everything he ever wanted. And he would have that if not for the odd personal effects that politics sometimes cause. All that Luis Tiant really wanted was for his parents to see him pitch. And all these years, this simple desire was thwarted for reasons of intentional political ignorance. An embargo was an embargo, and not so much as one baseball player's mother would be allowed to slip through.

And suddenly, Luis Tiant, Sr., is sitting at the baseball stadium in Boston, watching his son, star hurler Luis Tiant, Jr., getting blasted by some no-account team from California. And it turns out that the elder Tiant threw out the first ball, doffed his baseball cap to the crowd, and shook hands with all sorts of big shots, and it was all over the newspapers. Luis Tiant, Sr., had been a pitcher for the New York Cubans of the old Negro American League from 1927 to 1948, and he was welcomed back as a baseball insider as well as a celebrity.

Luis Tiant had not seen his parents since the imposition of the sugar embargo. Last victims of the cold war, first beneficiaries of detente, the Tiant family had been reunited. The State Department was meddling in my territory. And the New York Cubans of the Negro League were destroying my confidence in the depth of my own esoterica. Swift and decisive action was all that I could think of for myself, but first I would have to finish in the library.

Some evenings, I was fortunate enough to be only human, and left the library at dusk. Then, at Sammy's arrangement, we would go around and visit old friends who had remained in Rochester. They were people I once knew well, and whom I now approached as a stranger.

On alternate evenings, Sammy and I visited Walmbs
and Corky, those who stayed behind. Corky had been to
the Peace Corps and Vietnam, and Walmbs had been to
countless hockey games in Boston, but in terms of the
no-nonsense concept of domicile, they had never left
Rochester.

It was about fifteen years ago that, after two nights
of being listed in missing-persons reports, Walmbs
turned up, recognized by a police car for speeding, reckless driving, driving without headlights, and resisting
arrest, on the night he tried to outwit the police by driving through the golf course. It was Corky who had side-
swiped the station wagon of a vacationing family between
Scranton and the New York State border and who, in
court the next morning, pleaded innocent on the grounds
that he was asleep at the time.

Of course, these escapades happened years ago, when
we were all young and exuberant. They were not recalled
on our visits. Those who stayed behind were settled family men now. Walmbs was a machine repairer at Rochester
Products, the Rochester branch of General Motors, where
this year they were making carburetors. After years of
manufacturing brake-line tubing, the carburetor business
suddenly seemed more lucrative, and the shift was made.
Carburetors were in short supply, and Rochester Products
was coasting through hard times in typical Rochester
fashion, unscathed. Corky was a carpenter, now unemployed, but he still had an expensive racing car left over
from better days. He was not complaining.

Both Walmbs and Corky had spent the postwar era
in far more traditional ways than I, sowing wild seeds
in youth, then giving diligent attention to jobs paying
the highest wages for manual work in the history of
mankind. Walmbs had spent several years in the drafting
rooms of the design department at General Motors, but
he had given up design to pursue his first love, machine
repair. It was a financial sacrifice, but Walmbs had fol-

lowed his heart. Even after the financial sacrifice, Wamsly was earning five times as much as I had in my "peak years." Such was the material expectation of ordinary citizens who matured in the postwar era.

Both Walmbs and Corky had lived in Rochester for all of the fifteen years that I had been gone. And where I had expected to find a pride, I found an uneasy embarrassment. Each apologized for still living in Rochester. I had gone away and they had not. But I was now a public charge, subsisting on New York State Unemployment Insurance Benefits, and no candidate for envy. What they did envy was that I had gone to Washington, and New York City, and had lived in Europe. They had let their youthful years slip by as they earned large sums of money in Rochester, and they wished that they had traveled as I had.

And so we sat, discussing hockey games, traffic accidents, and the people and automobiles of the days when we knew each other better. I envied the continuity, if not the stability, of their lives. And they envied the sights I must have seen as I moved from place to place.

We had acted in opposite fashion, and yet these old friends had no more roots or home than I did. They didn't even have the dream. The Rochester of the postwar era, so carefully preserved in my memory, by absence had been continually revised in their minds to deal with changing present circumstances. They laughed when I suggested the Towpath Inn for a beer, and the Twenty-Five Club for a hamburger. Those places had been closed for ten years.

Walmbs spoke of his desire to leave Rochester. He had tried to transfer to the General Motors plant in Australia so that he could both travel and retain his eight years of seniority. At General Motors, it's thirty years and out. Walmbs could retire at the age of fifty-one and he knew it. But now hard times have hit the automobile industry, and there are no vacancies in Australia. Walmbs has resigned himself to waiting for a transfer

[97]

to the radiator factory in Lockport, New York, which will at least be calm and quiet after the hubbub of Rochester.

I absorbed stories from Walmbs and Corky and waited for a point of contact that never occurred. We didn't live in the same world any more. The notion of job seniority always seemed a joke to me. And here was Walmbs, living in a world where seniority was of greater value than mobility. It was a world where it was possible to circle the earth and still keep the same job on the assembly line. It was a truly mobile society, a truly pervasive empire, and a brand of wanderlust that was not my own.

I could not console either Corky or Walmbs. I had left and they had stayed, but there was a lesson we shared. This time geography didn't make any difference. Working for General Motors, or the State Department, or eating berries in the forest: it was all the same because we carried whatever it was with us, and when the reality of historical events continued to wear it away, it disappeared.

War babies were raised in a mass society, consciousness was collective. And when that consciousness disappeared, even for those who stayed home, it disappeared. And we only recognized it when it was gone.

And all of this understanding was what I shared with Walmbs and Corky, and probably even with my family, but it could not be discussed. Each time I pointed out an anachronistic feature of the postwar era, or a salient change characteristic of the new age, I was interrupted and swept away by a defensive hospitality. A piece of pickled fish, a bottle of beer, or a glass of tea, and didn't I want a piece of mandel bread or a graham cracker to go with it. No one was ever puzzled, no one gave me an argument, and no one threw me out. But everyone thought that memory was strictly functional, history strictly academic, and baseball only for children. Any evidence to the contrary was greeted with a blank. What I had to say was incomprehensible. And so I bid them all goodbye and reassured myself of the necessity of going it, if not in the isolation of the microfilm-reading room, at least alone.

An historical era is identified when everyone has felt its effects. The postwar era is unusual in that it ended so suddenly. We have come to identify it not by its effects, but by our realization of the significance of events that happened a long time ago.

It was two years ago that I waited in line with sixty-six other automobiles at the gas station, and felt that neither the American spirit nor the American economy would survive this introduction to the notion of shortage. The cold war mentality which had built and administered an empire rested on the knowledge that more and better of everything would always be available. This was the emotional basis for our cultural considerations of the reasonable limits of everyday life. When it came to material abundance, everyday life in the postwar era was totally beyond the pale. Out of bounds to a point of instability.

My assumption was that the material security of the postwar economy had cracked, and the emotional security of the American consciousness would follow quite quickly. But it never happened. Instead, people simply adjusted to the uneasiness, and I did too.

And then I had a dream, and I understood in a new way that an era had ended. I was driving south on the New York State Thruway, just past Albany. It was a hot summer afternoon. I was doing about seventy-five miles an hour. In my rear-view mirror, I noticed the shadow of something moving up behind me, very fast. As it sped past me, I looked out of my window and saw the knee of an enormous dinosaur. It was as large as a commercial airplane, its skin was all wet and shiny, and its eyes were determined. A huge leather harness connected the shoulders of the front legs, as well as the rear legs and wings, to a tractor-trailer it was pulling.

[99]

Although conforming to the laws of the New York State Traffic code, and practicing lane discipline, the beast seemed totally lacking in grace and coordination. It was simply through size and sheer power that it maintained a speed of what must have been well over a hundred miles an hour. And there was no driver, so this thing knew where it was going.

As this vehicle lumbered past me, I noticed the lettering on the side of the trailer. Beautifully painted in ornate victorian letters it said, The Great Atlantic and Pacific Tea Company. What moments before had been an ordinary drive was suddenly shattered.

The threat of economic disaster had been beaten at its own game, I dreamed. An unscrupulous Samoan teenager, employed as a runner for a tropical-fish smuggler, fell asleep on the Greyhound bus enroute to a tropical-fish store in Miami Beach, Florida. The four tiny obscure-species lizards he was carrying escaped.

The lizards multiplied and became the menace of Florida. They hopped from pond to pond, eating everything in sight and multiplying. When they finally began to group and head north, people began to take notice of them. The biologists, astrophysicists, and plastic surgeons got interested. The lizards were captured and examined. They were studied and experimented upon. Failure alternated with success in the experiments, but eventually a source of capital was located, and the lizards were bred and domesticated. And slowly they began to replace the internal-combustion engine.

I awoke dry, but in a metaphorical clamminess that always accompanies fear without sweat. I had dreamed a dream of the next era. The vision conveyed by my dream showed my acceptance of the kind of drastic solutions that have characterized the American approach for the last century. Solutions to environmental, economic, and social problems are found through drastic and even startling change, just as they have always been. Only in this dream, it was I who was locked into the postwar consciousness. I was the one who feared the extremes to which new directions might be taken. Convention had blinded my imagination, and my dream was reminding me of that.

Asleep or even awake, I didn't know what was coming next. So constrained was I by my postwar roots, that I felt no instinctive or emotional bias. It no longer seemed unlikely that the domesticated dinosaur would be the new direction for technology. I was the creature of another era, and my instincts could no longer be trusted.

In the postwar era, change was always good. There was the trauma that goes with every change, but we braved that knowing that when the trauma was over we would be changed and we would be better. And so we changed our hair-dos, our diets, our machines, and we changed our culture. We replaced Hollywood with the music business. We replaced art history with Hollywood. We replaced a weekend in Miami Beach with drugs. And for religious affiliation, we substituted diet. Chance acquaintances became family as we changed cities and commitments with frequency. And even where we couldn't change institutions, we changed the social roles within them. And each cultural shift has been accompanied by changes in the structure of our social relationships, with each of these structural changes causing traumas. And even these traumas are minimal when compared to the ravages that pure change brought with the extended rearrangement of our families, our friends, and our lovers. We changed all of the people we knew, and the places we knew them. By the end of the postwar era, we had too many distinct peoples, and places, and relationships to even hold them all in memory. Emotional abundance, which seemed such a good idea one magical summer, took us to the brink of madness.

Now that the era has ended, and its consequences have backed up on one another, we are left trying to search our hearts and understand how we ever came to be here. As the postwar era was characterized by limitless dreams and frustration, so this new era is one of limitless fantasy, no dreams, and exhaustion. The breakdown of technology, once a sociological postulate, is now a practical problem of everyday life. Destiny has become less manageable, and consequently life has become less anxious, less complicated, and more difficult. And in these times it seems perfectly acceptable to crave the relief of baseball.

The political drama of the postwar era is in hibernation. The culture survived, substantially more weary than before. The supreme sacrifice of moral confrontation, we can now see, was energy and optimism. I was able to maintain my defenses throughout the postwar era, but I now became, once again, vulnerable to baseball. Weary souls were seeking no more than amusement. Tired and discouraged people didn't seek transcendence, they sought escape. Given the state of the culture, what could be bad about baseball?

One evening, Sammy and I went to a Red Wing baseball game. Some things had changed and some hadn't, but the experience was baseball, and mainly as I had always known it. The field was real grass and as perfectly manicured as I remembered it from childhood. The scoreboard was traditional rather than electronic. The score was told in painted fluorescent letters and numerals, just as it had always been.

The uniforms were new, now much more like sexy pajamas and much less the casual plus fours of my childhood. The change in uniform style often makes the big-leaguers I see on television seem like baseball astronauts, but in Rochester the no-buttons, no-fly, clinging double-knit uniforms illustrated only the acceptance of that seamy side of life that used to be known, but denied.

The Rochester Red Wings hosted the Charleston Charlies, whom I had never heard of. A quick glance at the program and I realized that except for the Red Wings and the Syracuse Chiefs, who were out of the league when

I left it, I had never heard of any of the teams in the league. Tidewater Tides, Toledo Mud Hens, Memphis Blues. Not only no Havana Sugar Kings, but no Miami Marlins, no Columbus Jets, no Canadian teams, and no Buffalo. Mobility and change had cut deeply into the geography of the International League, as they had into all of life.

If I had been a bit more trusting of the elegance of the universe and the grand order of it all, I would have known exactly who the Charleston Charlies were. They came to Charleston, West Virginia, in 1962, when a deal with San Juan, Puerto Rico, fell through. The year before, they played under the name of the Jersey City Jerseys, and drew only 62,000 fans for the season. Jersey City is no place for a baseball team. In fact, Jersey City would never have had a baseball team, except that in the middle of the 1960 season, clumsy cold-war politics stumbled into Cuba, and the Havana Sugar Kings had to be put somewhere safe, quickly. And Jersey City was both available and committed to capitalism.

Here were the coconspirators, with the metaphorical culmination of their plot taking place before their very eyes, and they, being both ignorant and caught up in a baseball game, were not even noticing. I hadn't thought of genealogy, so I didn't recognize the Havana Sugar Kings twice reborn. Thus, I didn't know enough to declare this game for detente.

It was baseball without implication. Even baseball in ignorance. But it was good baseball.

The Red Wings scored a run in the first inning, but by the fourth inning were behind 2–1. They continually threatened to tie the score and left two men on base in the third, sixth, and eighth innings. Both pitchers pitched complete games. The Red Wings lost, 2–1, but there was some very nifty baseball to drop in on after fifteen years.

The circumstances of the game startled me in unexpected ways. Who were these grown men, still playing

[103]

minor-league baseball after television, airplanes, and changing values made its existence nonviable? They didn't look as young and carefree as I thought they would, and what else were they doing here? What does it mean to be batting .220 in the minor leagues, now that the postwar era has come and gone? The minor leagues as preparation is not available justification to a lousy hitter. And there are plenty of lousy hitters in the minor leagues. The only possible explanation for the situation is a love of baseball. It still exists. There is still a baseball without fame or money or a demand for advertising endorsements. In the era of millionaire athletes, there are still professionals who are playing simply because they love the game more than they love shifting crates at the local warehouse, even if the pay is less and the work is seasonal.

The reality was more interesting than the explanation. Here was a hokey small-time operation, flourishing long after I had accepted the decree prohibiting all hokey small-time operations.

I had been away a long time, and things hadn't changed much at Red Wing Stadium. And because they hadn't, the place was as strange and exotic as a Trans-Siberian Railroad café in Vladivostok. Strange not because it was unfamiliar, but because it was out of the past, and did not fit the cultural context.

I enjoyed the game, and I enjoyed being in the stadium. I took great pleasure in marking the little boxes in the scorecard with the baseball shorthand I hadn't used since childhood.

And there was a special comfort I took in the joy of the event. I knew how to keep score, I knew where the toilet was, and I knew how to speak the language. I was a seasoned traveler who knew the local customs. I was trusted by the natives. I could mingle freely and pass as one of them.

In the scorecard, just above the listing of the Charleston players, was a picture of Frank Horton.

"Best Wishes from Your Congressman, Frank Horton."
Alongside it I wrote "attendance: 2,313" as it was announced over the loudspeaker. I knew the rules of comportment. I knew the character of Frank Horton. And it
pleased me to be on top of the situation.

Red Wing Stadium was, like it or not, my homeland.
And I liked it. In spite of my preference for being intellectual, ambitious, and above all, serious, I felt an alien
pride about how I had spent my childhood.

The postwar dream of relevance to, and applause
from, the abstract of American society was finished.
Political and moral judgmental grudge-settling now had
to be done for its own sake. Education, even law school,
was no longer a bridge. There were no more tickets to
the top. Virtue had once more been isolated as its own
reward.

With the end of the postwar era, the mystique of
status and authority began to vanish. Relevance, fame,
and fortune no longer seemed matters of genius and
mystery, but rather circumstances of either bewildering
luck or crooked dealings. The thrill lingered on, but the
awe disappeared with the mentality that fostered it.

And so the nature of everyday life moved on. Alternatives for behavior became less and less a matter of
consequences and more and more a matter of substance.
"Do-it-yourself," once the slogan to create pride in pro-
ductive activities, had shifted, and was now applied to
consumptive modes.

We used to talk about the movies, and now we just
look at them. We used to analyze the lyrics, and now we
just listen to the music. We used to decide how far we
were prepared to go, and now we just let it happen.
Having the experience is now more cherished than having a position on the matter. And in that complex switch,
I reentered the world of baseball. From within that
world, I am quite willing to admit that I prefer the
microfilm-reading room to chasing down my Uncle Hymie
for his side of the story. I would rather spend a Sunday

afternoon at the baseball park than in the uneasy company of my relatives. I would not dare go back to Rochester and pick up my past life, but for baseball I have time and patience, and the will to go back.

The Cuban detente–Havana Sugar Kings–microfilm reading room obsession was not a quirk, but a decision. And against all that I have learned about reason, justice, and significance, not to mention goodness, truth, and beauty, I am still interested in baseball. And how that came to be is one of the stories that my own history tells me.

Here in the microfilm reading room, it is the spring of 1960 and bloom time for the cold war. Soon Eisenhower will harden Cuba's heart while the American media turn the romantic revolutionary into the bearded demagogue. America will continue to pause, at home, at work, or on the way, but it will never again be Cuban sugar that refreshes. Dr. Fidel Castro will move from the lecture halls of fancy East Coast universities to the satanic fears of fundamentalist preachers.

It was a long time ago last summer that Frank Verdi's skull was creased by a bullet in Havana. That symbolic wound will never have its chance to represent a nation's feelings, but arms will be twisted, Fidel Castro will say uncle, and organized baseball will jilt its adoring Cuba. They will take away our beloved rhumba, gambling and whoring, and United Fruit Company plantations, and we will take away their beloved baseball team.

The 1960 baseball season opened on several strange notes. On opening day, Caryl Chessman was executed by the State of California, having smiled at an unidentified red-haired woman a moment before. Russia shot down a U-2 spy plane containing Francis Gary Powers, who, despite his training, forgot to swallow his poison pill. Even in a Republican home-town newspaper, the distinguished Dwight Eisenhower could be seen to be losing his dignity, right and left. He denied, then admitted, then justified, and finally threatened more of the same. And it all went on at star time in a concert of cold-war diplomacy. A Soviet spaceship flew far above the proceedings. The hero of World War II was visiting his adoring fans in Paris. And every general had booked a visit to his enemy's tent in the immediate future. The newspapers were filled with PARIS WELCOMES IKE/PARIS JEERS NIKITA contrasts, and cartoons of Khrushchev, with neat lettering, usually on his behind, saying "The Real Aggressor." The verbs in the headlines were always BLASTS, THREATEN, RETALIATE, WARN, BLAME. It was RUSS against the U.S. every day for weeks.

May 24, 1960. HAVANA, RICHMOND SPLIT

May 25, 1960. GIANT U.S. SPY SATELLITE ROCKETING AROUND EARTH. CAN SPOT ENEMY MISSILES. OPENING A NEW CHAPTER IN THE RACE FOR SPACE

May 25, 1960. HAVANA DEFEATS MIAMI, 11–7

June 1, 1960. CIA'S CHIEF DULLES CLEARED OF BLAME IN SPY RING HASSLE

Chairman of the Senate Foreign Relations Committee William Fulbright (D-Ark.) cleared the CIA yesterday of all responsibility for the controversial policy decisions in the U-2 spy affair.

Not a single word uttered in the five and a half hours of Dulles testimony will be released to the public. Sealed and bound, it will be locked up in committee files and the stenotapes and duplicating masters will be burned.

Dulles, whose white brush mustache and handsome bespectacled face is a Washington landmark, declined to say why the flight of Francis Gary Powers was ordered. . . .

June 2, 1960. MAY RAINS HURT FARMING, BASEBALL

June 5, 1960. U.S. ENDS CHILLY SILENCE,
CALLS KHRUSHCHEV'S SLUR AT PRESIDENT
DISGUSTING
Ike said, "No nation in the world dares attack
the United States and they know it."

June 6, 1960. IKE DENOUNCES EPITHET
USERS IN SLAP AT MR. K

June 11, 1960. ROYALS TOP CUBANS ON
HOMER IN TENTH (attendance: 1,400)

Years later, my mother would accuse me of dressing like a communist when she noticed that I was wearing a sock with a hole in it. I was flattered at the notion of not only feeling, but looking, like a communist. My own small legacy of the McCarthy era. Reading through the headlines, I see that I wasn't the only one. The harvest of that seed of national guilt and insecurity was abundant.

McCarthy was dead and the purges were over—if not forgotten, at least repressed. In the process of making itself secure, America created, out of its own fear and arrogance, a colossal enemy anxiously crouched at the borders, crazed, and about to pounce at any moment.

It was the duty of every serious newspaper to remind its readers of the impending threat. No rhetoric could be too crudely alarmist; the only danger was complacency.

One plaguing problem in the twilight of the Eisenhower era was that the McCarthy fad had run out of hysteria. The rhetorical style that once made Americans spring to preparedness had lost its impact. It was now merely familiar.

In the suburbs of Rochester, the attempt to solve the familiarity problem led to the bomb shelter. A sensible fantasy that avoided hysteria with all the seriousness that attaches to any dealing in real estate. I remember the staid and serious gathering of all my suburban neighbors to decide on the building of a community bomb shelter. It was the first and only time I saw the entire neighborhood together in a public forum, but it was a very low-keyed event. The construction of a streetlight or a stop sign would have aroused greater passion. There were no anticommunist outbursts, no mention of the Russians, even. That the bomb was coming was inevitable. All that had to be decided was whether to survive collectively or individually. The meeting was dominated by a pervasive boredom. The capacity for frenzied paranoia had been exhausted.

In character, my patriotic American neighbors decided that they would rather not survive in each other's company. A few of them actually did go on to build backyard bunkers, which years later they would describe as wine cellars. Most of them settled for keeping a case of canned fruit and thirty gallons of drinking water, changed every three months, in the basement. None of them would admit to this today. The old-fashioned always looks slightly ridiculous, but the bomb shelter is a special source of embarrassment.

June 12, 1960. (editorial) WHAT WILL BE-
COME OF CUBA'S FUTURE IF NOTHING IS
DONE TO HALT FIDEL CASTRO'S PROGRAM?

As things are going, the island country in the Caribbean is more likely to become a thorough Communist dictatorship with every movement of the citizens under government surveillance....

June 18, 1960. (AP) The United States is preparing to indict Cuba before the Organization of American States for a long list of diplomatic sins ranging from slander to plots to embarrass this country, diplomatic sources said yesterday....

June 18, 1960. HAVANA AT MONTREAL,
RAIN

June 19, 1960. TWO CUBA DIPLOMATS OR-
DERED TO LEAVE THE U.S. IN 48 HOURS,
ACCUSED OF ARMS SMUGGLING AND
ESPIONAGE

June 20, 1960. (movie ad) HANNIBAL ... and his fantastic elephant army that clobbered half the world . . . starring Victor Mature, now at the RKO Palace.

June 22, 1960. IKE CALLED "MANIAC" AS PEIPING OPENS WE-HATE-U.S. WAR

June 22, 1960. CUBAN NEWSPAPERS DE-NOUNCING MONROE DOCTRINE

June 22, 1960. (movie ad) Jump on! Hang on! Here comes the avenging Hannibal and his crazed elephant army! (And heaven help anyone who gets in his way.) "What my elephants can't conquer, I will conquer alone."

June 22, 1960. CUBANS WIN 3–2 BEHIND SANCHEZ (attendance: 964)

June 23, 1960. DEMOCRATS OK IKE ON MOVE TO CUT SUGAR FROM CUBA

June 23, 1960. U.S. BUILDING UP CASE AGAINST CASTRO

by Francis L. McCarthy, UPI Latin-American Editor

. . . The United States is building up the historical record of its relations with the Fidel Castro regime in Cuba, in the event any "police action" against that country should ever be necessary. . . .

. . . Under present hemisphere security treaties, Latin American nations are committed individually and jointly to resist the encroachment of international communism by all means. . . .

. . . American diplomatic protests trace not only unparalleled U.S. patience and forbearance in the face of almost savage Cuban provocation, but relate the tragic tale of a God-fearing people being sold down the river to atheism.

They portray a self-proclaimed Messiah, leading his people not out of the wilderness, but into the hands of their arch-enemies with a brutally cynical disregard of their religious and political beliefs.

June 25, 1960. CASTRO HINTS TAKEOVER ALL U.S. INTERESTS

June 25, 1960. George V. Allen, Director of the United States Information Agency, told a House Foreign Affairs subcommittee that communists are spending $100 million in a "Hate America" campaign spearheaded in Cuba.

June 25, 1960. Senator Kenneth B. Keating, Rochester Republican, declared the Senate Internal Security subcommittee has evidence that 1,000 Chinese communists have entered Cuba to enlist the support of their 30,000 countrymen there. . . .

Keating proposed O.A.S. action to inform Castro that: "Responsible governments do not countenance his piratical techniques, his open courtship of communist tyranny, or his abysmal disregard for democratic processes. . . ."

And so the season progressed. No mention of Cuban agrarian reform, tendencies toward expropriation, or the attack on the cultural decay that Havana represented. But, from the other side, a steady and orderly move away from saying nice things about the Castro regime in Cuba. And then the final decision and a committed campaign. A story with the byline of UPI's Latin American editor, Francis C. McCarthy (who, by the way, scooped everyone back in 1956 with his mistaken report of Castro's death) gets to "the tragic tale of a God-fearing people being sold down the river to atheism." A United States senator calls Castro a pirate who courts tyranny and disregards democracy. A point of no return has been passed. Within the style of the rhetoric is the end of America's fascination with the personality of Fidel Castro. The honeymoon is over, and all that remains is for the specific political events to play themselves out.

The American people were growing bored with global fears. They consoled themselves with their new electric toothbrushes and frozen TV dinners. Military fantasies began to shift from first-strike capabilities to the movements of a jeep driver stationed in Germany, Pvt. Elvis Presley. As the public faded, the government and its financial and industrial patrons caught their second wind. The decision had been made, and no mentality as tough as America's ever goes back on a decision. From now on, the isolation of Cuba would be seen only as the inevitable movement of progress. And to make that inevitability certain, the dike was opened and a flood of assurances poured into the American press.

As spring crossed into summer, the status quo was maintained but it was no longer stable. America was begging God to save Cuba from communism, and threatening to help with the dirty work. Hannibal was gallivanting across a downtown movie screen and teaching Rochesterians the value of being mighty. And the American government was making its decision to finally lose its temper in Cuba. And far away from all this, but at its geographic center, the Rochester Red Wings breezed into Havana for a four-game series.

Havana shut out Rochester in the first game of the series on the three-hit pitching of Miguel Cuellar. George Beahon was quick to notice in his report of the game that Howie Nunn, an ex-Red Wing, now of the Havana Sugar Kings, had dyed his hair red. "Switch caused considerable comment around the batting cage last night," said Beahon. Perhaps an oblique comment about the decadence that overtakes good, clean-cut American boys when they wind up pitching in Havana. Perhaps not.

And Havana shut out Rochester in the second game. A bad start for the Red Wings, but still no diplomacy in sight. Or, stretching things a bit, almost no diplomacy in sight. In his story of the second shutout, Beahon did slip a rather odd analogy into his criticism of the Red Wings' hitting: "Waiting for the Red Wings to score runs on this trip, a guy could miss planes, trains, and the night boat to Miami."

Could the witty sports prose belie that somewhere, somehow, George Beahon knew that there was a reality to the fear of getting out, because this was the last road trip to Havana for any American baseball team? Was the hard-nosed reporter, at this very moment, rushing around the bars and byways of Havana saying sentimental goodbyes to tipsters, contacts, friends, and sweethearts he had known in the happy-go-lucky posture of the professional sportster? Now he would have to reveal himself as a shrewd and calculating man as he rushed through the twilight world of Havana, explaining that American patience had run out for Cuba.

Or was he simply an earnest sports reporter from Rochester, concocting good copy for his story, without ever considering the possible unconscious sources of his wit? Did he or did he not know something?

There wasn't ever time to answer the question. Organized Baseball made no special cases. And the sports pages pretended that such a thing was conceptually impossible. Baseball was doomed in Cuba. Such was the nature of progress. Baseball was about to leave, and a real revolution—a radical restructuring of Cuban society—was about to begin.

June 27, 1960. MUNITIONS BLAST RIPS HAVANA. RED WINGS LOSE FIRST GAME, TIE SECOND

Havana. (Special to the *D & C*) There were explosions inside and outside of Gran Stadium last night. The most costly explosion for the Red Wings came off the bat of Felix Torres in the seventh inning of the first game. Torres sent an Artie Kat pitch over the left-field wall with Borrega Alvarez on base to give the Cubans a 6–5 decision in the opener of a twi-night double-header.

The Wings scored in the top of the ninth to tie the second game 3–3. The game was halted after nine innings, by curfew, and will be resumed on the Wings' next visit here.

A deafening explosion at 7:55 P.M. shook Havana and cut off electrical power to Gran Stadium, delaying the start of the opener by an hour and a half.

Contacted by phone at 8:50 P.M., George Sisler, Rochester general manager who was with the Wings in Havana, said, "About five minutes before game time there was a terrible explosion. It shook the

ballpark but it wasn't close enough to injure anyone at the park. . . .

"Following the explosion a huge cloud of black
smoke rose over the city. Right now, nothing seems
to be happening. We're waiting for the power lines
to be restored so the game can be played. Lights
seem to be on elsewhere in the city."

It was later learned that a munitions dump had
been blown up.

The explosion killed two people and injured some two
hundred. Premier Castro, on his way to the baseball game
after finishing a four-and-a-half-hour television broadcast, rushed to the scene. En route, the automobile carrying Castro was hit by another car. Dreams of the CIA
waylaying Fidel Castro on his way to the Red Wing game
dance in my head, but no one was hurt in the car crash.

The following day, an anti-Castro religious organization, La Cruz, claimed that its agents had caused the
explosion. It would certainly be naïve to assume that some
branch of the American imperial secret police did not
have a few fingers in the pie that caused the explosion.
But it would be presumptuous to assume that it did.
Either way, it is not really a question of fact, but a matter of divining entrails. The bulk of historical evidence
seems to show that in situations that parallel what was
going on in Havana that day, large numbers of political
agitators and informers are running loose, with no clear
knowledge or conviction about who it is that they are
really working for. Most prefer to be on both sides,
rather than on either one.

Certainly the loss of electricity in the stadium for
ninety minutes could not be compared with shooting the
visiting team's third-base coach in the head, but it's not
as if more outrageous capers with even more obtuse
motives did not happen every day in the course of ordinary cold-war politics. But it is certain that there is no
"scoop," in the newspaper sense, to be found here.

No scoop to investigate, and no poetic spring to consciousness. The second game of the double-header was tied 3–3 in the ninth, and remains uncompleted. It was the last game ever played by an American team in Cuba. No one knew it at the time, but this was it.

But I was sitting in the microfilm-reading room, and I knew it. I knew that this was the last game in Havana, ever, and it was also my last chance. The double-header was the last central event around which to build a coherent and educational framework. In the grand hope for a history within the history of the Havana Sugar Kings, this was the last opportunity for any information or inspiration that might lie in the unknown. This was the last newspaper to read, this was the last piece of the whole story.

And after I read it my muses remained silent, while history, having dashed my hopes with a Latin flair, trundles along. And I must watch it disappear into the distance. I have my two cities and their respective baseball teams, but wherein lies my tale? I have the very acme of dramatic events occurring in the 1959 season and yielding no consequence or aftermath beyond the resignation of the Red Wing manager. I have the profoundly significant events of the 1960 season, loaded with aftermath but growing out of no identifiable dramatic incident. Baseball was unaffected by the explosion, but it did leave permanently afterward. Historical events, attitudes, and sequence are destroying one another's continuity. At a time when all sorts of loose facts and notions should be congealing, plot is dissolving.

And then I realized that I didn't care about plot at all. What I was looking for were signs of the times. What I wanted was a historical sense of understanding. And all I really cared about was reflecting history through my state of mind.

That history must unfold through dramatic events is not necessarily true. The fantasy of the investigative reporter cannot find fulfillment in the sports pages of the local papers. I was finding something personal that was every bit as sensational to me as an uncovered historical scandal would be to them.

I worked my way through baseball season after baseball season. I jolted my memory. I found rich veins of drama and startling coincidences of historical juxtaposition. I found baseball games filled with shootings and explosions, joy and sorrow, celebration and remorse. I found more than I dreamed was there. And I found all this when I realized that the context of events is every bit as significant as their future consequences.

In times when everything is up for grabs, patterns and order become more important than facts. This is a time for arrangement, not decision. The time for clear metaphors and allegiance to them has passed. The new sides have not yet declared themselves.

I found, in all this, that plot was neither available nor desirable, and that my own story was both more interesting and more accessible. The newspapers would not supply the structure, but they did create a space in which I was hearing, for the first time, the story of my life, told by my memory.

Because I appreciated this, I carried on, even as I complained to myself. The reading of the microfilm never needed justification. The process was too evocative to stop.

Back at the point of action, in the microfilms, Cuba is getting pounded with cold-war platitudes. Even baseball is beginning to show signs of mobilizing. And Frank Horton, of all people, coincidental to his position suddenly becoming politically sensitive, has been promoted. George Beahon, still in Havana, moved from sports to page one.

June 28, 1960. U.S.–CUBA GAP WIDENS
DAILY; REDS POUR IN
    The breach between the U.S. and Cuban governments widens every day. And the world's foremost communist organizers are pouring through the gap in droves.
    ... Reds from China, Czechoslovakia, Yugoslavia, East Germany, and Russia find an open

door when they seek Fidel Castro, his brother Raoul, and the key government commie, Ernesto (Che) Guevara. They have talked and visited together many times. In our own hotel, the Copacabana, 14 Russians live together, ostensibly working with Cuba's agrarian reform. "Their only job is to hate our guts," said one U.S. newsman.

... During the last six months in Cuba, 29 strong propaganda pieces have been written and printed in a total of five million copies. Next year's press quotas call for a printing of 100,000 booklets. For Cuba? Impossible. Cubans couldn't absorb this much. It is for the 21 other South American republics.

In the baseball stadium, Castro was available on television after the game. The set was in the bar section of the club. There were three people in that section. Twenty-five or thirty others shunned the magic lantern and sat in a separate section where service was much slower. . . . It was obvious why they chose the other section. Embassy people considered this significant.

All agree on one prediction. An uprising, with bloodshed and lots of it, before the year is ended. Meanwhile, Americans rush out. Communists rush in. It is indeed a depressing situation. And the fate of all the Americas could depend on future events in Cuba.

June 29, 1960. U.S. KILLS PROFESSIONAL
SPORTS BILL

A bill to put professional sports under the government's antitrust laws was defeated. Frank Horton, only Monday named Executive Vice-President of the International League, said, "A great victory for organized baseball. It was a bad bill, legislative-wise, and would have left the question as to how baseball would operate to be solved by the courts."

June 29, 1960. HAVANA BOMBS FADING
BUFFALO BISONS 15–3

June 30, 1960. CASTRO REGIME SEIZES
TEXACO REFINING PLANT

June 30, 1960. CUBANS BOMB BISONS 7–4

[117]

**July 1, 1960. HOUSE VOTE HITS AT CUBAN
SUGAR**

**July 1, 1960. CUBANS NIP BISONS 6–5 FOR
SIXTH STRAIGHT WIN**

**July 2, 1960. CUBA GRABS TWO MORE
REFINERIES, FACES ACUTE SUPPLY PROB-
LEMS**

It is Sunday morning, July 3, 1960. The Havana
Sugar Kings are away on a road trip, from which they
will never return, although there is no mention of it yet.
The next phase of the mobilization begins in the morning
paper. The future is being shaped rather than predicted.
For the first time, politics and baseball merge into a single ideology. The rhetorical attack is intensified, and it is
all happening on the sports pages, in George Beahon's
column.

**July 3, 1960. WINGS KICK AWAY 10–6
GAME TO CUBANS**

This man was a career diplomat with experience
in many foreign offices. He shook his head as he discussed the situation. It's just about impossible to
play the diplomatic game with Fidel Castro. He simply does not play by the rules, and leaves you almost
helpless with normal procedures.

Another man was close to the Cuban government, and speaking carefully. "Your International
League is finished in Cuba. Why do you think Lt.
Guerra Matoss (director of all sports and recreation
and a revolutionary here) is traveling in Europe today? He is arranging to bring all sorts of European
soccer teams here in an effort to popularize them.
Because the commies want no associations with the
U.S., economically, culturally, educationally, or in
any other way, and that includes your International
League."

... Last December, the International League
drafted an escape plan which would give directors
the right to move the Cuban franchise in event of
an emergency.

[118]

In January, the directors presented the International League president, Frank Shaughnessy, with authority to move the franchise in event of an emergency. In any event, Bobby Maduro, the Cuban sportsman who is caught directly in the middle of the situation, would be powerless to resist such an emergency move. Maduro has been good to the league and good to baseball; he has been better to the league than the league has been to him. He warrants any and all consideration that has been and may be forthcoming to him.

The ink on this emergency legislation was barely dry when one man took measures to work out the solution.

Still before the 1960 trouble season opened in Havana, Gabe Paul, the Cincinnati Reds front-office leader, stepped secretly into the picture.

If the International League found it necessary to discontinue play in Havana, the foresighted Paul privately guaranteed the continuance of the International League as an eight-club operation. He would personally operate the franchise in Jersey City's Roosevelt Stadium.

. . . Unless International League president Frank Shaughnessy decides to quit dodging the issue, throws off his ostrich feathers, and finally exercises the power presented him.

Shaughnessy has one week—the duration of the Sugar Kings' trip—to do what he must do. Thus far, he has ignored the escape button.

He has a choice. If he finds a half season in Jersey City too complicated to make a change at this late date, he may decree that the Cubans become a road club for the rest of the 1960 season.

If the Cuban government, which could break diplomatic relations with the U.S. within a week, takes too hard an attitude, then the Cubans might drop out of the league. In which event, every remaining game would be wiped out of the schedule, thus creating serious travel and scheduling problems.

The point here is that Shaughnessy and the league have ample anticipation of the current mess.

Thanks to Gabe Paul and other friends, escape plans became available.

Apparently, however, what the U.S. government worries about does not worry Frank Shaughnessy, who observes all this from his smug third-base box in Montreal, Quebec.

That's exactly where Shaughnessy will be, in Montreal, when Toronto plays Havana next July 26. Last year's near tragic shoot-em-up in Gran Stadium could be excused. There was absolutely no malice connected to this simple celebration.

They are so emotional that next July 26, they may even be taking an entirely different view of the goings-on, ever playful, between Cuban and American athletes. By that time, the Cuban sugar quotas to the U.S. probably will have been slashed to a minimum. Because the U.S. finally is taking a different view of the situation in Cuba.

Reducing the sugar quota could have one direct effect in Cuba. It could take the bread from the mouths of Cuban babies. By that time, the hate-America campaign being directed and executed by communists in Cuba could get through loud and clear. Perhaps not loud enough to be heard in Montreal, but acoustics in Gran Stadium are remarkable.

And now, after all my diligent days in the microfilm-reading room, and after all my diligent years of reading the newspapers, George Beahon suddenly bestowed the knowledge that discredits most of my thinking about this situation. And at the same time, what he has to say isn't itself true. Fidel Castro, who saved the team when it was about to leave Havana for financial reasons, and who proclaimed baseball a part of the Cuban people, now wants, according to the papers, to get rid of the International League. And Fidel Castro, who pitched in exhibition games while in office as the head of state, now wants, they say, to replace baseball with leftist soccer.

And George Beahon also tells us that the exemplary behavior on the part of the International League at the time of the Frank Verdi shooting incident was not all that noble, and in fact was no more than the calculated showing of as few cards as possible. The truth is that the International League had secret meetings, plotted against its members behind closed doors, leaked certain secrets at opportune moments, and in general acted out the cold-war fantasy of emergency response to the eternal threat of communism, just like any regular American business.

The paroxysm of guilt that Frank Verdi's shooting caused between my memory and my sense of self was no more than the effect of a successful public-relations presentation. The league smelled like roses because it got exactly what it wanted. My devotion to the newspapers is now revealed as no more than a willful submission to the self-serving pronouncements from the people who made the money off baseball. The joke is only on me. And the joke exists only because, against my knowledge to the contrary, I chose to take this issue seriously.

And, as if that weren't enough, I find out, now that it is far too late, that it is Gabe Paul who emerges as the gray lackey of imperialism that rightfully should have been Frank Horton. Gabe Paul is Joey Paul's Uncle Gabey. A Rochester boy, and one of Jewish Rochester's greatest success stories. And now he turns out to be the Eichmann-like administrator who deals with the realities of implementation for organized baseball. Gabe Paul, who worked his way out of poverty by selling programs at the Bay Street Stadium long before there was such a thing as the Rochester Red Wings, who worked his way up to become an often-quoted-in-the-newspapers big-time baseball executive, who honored Red Wing Stadium with his occasional visits—this same man actually set up the move to take the Sugar Kings out of Havana, and deposit them in Jersey City. *Oi vey!*

July 5, 1960. TEEN CRIME, MARIJUANA
LINKED IN U.S. SURVEY
A year-long study by a Senate subcommittee pictured a sizable segment of American youth as trou-

bled, drug-addicted, crime-oriented, and preoccupied
with sex.

July 6, 1960. U.S. HITS CUBAN OIL SEIZURES, IMPORTS OF SUGAR SUSPENDED

Here, at least, is the *Democrat and Chronicle* singing. First it tells me that my government considers me
troubled, drug-addicted, crime-oriented, and preoccupied
with sex. If there was ever a time when teen-agers
weren't any of these things, this was it. The Senate subcommittee just didn't understand what ordinary life was
like. Institutions had calcified, leaving our governors remote. The link between citizens and their governors was
already gone.

And then, the next morning, the entire Cuban story
is summed up in one headline. "Imports of Sugar Suspended" covers everything. Cuba produces sugar, and if
we don't want your sugar, we don't want anything, especially baseball.

Over on the baseball flank, sportswriters were rushing to participate, personally, in the cold war. And they
responded, like anyone else, by going over the top.

July 6, 1960. (*The Sporting News*) CUBA'S POLITICAL CLIMATE IS NOT SAFE FOR ORGANIZED BASEBALL *Operating Club in Havana Is Called Incompatible with Ideals of America* by Dan Daniel (*New York World-Telegram & Sun*)

International League baseball in Havana is an
island of freedom in a sea of communism, Soviet af-
fliction, and Castro terror. Everything about the operation of the ball club in the Cuban capital, from
its membership in the Cincinnati farm system, its
American talent, and competition with seven teams
from the U.S., to the free and untrammeled enterprise which the league race represents, is alien to the
sticky atmosphere created by Castro.
... When the proposal to drop Havana from the

International League first came up last March, Bob
Maduro, owner of the Cuban team, and sportswriters
in Havana protested that an effort was being made to
embroil neutral baseball in politics.

Commissioner Frick went to the capital and discussed the Cuban situation with Secretary of State
Christian A. Herter. At the time, the administration
was very forbearing and still hopeful that things
would quiet down in Cuba, but conditions have wors-
ened.

... The United States has done big things for
baseball in Cuba, and Cuba has given our major
leagues many spectacular players, among them Ores-
tes Minoso, Camilo Pascual, Pedro Ramos, Adolpho
Luque, Mike Gonzales, Armando Marsans, and Mike
Almeida. The last named and Marsans, who joined
Cincinnati in 1911, were the first Cubans in the big
leagues.

However, the climate in Cuba is no longer
healthy for our national pastime.

The obvious problem with this kind of information
is its style. But there are nagging subtleties that are
more disturbing. There is the lure of Latino veneer. Havana as sin city, and what a wonderful place to sneak
around. And everyone there was most probably sneaking
around all the time. Then there is the lure of baseball,
which has become my own particular weakness. But
above all is the constant and overwhelming availability
of intrigue.

Christian Herter, Gabe Paul, Frank Horton, "Shag"
Shaughnessy, George Beahon, and the rest. These are all
distinct pieces. And though they show no sign of converging into a puzzle, nor will they go their own separate
ways. And this leaves me with neither intrigue nor the
ability to accept the news and stop searching for intrigue.

Baseball did leave Havana. And those who arranged
that are collectively guilty. Since no one acted in any way
that would metaphorically summarize their feelings,

there can be no specific charges. And the outrage that grows out of this story remains amorphous. And for some incomprehensible reason, I find that good enough.

July 6, 1960. NIXON REJECTS U.S. NAZI
SUPPORT

Vice-President Nixon repudiated the support of George Lincoln Rockwell, head of the American Nazi Party, and "the evil he represents."

July 7, 1960. BASEBALL'S AXE FALLS ON
CUBA

The International League has played its last game in Cuba. . . . Harold Cooper, the Columbus general manager, is firm in his thinking. "Castro says he's ready to grab all U.S. industry. So far as I'm concerned, this could mean my ball club."

July 8, 1960. AMERICANS FLEE AS SOVIET
OIL REACHES CUBA

July 8, 1960. HAVANA FRANCHISE WILL
BE MOVED IN FEW DAYS: SHAUGHNESSY

Earlier yesterday, Frank J. Horton, president of Rochester Community Baseball and executive vice-president and legal counsel for the International League, advised Shaughnessy to "invoke the provisions in the bylaws declaring a state of emergency in Cuba and remove the franchise."

In Havana, according to the AP, Bob Maduro, owner of the Sugar Kings, said he knew nothing about a switch of the club to the U.S. Maduro called the report pure speculation.

July 9, 1960. NEGRO TROOPS REBEL, RUN
WILD IN CONGO

July 9, 1960. JERSEY CITY NEW HOME
OF CUBANS

July 16, 1960. (*New York Times*) The return of International League Baseball to Jersey City after a ten-year absence was marked tonight by perfect weather, a mayor who insisted he could throw a curve, a twenty-pound cake made with a quart of

[124]

rum, and the appearance of a beauty queen whose
enthusiasm for baseball cost her a job.
    ... The existence of a large Spanish-speaking
element in downtown Jersey City is being counted on
by the club to increase attendance. ...

And so the Havana Sugar Kings became the Jersey
City Jerseys. It never made the front section of the newspapers. Buried in the sports section, it was played strictly
for laughs, though not a laughing matter. It never had
any historical impact. Cuban baseball disappeared quietly. It was as if nothing happened. And though this is
neither the time nor the place, nor is it my proper intention, to mention it, something awful did happen.

America is a very materialistic culture where everyone works very hard to accumulate as much as he can
and to notice who has accumulated how much, lest he
himself fall behind. And in the strife of this endless
backbreaking accumulation, there is a little haven called
baseball.

Baseball is beyond everyday reality. American politicians, businessmen, and sportswriters couldn't see this,
and Fidel Castro could. And it is a shame that this was
never mentioned. And a scandal that no one in America
ever knew or ever cared about what went on in Havana.

July 9, 1960. (*D & C*) Fidel Castro, Cuban
prime minister, lashed out at the International
League transfer of the Havana franchise to Jersey
City. He called it another aggression against the
Cuban people by Americans.
    "American players when they came here got
nothing but respect and admiration. The people
treated them cordially and there is no record of
attacks on players of any kind. But violating all
codes of sportsmanship, they now take away our
franchise.
    "It's another oppression they've committed. We
never told our players not to play in the U.S. in
spite of attacks against us there."

[125]

Maduro received the news with bitterness. "The International League is making a big mistake. Baseball was a strong link between the Cuban and American people and it should never have been broken. It's always been safe for U.S. players in Cuba and it's safe now.

"I don't know what I am going to do. The whole thing is outrageous."

And finally, the newspapers gave out. I lingered on the relocation to Jersey City, but I could no longer prolong the search through the microfilm. The name Havana had disappeared from the sports pages. There were no more places to look, there were no more reasons for me to stay in Rochester.

For days I had assured Sammy that I had only a few more hours in the library and we would leave town by the following noon. And each evening, I would appear at his doorstep, slightly more bloodshot in the eye, slightly more shaky on the true history of the Havana Sugar Kings, and certain that the research was "almost" finished.

Now it was done, and I was leaving. I had insulted nearly everyone by demonstrably preferring the microfilm-reading room to their company. Not to mention that I never finished the painting, over which I had given, and now devalued, my word. But it was a small price to pay for the kind of experience I gained.

What my imagination had helped to create was a caricature of political activity, more caricature than cause. And though history has taught me that caricature is a most vivid political art, what I used to refer to as "direct action" just didn't seem possible. Who could I approach with a straight face?

I had done my homework, and it didn't suggest a political organization, even though a political organization was precisely what was needed. I consoled myself with conclusions reached in the public library. This was not the historical moment to be seized by those most easily unglued when the postwar momentum slowed. This was not a time for those first floaters to be serious political actors. This was a time for self-understanding.

But I never did figure it out, and truthfully, I never tried. In fact, my mind was drawn less to the notes that I had taken than it was to further research. There was Luis Tiant, Sr.'s old team, the New York Cubans of the Negro American League. The twenty years of sports sections of the appropriate black newspaper are available on microfilm. And so is the English-language newspaper called the *Times of Havana*, published between 1957 and 1965, and the English version of *Gramma*. And a 1945 report on the effects of suburbanization in Rochester, New York.

The world within me was as limitless as the world outside. I could go on subjecting my memory to jolts of recognition forever. I could present the menu from my bar mitzvah dinner, which consisted of the finest kosher half-capons money could buy.

And believe me, I can remember very well the specific details of the trip I took with Richard Fleischer and his mother to see the Red Wings play a double-header in Buffalo. I was shocked to see my beloved Red Wings in the gray visitors' uniforms that I had come to despise. In the second game, a Red Wing pitcher named Gary Blaylock came into the game and gave up six straight runs without getting anybody out. I felt enraged at Cot Deal, the Red Wing manager. How could anyone have left Blaylock in for so long? I vowed I would never attend another Red Wing game as long as Cot Deal remained the manager. A source of alienation, perhaps worthy of analysis? A strand of a thread that might forever yield potential meaning?

No. It is time to stop. And time to admit that I learned as much from hiding in the library as I did from what I read there. Further research may be unstoppable, but it is not necessary. The lesson is already clear.

History belongs to everybody, and you can have it

[127]

any way you want it. There is no verification beyond
your own preference for it. And you can feel absolved
or punished by history, as you choose, but you will never
be able to find out by looking it up.

And so there can be no point to the journey other
than the taking of it. Somewhere between the poles of
wisdom and curiosity there is always some value that
attaches to the truth. And the truth of this dream of
home, roots, and tradition is that there is none, particularly. Baseball's serene domination of my childhood
masked a time that was as cruel and nasty as the present.
And what's most startling about that time is just how
heavy-handed the crudeness seems. That we remember
it as a field of daisies on a summer afternoon has everything to do with how embarrassed we are by present
circumstances, and nothing much to do with how it was
back then.

And yet all this is commonly known by intuition, and
there is a sense in which I certainly knew it or I would
never have dared to read through those old newspapers.
And my cultural peers certainly know it, and that's why
they worship the Howdy Doody Cocoa Mug, the Mickey
Mouse watch, and Marilyn Monroe, rather than that past
era itself.

Memory always serves the present. The idyllic dream
of home and roots tells us much about the state of the
culture and who is doing business in it, and not much
more. There is no reality without interpretation, and no
interpretation that does not serve motive. Which is another way of saying that nothing is ever what it seems
to be, quite, and the more often we are aware of this, the
less frequently we will see ourselves as fools.

Gran Stadium has been renamed the Stadium of the
Heroic Vietnamese. American baseball teams will play
there again, much sooner than anyone would think. And
I will pay attention and accept it all as significant and
part of my life. That is the kind of person I am, and more
than that I will never know.

PART

2

I have acquired the habit of rising early in the morning. Bundling up against the dew, I leave the house before sunrise and trudge through the woods surrounding the house, until I come to the top of the hill. And there, in the majesty and solitude of nature at dawn, I watch the rush hour. I stand, in organic purity, feeling far above the sins of capitalism and technology and consumption, while below me the cars rush, bumper to bumper, at seventy-five miles an hour, toward New York City. They are on their way to create and maintain a crazed mechanism, which provides for the few at the expense of the many. Meanwhile, I am in the woods, far removed from this process in every way but physical proximity. And whereas I would meditate, no doubt, if the circumstances were less suburban, instead I watch the cars. And the cars remind me that they are rushing off to create the very institutions that provide for my welfare, and dangle before my insecurities the ambivalent promise of total security. These cars are all speeding to New York to strike it rich, but they are also tentatively promising, to the man on the wooded hillside, a series of checks, if and when they decide he is in need. Maybe.

I know that I am not separate from this rush hour, nor immune to its madness. And I also know that this madness has not ended.

This knowledge became a systematic distraction, and I began the slow transformation from baseball devotee to plain loafer. I thought I had ended my story. I thought a process that had threatened to take over my life had been arrested. I did not want to carry on until I lived in a world where the planet itself was merely a replica of a baseball. But left to itself, my story was not dying, but germinating.

It seemed a wonderful idea. My senses, both common and paranoid, failed to intervene, and a moment later, I was on the telephone to Rochester, New York, arranging an appointment with George Beahon, the former *Rochester Democrat and Chronicle* sports reporter, who only a few months ago was built into a heroic image of my childhood by my labors in the microfilm-reading room.

But this was a different time and a different commitment. I was going back to Rochester to end my story. Just as my trip at the beginning of the summer had jolted my sensibilities and symbolically opened this strange path through my past, so this trip would close it. If fortune bestowed the gift of historical surrealism, I might get to the bottom of the matter. Without such a gift, the matter was bottomless. And so I went to Rochester once more, this time not so much for examination as for conclusion. I was determined. Even if only symbolically, I would lay my burden down at exactly the same spot where I had picked it up.

Now, why did I pick on George Beahon, I wondered? Baseball is a strange world that make no distinction between childhood and maturity. And George Beahon is the fulfilment of a boyhood fantasy that exists in a world that does not know the shame of being childish. And now, walking through the maroon curtain will be the man, now a successful broadcaster in Rochester, New York, whose dispatches from Havana to the *Rochester Democrat and Chronicle* I followed as a boy. Yes, the journalist who covered the Rochester Red Wings during your child-

hood, the originator of Dugout Diggins, himself, Mr.
George Beahon ...

But why seek out George Beahon? Why not my
uncles? Why not Howie Nunn, the Havana relief pitcher
who mysteriously dyed his hair red? And why not Frank
Verdi himself, who after his historic shooting went on
to manage the Syracuse Chiefs? And why not aim, if not
deeper, then at least higher? Why not talk to Fidel
Castro?

In fact, talking to Fidel Castro would be easier.
"I understand, Dr. Castro, that as a boy, you wrote to
Roosevelt, congratulating him on his victory in 1940 and
asking him for twenty dollars?"

"Sí. I did. The State Department replied, thanking
me, but regretting they could send no money. I posted
their letter on the schoolhouse door."

But I was going to see George Beahon. I knew that
my encounter was impossible to prepare for. Some piece
of a past I had so carefully and so recently constructed
was at stake. I knew that however foolish or empty-
headed I felt at the time, my mind would hear what it
needed to hear from George Beahon. After a baseball
season of diligence, my identity was no longer fragile.

And so I convinced myself that the substance of our
meeting wouldn't matter. It was a straight case of a
journalist's old memory versus a recently refreshed version of the same material, courtesy of the microfilm
reading room mania. It was an arena of my own construction. Whatever the victory consisted of, it would be mine.

Meanwhile, I had my own curiosities, and, oh my God,
the most idle and tangential of all possible daydreams
was soon to be answered. What did this guy look like,
and was he intelligent? What did he think of his own life?
And if I was particularly lucky and observant, I might
get to see the effects of baseball on a man who had lived
his life, and earned his living, within that world. Yes, I
was excited, but I knew that my own curiosities were too
personal to be answered meaningfully for any outsider,

not to mention a daydreaming total stranger with a weakness for analytic fabrication.

I knew now, as I hadn't known before, that my curiosity had, out of habit, focused on values that no longer made sense. When I was ten years old I could write to the sports pages and ask him what it was like. And I could get a reply from Mr. Paul Pinkney. I never understood anything about Mr. Pinkney. But still, enough substance remained for Paul Pinkney to present his life to me, without embarrassment, as a reasonable social outing. And now, at a time of mass isolation, where even the notion of meaningful self-judgment remains only as a relic of the past, I was returning to ask George Beahon to judge the logical and the illogical extension of my childhood dreams. George Beahon himself was a logical extension of my childhood dreams. What was I doing?

What I failed to realize was that Rochester was caught in a historical time warp different from my own. As a culture in transition, Rochester is, despite its aggressive retraining programs, still reliant on the postwar mentality. Like any good industrial town, Rochester is addicted to the present, but its attitudes aren't. And I, making my way to George Beahon's place, represented the contrary. By virtue of my physical absence, I could rely only on the present. And like any good returning émigré, I was enchanted by and powerless to resist the memories.

It was called the cold war by some. It was cold, but it was not a war. It was a calmly rational mass insecurity bordering on hysteria, but it was not a war. In the increasing material security of the postwar economic boom, the strange bedfellow of pervasive insecurity appeared. Economic relationships became primary, and all other relationships became secondary. Technology kept this secret by masking human interdependence as the central necessity for the continuation of life.

And now, when all vital relationships are masked by technology, and when the available economic roles

[134]

prevent us from seeing through this, and all values are merely personal decisions, I am going to ask George Beahon to answer, from baseball, the question of the meaning of life. How on earth do I expect him to know what his life is about, even if he is prepared to tell me?

It turned out that George Beahon had left the newspaper business several years ago to take a better job as the public-relations director of a shopping center, or something. The whole thing fell through, but some of the old boys got together and pulled strings. And George Beahon was now doing the sports slot on the news at the local television station.

I was early for our appointment. Mr. Beahon had not yet arrived and I, still adjusting from the blizzard, decided to get some coffee beforehand.

What I wanted was simply directions to a cup of coffee. And I was taken by the hand to the kitchen, where I boiled some water and made myself a cup of instant coffee. And right there in the kitchen, all the television stars of the local news show were shaking my hand and asking my name, and it was all very friendly and humane, and nothing whatever to do with either the Rochester or the America of my expectations. And neither was it foreign—these were the social manners of the middle-sized industrial towns that disappeared with the postwar era. These were the manners of my childhood, and what were they doing here?

Just as memory and reality were about to change places, George Beahon strolled in, smiled at me, and shook my hand. We went off to the plush leather chairs of the conference room to have our chat. Mr. Beahon was dressed in a color-coordinated coat and turtleneck sweater. He wore a white plastic belt, and suede-and-plastic maroon shoes. Around his neck there was a gold chain, and awkwardly hanging from it was a large gold seagull. Visions of demonic small-town businessman hepcats danced in my head. I was afraid that we wouldn't have anything at all to talk about.

All else failing before I opened my mouth, I settled
for simply uttering the names of old Rochester Red Wing
players. And George Beahon replied to each one, with
neat sports-page clichés, in exactly the same style as he
had used when he wrote.

"Harry Walker, ask him the time and he'll tell you
how to build a watch. His brother Dixie was kind of
flaky. Dixie would never admit it now, but when he
played for the Dodgers, he tried to lead a strike against
Jackie Robinson. Eddie Kasko, he was the smartest.
Jackie Brandt, you probably heard this story someplace
else, but I promise you it originated with Jackie Brandt.
He made the whole team drive twenty miles outside of
Miami to this ice-cream place that served forty flavors.
And he ordered vanilla. He did it on purpose, too."

And so the time passed and I began to like George
Beahon. I forgot about my preference for a dingy bar
with a Spanish jukebox, and accepted the atmosphere of
a life-insurance sales warm-up that I found myself
caught in. It was not exactly the rime of an ancient
journalist, but there is a special warmth that comes
from sharing the memories of old ballplayers, and I was
enjoying that feeling.

What was the difference between the ballplayers of
those days and the ballplayers of today, I asked. And
George answered me. "In the old days, some players
drank, some didn't. Some gambled, some didn't, some
fooled around, some didn't, and some read books, and
some couldn't. But today, they are all mod."

"What?" I said.

"Mod," he said again.

"Well, what does that mean?" I asked.

"You know," he said, "mod."

I had no idea what he meant by the word. We silently
stared at each other for a moment longer than was acceptable. I had no choice but to ask my question then
and there. I had hoped to wait until perhaps our third
meeting. I had hoped to ask this question through a

drunken haze with some rhumba music in the background. And there I was, fifteen minutes after the beginning of our relationship, and I had to ask it or leave.

And so I said, "Tell me about Havana, George."

Havana, according to George Beahon, was everything I had hoped for. Well, your playboys all loved the road trips to Havana, but some of your straighter, clean-living boys hated it. The gambling in the casinos was all crooked, you know. All fixed. Batista was in on the take. That town was wide open, and ballgames didn't start until nine o'clock, so you didn't have to get up before noon.

The more we talked, the more I grew to respect George Beahon. His style was not my own, but underneath the veneer of small-town noncelebrity television announcer was the hard-bitten heart of a tough old journalist that had nothing to do with the versions presented by Hollywood or literature. World-weary and slightly cynical, George Beahon served no interests and played no games. This was the heart of the matter and I was getting it straight from the man at the scene. The trouble with the Havana teams was that they always felt slightly inferior, socially, to the other teams in the league. And sometimes this came out as arrogance. The problem was partly due to the cliques. There were the white American players, the black American players, the Cubans, and the other Latins. And that's not exactly a team.

Frank Horton. He was a working president when he ran the Wings. He got quite involved in the running of the league; it was no honorary job. Hey, one time Frank Horton was down in Havana for a game. When he was introduced to Fidel Castro he said, "I'm a politician, too," and shook his hand. "Castro spit on the ground, turned his back, and walked away. He had contempt for us.

"You know this myth about Castro being a great pitcher? It's not true, he's a horseshit pitcher. I saw him pitch that exhibition game the same night as the Verdi thing, and he had a big gut. He may have been in good shape when he was up in the mountains, but by the time he took Havana, he was already flabby. He had no motion. No speed and no control. He couldn't even find the plate.

"No, the Red Wings were treated fine at the ballpark, but in the hotels and restaurants, soldiers were always bumping into you with their rifle butt. You could just feel the hostility to Americans.

"No, Frank Verdi didn't appear to be shot. He didn't fall down. You know, we left Havana that night, and I tell you, there was a panic at the airport. Lots of Americans decided to get out that night. It was pretty rough. George Raft ran a casino down there, I don't know how they let him out alive. . . .

"I'll tell you the man in Havana I admired the most. It was Preston Gomez, the last manager of the Sugar Kings. He was very, very good.

"Politics in baseball with Cuba? No, I don't remember any meddling by the government. I did some page-one reporting, and I don't remember anything, but maybe George Sisler can help you on that. He was the general manager of the team, and he was down there for the last game."

Now, secret lives are not necessarily perverse. Secrecy can be its own rationale and its own aesthetic. So it wasn't that I didn't know better, but my desire for political intrigue knew neither bounds nor political reality. And so, I pulled my chair closer to George Beahon, and in a last stab, I asked how he could explain the resignation of the Red Wing manager, Cot Deal, just after the so-called shooting of Frank Verdi.

He didn't resign, he was fired, George told me. Scouts for the Baltimore Orioles were in the stands in Havana. Cot Deal came out to the mound for the second time in an inning, and some young pitcher talked himself into staying in the game. The scouts thought Deal was wrong and they canned him. That's all there was to it.

That concluded our business, but we carried on

chatting about old ballplayers for pleasure. "Deeply religious man, Jack Fasholtz, he was a preacher in the off-season. . . . Keegan lives in Rochester, somewhere in the suburbs. . . . Yes, Billy DeMars coaches for the Philadelphia Phillies. . . . Last couple of years, Cot Deal's turned into a religious, well, I'd have to call him a religious fanatic. . . . Tommy Burgess, he manages the Tidewater club now, but until last year I didn't know he was still in baseball. Dick Ricketts, he's an employment recruiter for Kodak. His kids are going to be great basketball players.

"I don't know what happened to Rocky Nelson. Yes, he was a very great ballplayer. I guess he was just allergic to a major-league uniform.

"Gabe Paul? Yes, I know him. He started as a batboy, went to office boy, road manager, general manager, and on to the major leagues. Rochester has always been a jumping-off point for baseball executives, because it's the only minor-league operation to pay its own way. Rochester is special in baseball. It's always first or second in attendance in the minor leagues, a real baseball town. Maybe Mexico City, where admission is half a buck, is ahead, but no place else."

And so we chatted on, and eventually it was time for the news. Time for George Beahon to go back to work, and time for me to exist in Rochester. On my way out, George Beahon told me one last thing.

"You know, when I was a boy, I dreamed of playing in the major leagues, and then when I got a bit older, I dreamed of playing in the minors. After that I dreamed of playing on a college team. In the end, I wound up in pick-up games in Genesee Valley Park, but to tell you the truth, those games felt as big as anything I have ever done in my life."

In the world of baseball, the only legitimate activity is play. And so the only legitimate life style is to be a player. And so, by emulation, proximity, and desire, everyone who embraces baseball becomes, in some way, a baseball player in personality. Journalists, fans, hot-dog sellers, and front-office executives, like everyone else, age and retire, and linger at ballparks and television sets. And they gather because they share not only baseball, but an attitude toward it. And so they meet and reminisce, and recall the glories of the old days. This is part of the life, and to partake of it you need only care about baseball. That's why George Beahon was so willing to see me. That is why he was so able to tell his story, even in the face of my inability to come to terms with a coherent notion of an interview.

And so, while I didn't find out much about Havana, I did find a link that connected myself to George Beahon, the players I worshiped as a child, and everybody who follows baseball. George Beahon was an aging ballplayer, and so was I. And so were we all. And whatever the differences between the reality of my life and that of George Beahon's, it was a natural thing for us to meet and, remembering the old days, shoot the breeze.

The ghostwritten autobiographies of aging baseball players are, in one sense, all the same. These players have a need for money and recognition, the two things that came most easily in their playing days. But when the time for memoirs comes, so does the knowledge that whatever their efforts, they can never recapture what they have lost. And so these autobiographies begin in disappointment, frustration, and bitterness. The motivation is to expose professional baseball to its adoring fans as the agony, pain, insecurity, and bewilderment that it is. And, having done that in the first chapter, the author runs out of bad memories and is forced to turn to pleasant memories and anecdotes in order to complete his own story. In doing so, he brings himself to a state where he confesses that he loves baseball and always has, whether or not baseball loves him, and that he would do it all over again in exactly the same way, the bad memories notwithstanding.

This was George Beahon's story and it was mine,

too. Baseball is business. And that business spins webs of illusion to draw loyal paying customers to itself. To partake of shared illusion is the definition of play. And so children are most susceptible to baseball.

Maturity does not destroy the capacity for play, but it does dispel illusion. And disillusion leads to cynicism. As I can see through the myths of baseball from the outside, so George Beahon can see through them from the inside. But the cynicism is about business and the frailties of mortals. The illusion of baseball cannot be dispelled. And so, despite the cynicism, we remain unable to refuse the playful notion of pure grandeur that is baseball. And we are glad for it. Cynicism, I learned from George Beahon, is no fun, and baseball is.

I was changed by my meeting with George Beahon in the way that you are always changed when you meet an honorable human being. Back in the postwar era, George Beahon was a professional tool of imperialism. But he, like everybody else, had come a long way since then. And though his politics and his style were definitely not my own, at a time in history when personalities are mannered to conform to a specific range of choices, George Beahon fitted none of the categories that I feared or mistrusted. His was not exactly the romance of the old journalist, but neither was he a modern corporate executive. The hysterical overstatement of postwar-era journalism was unbelievable, but now, I believed George Beahon.

Throughout the summer my thinking had been diligent and rigorous, but I had begun with many misconceptions. The International League was not the fleabag bus route of the low minors. It was always first-class trains and fancy hotels. The players were not particularly hungry. Old players, finished in the majors, always did, and still do, play in the minor leagues. This is the love of baseball, but it also fills out pension requirements, and this is a different kind of love affair than the one I remembered. Baseball for love was a thing of the first three decades of the century, but not a thing of my childhood. Fifteen years ago, players used to break down and cry when they lost the big game, but those players were paid bonus money for big games. According to George Beahon, when the Red Wings lost the pennant in a special playoff game this year, there were no tears in the clubhouse, but there was also no bonus. And tears flow more universally over lost money than over failure.

Baseball has changed. Modern players are smarter and more sober. In the old days, players gratefully took whatever they were offered. Now they know what they want and they are not afraid to ask for it. And nowadays, many of the players have gone to college. Apparently, on a statistical basis, it makes the pitchers smarter. And, of course, modern ballplayers are all "mod." In the old days, when I was a boy in the grandstand, some players conducted their private lives in a manner exceeding the limits of decency for a public figure. And other players of that era lived quite quietly; some even lived righteously. But today, they do everything all the time, and nobody thinks anything of it.

In the old days players hung around longer. It did not seem unusual when Steve Bilko played seven seasons for the Red Wings, before and after his successful major-league career. People knew him around town, fans knew him. Today, it's in and out before you learn how to spell their names.

In the old days the league was filled with big cities. Toronto, Montreal, Ottawa, Buffalo, they were all large enough to support not only a team, but an active night life. Towns had character for the players that played in them. Now they play in empty lots between dinkwater cities, and the loyalties and feelings of the fans are quite different. Rivalries used to be real. Buffalo hated Toronto and Toronto hated Montreal, and those games really meant something. That's all gone now.

And clearly, though I knew what it was to be a baseball fan in those days, I knew nothing about what the players' lives were like. And now I knew. Now the

romantic ideal of baseball above life would have to coexist with the realization that baseball *is* life. Older
players played just hard enough to get a job, and young
players were filled with enthusiasm, and that is how life
is, romantic about baseball or not.

George Beahon set me straight. And, oh dear, I had
opened up another vein of pure inquiry, but look at the
gems he handed me to begin with.

The secret dream I have always harbored of insulting Frank Horton had already been taken care of, on the
spot, by Fidel Castro. And local boy wonder Gabe Paul,
the cosmetic surgeon who healed the league when Havana
was amputated, it turns out has no friends in Rochester.
Gabe Paul's dream in life was to close down the minor
leagues and replace them with intrasquad games, played
by promising youths at concentrated baseball camps in
Florida. This was not a way to win friends in minor-
league baseball. This was a sin for Gabe Paul, larger
than I could have imagined.

I had been told of gilded corruption and decay in old
Havana before. But this time it was told without romance, and with the fear of being a white American.
Perhaps this was baseball's side of the story. Or perhaps
it was just the effects of political images on memory in
a mass society.

Anyway. Just by contrived circumstances, I happened to be in Rochester and I began to wonder. Who
were these aging ballplayers who dreamed the same
dream as all of us, but whose lives grew into the dream
when everyone else was outgrowing it? And because I was
back in Rochester, the question broadened. And who was
I, the aging ballplayer who retired to become a spectator
at the age of twelve and never gave it another thought
until the dawn of the corporate era caused the need for
a historical realignment?

Who were these people who lived their lives within
the world of baseball? Because I, in the form of my childhood dreams, am one of them. And I know now what

[143]

these childhood dreams mean to me, but what of those who lived a life that is a childhood dream come true? What does it mean to live a childhood dream past childhood, and into the disillusion that comes with age? Childhood dreams are usually abandoned and forgotten, but for ballplayers they must, one day, be shattered. How could I possibly know about these things from the grandstand? I had seen George Beahon on Friday, and on Monday morning I would see George Sisler, Jr., the Red Wing general manager who had been in Havana on all the right days. For the weekend, I was a restless innocent.

Restless, that's true, but not quite innocent. For the weekend, I was the errant son, back from his fruitless travels. And I brought to my parents' household, along with foolish ideas, the gloom of extended unemployment.

My dreams and analysis of baseball were constantly interrupted by questions pointing to the instability of my financial future. "But I can't look for a job," I countered weakly. "What about my research?"

As tempers rose, the situation moved from abstract to concrete. Parables and the wisdom of homespun sayings were replaced by a hard offer from a prominent friend of the family who happened to be a popcorn baron. And I was driven to articulating my commitment. "A man on the verge of translating the Rosetta Stone of his life does not sell popcorn at the movies until two o'clock in the morning for $115 a week!"

Children act on sheer impulse. And as they get older, increasingly, even against their will, they act for reasons. Eventually, as mature adults, they begin to need reason in order to act at all. We grow up, as it is called, not by necessity and not by desire, but by experience. If experience is, as it is for baseball players, merely an extension of childhood impulse, who needs a reason?

Children who are good at baseball need never grow up. To the childhood dreamer, this is the best life of all.

In the suburbs, children don't know what work is.

[144]

It is something done in secret, far away. But everyone knows what a baseball player does. He plays baseball all day long, just as children do. The baseball player is an adult, and yet he remains, in the eyes of children and adults alike, a boy.

A chance to fly in airplanes and sleep in hotels, to ride elevators and taxicabs, and to buy the newspaper just to read about yourself—could any young lad leave home with an exit as grand as baseball? Could any life compare?

It must be like heaven on earth to be a baseball player, and yet I do not come to the subject from the barren reaches beyond left field. I have learned the functions of desire in the discovery of truth during my baseball season of rediscovery. And I know that heaven and reality are never the same place, whatever the internal geography.

The childhood dream of playing baseball is one thing, and the reality is something else again. The two are as different as the social surroundings that create them. I have spent my life chasing dreams, all the way from being a baseball player to the glorious dream of revolution. And I have come all that distance to find out that, although responsibility may be a matter of moral judgment, truth is always personal. After a life spent pursuing idealized forms of living, and trying to fit my own eccentric character into those forms, I finally came to realize that the forms themselves were my own creation.

And I know that I look at baseball, and perhaps even at life, through the eyes of a child fan. That is my history. And the truth of the matter is that my envious curiosity about the lives of these baseball people is how I want things to be, because I know too much about the game to believe otherwise.

There is no way to train yourself to hit a baseball. If you can hit a baseball there are all sorts of things you can do to train; hitting the ball is a matter of reflexes, and the speed of these reflexes comes and goes, even within the same body. Hitting a baseball is something that some people do better than others, and that a few people do very well, but no one knows how or why they can do it. Hitting a baseball is a mystery.

Anyone old enough and good enough to play baseball professionally has already spent the entire focus of his childhood in practice, if the game holds such a concept. Experience is the best teacher, of course, but in baseball, the determining factors are always indeterminate until the game is over. The decisive moments appear only in retrospect, and this makes it difficult to prepare for them.

In baseball, necessity becomes available for recognition only at the moment of its execution. In baseball, the philosophical question "What do I do now?" can only be successfully answered by an instinctive reflex action. And we know, from life, that for such situations there is no possible preparation.

American children, if they are so inclined, learn the rules of baseball. How to play the game must be learned. But how to save a step or an instant by doing it before you decide—that is more difficult, even a bit mystical. No one knows how it works. Even the people who possess the phenomenal knack don't really know what it is, or why it exists.

All baseball stems from childhood dreams, but when baseball is life, and not fantasy, those exuberant dreams must rub against the embarrassment of mature personality, leaving every old ballplayer wondering how he got completely caught up in something that is so totally a part of youth. And, of course, this leaves old ballplayers, and their journalists, world-weary.

What George Beahon was trying to tell me was that, of course, his was a wonderful job. Havana was a certain kind of good time, but baseball, like baseball journalism, is a thing for the young. And while it all seemed wonderful then, it doesn't now, because we have seen too much of life to be able to suspend our carefully wrought sense of disbelief.

Broken-down bus rides, fleabag hotels, sandwiches for food, all the trials and sacrifices of the developing ballplayer in the lower minor leagues never bother the teen-age hopeful the way that they bother the middle-aged memory of those times. Memory is the defining characteristic of age, but the glories of one's own past cannot be rekindled just by examining them. The dreams of youth remain, preserved in memory, but we want different things from our dreams now that we are older.

There is something unique about the way people look, and talk, and act in Rochester. And this industrial town in upstate New York is my home town, so these native customs are as personally familiar as they are anthropologically exact. And George Beahon had drawn me back to it. What struck me most about him was not his information, but his lack of pretension, and his lack of an air of expertise. He told me everything with the disinterested deadpan delivery of a stranger in a bus station. There was no boasting, no flattery, no desire to create an impression. Just plain, uncalculated conversation to pass the time and remove whatever ignorance no great effort was necessary to remove.

And it seemed so charming when compared with big-city life in the corporate era. A town of peers, where wealth and status were neither outwardly visible nor looked for. A town where a television journalist and a baseball fan could meet and talk without even wondering why the meeting was taking place.

What was it about this particular small-town culture and habit and style that made it so necessary for me to get out, since what remains of Rochester seems so pleasant, and nice, and decent? What formed a generation of Americans who could identify themselves as adults only by going away to the crummy apartments and anomie of the big city? How could a place so awful seem so nice?

My dilemma cried out for memory and I was off again. My first stop was the Joseph Avenue public library. As a child, one of the great highlights of every week was being bundled into my father's Chevrolet and taken to the Joseph Avenue public library. From the outside, the building was exactly as I had remembered it. Victorian storefront windows, a side entrance, and at the back, a parking lot with only four spaces, which was never full. Today it was empty. The neighborhood had changed, but not much. Opposite the library, Soloman's Bargain Store was architecturally intact, but it was now called the Christian Community Church of Rochester.

As a child, while my father leafed through the magazines, and my sister contemplated her next selection in the Black Beauty series, I headed straight for the baseball shelf and looked for the novels of John R. Tunis. And now, even after all these years, it was a familiar route.

The shelf, however, was empty. I looked in the card catalogue under the name Tunis, but none of his novels was listed. John R. Tunis holds the combined distinction of having written over thirty separate baseball novels and being the author of all my favorite books, as selected during the years of the first Eisenhower administration. Every single Tunis novel I ever read I borrowed from the Joseph Avenue library, and now they were not there.

Rochester and its Joseph Avenue public library were the provinces. And in the provinces, things are built and destroyed a bit more slowly and a bit less thoroughly. This was no pocket of cold-war-era culture, this was a derelict cultural form scheduled for demolition, and slightly behind schedule. After all, someone had undertaken the physical task of actually throwing John R. Tunis out of the library. And that reveals a mentality that has nothing to do with the past and everything to do with the nature of modern market structures.

The key to the themes of all Tunis novels is stated

on a separate page, after the title. "The author wishes to state that all the characters in this book were drawn from real life." This is a book of object-lesson education. Good ballplayers are made out of good boys. Good behavior is both the means and the end of baseball. In all the Tunis novels, noble characters triumph over those without the will or fortitude to succeed. Strength of character is always the key to success. Heroes are constantly suffering moral trials, on the field and off. Time and again, they are brought to the brink of despair, but fortunes change suddenly in baseball, and in the world of the novels of John R. Tunis, the day is always won.

The books center around a mythical team of Brooklyn Dodgers. All characters have only nicknames. Spike, Fat Stuff, Razzle, Rats. The umpire is Old Stubblebeard, the manager is Grouchy. A large percentage of the books is straight dialogue. And the dialogue always consists of the rigid and formal patterns made famous by Hollywood movie fantasies of the all-American peasant. Lots of "Foller that ball, will ya," and "A pop-up to the catcher, shucks! Well, only one down," and "Holy Suffering Catfish!" Uniforms are always "monkey suits," bats are "war clubs" and second base is often "swiped" but never simply stolen.

At the center of the plot there is always a young lad. He is a good boy who is awed by and respectful of the world of baseball. He is kind and decent and honest, and modest and shy. And, it turns out, he is a phenomenal baseball player who saves the pennant for the team and brings fame and fortune to himself. There is always a crisis with celebrity, and it is always resolved, after a long talk with the manager, by the realization that baseball is what really matters. Honorable behavior off the field is just another part of keeping yourself in the best possible shape to play baseball. Philosophically, Tunis is just a short step away from John Calvin. He never takes that step, but it is a short enough distance to see how he would do it. Giving up your seat on the bus to an old

[149]

lady was necessary to good baseball, because it would be noticed in heaven. And tomorrow afternoon, as you came sliding into second base, heaven would remember what you did on the bus and make sure that you were safe. Good people do good works, and the World Series was the best work of all.

Tunis wrote most of his baseball novels before World War II. But as prototypical vignettes of postwar-era style, they are unsurpassed.

"This was the World Series. He thought of what it would mean, Grandma listening in, on the farm, the boys at the drugstore, and prob'ly old Mr. Haskins, the president of the First National Bank, who advised him not to leave his job and go wasting his time on baseball."

" 'Raz, your English is really something,' remarked Fat Stuff.

" 'Yea, and my Spanish is something too. Say, Fat Stuff, a guy I know who lived in Havana told me the Spanish have no word for shortstop. Whadd'ya think of that?'

" 'I wouldn't worry if I were you, Razzle,' said the old pitcher, 'neither have the Phillies.' "

" 'Catcher by the name of Jocko Klein, up from the Three I League to Rochester, and did better than all right there last year. He won't last here, though.'

" 'No? Why not?'

" 'Jewish boy. The bench jockeys will get to him. You'll see. They'll ride that baby to death. Besides, these Jewish boys can't take it. Haven't got the guts.' "

But Razzle wins the big game, and Jocko Klein, to my relief, becomes a star catcher. The secret of their success, and the success of countless other Brooklyn Dodgers, was that when crisis arrived, introspection followed. And introspection, with a little help from an authoritarian paternal figure of a manager, never failed to reveal a hidden source of strength and courage.

Tunis often calls it "pep" and "pepper," but more frequently he just says, "Be tough." " 'I had plenty of stumbles and tumbles. Only I kept on a-plugging. I didn't quit, see.' "

The standard American macho that was creating and sustaining an empire pervades Tunis. But these novels were written and read, for the most part, before World War II. Tunis wrote before the time when American guilt and material ambition went over the top of life. His books have a moral tone that was both authentic and quaint when I read them. And that authentic moral quality makes them more than just baseball books for boys. They were special to me as a child, and they are special to me now. And no matter how corny the dialogue, or how melodramatic the plot, I cannot judge them on their sins alone.

Now I can see the former governor of California, dressed in the uniform of the St. Louis Cardinals, peering off the mound for the signal from his catcher. It is Ronald Reagan, starring in a movie called *The Winning Team*, which in my neighborhood was always referred to as *The Grover Cleveland Alexander Story*. In real life, Grover Cleveland Alexander was a star pitcher who succumbed to epilepsy and alcoholism. At thirty-nine years of age, he was making a modest comeback with the Cardinals. He won the second and sixth games of the 1926 World Series, after which he went out on a stupendous bender, and for the all-important seventh game he was ill and hung over.

In the seventh inning, the Yankees loaded the bases with two out. Alexander was slapped together and brought out to pitch. He struck out Lazzeri on three pitches to end the inning. And then, still drunk and dazed, he held the Yankees for two more innings and became suitable subject matter for a Hollywood baseball movie.

This was among the best known of baseball stories. It has been endlessly retold in every anthology of the greatest moments in baseball. But, as everyone knows, Hollywood, in its heyday, had no lack of nerve.

In the film version, Ronald Reagan interprets Grover

[151]

Cleveland Alexander as a clean-living young man without a personality defect or a care in the world. On the day of the big game, he drinks a bottle of mouthwash, which he thought was water, and he becomes ill. Then, in the seventh inning, medically deficient but morally straight, Reagan comes off the bench for the famous strikeout. When I think of that kind of competition, my admiration for Tunis grows.

In his autobiography, Tunis says that he did not write his books for juveniles, but that they were read by children because only the young had not been corrupted and could respond to his notions of fair play and decency. He says that he was only a reporter who wrote what he saw. What he saw was sports, and it was, as he said, "seldom good and really clean in its effect upon those who watch and those who compete.

"We never learn to accept defeat as a part of maturity, that we cannot have our own way, always, or even often. How we face defeat and disappointment is a test of growth and part of the development of character."

Tunis was a baseball fan, not a baseball player. He knew baseball from the grandstand, not from the inside. And just as he was able to deduce entire personalities for the characters in his novels merely by watching real baseball games, so he taught me to do the same thing. What I learned from Tunis was how to make complete character judgments from watching baseball games.

What I was supposed to learn was that the arena of heroism was all of life. But I found no models for heroism in my neighborhood, so I invented them at the ballpark. Tunis taught me how. And that left me with a notion of heroism that understood moral living as the highest order, because ability grew out of character.

I read my John R. Tunis novels during the afternoons of the same summers that I went to all the Red Wing games. And it is as difficult to separate them from each other as it is to trace any aspect of identity to a single influence. But the Tunis novels were the easiest and most convenient physical objects to attach symbolism to. In my family, we had no family jewels, but we did have visits to the local public library. And so the higher metaphors of daring, courage, and bravery that I drew out of baseball from above, and the lower metaphors of baseball games that I drew out of hitting a tennis ball against the porch steps and, in fact, my entire capacity to enrich the meaning of the events of everyday life by the process of making metaphors, I attributed to the baseball books in the public library.

I returned to the Joseph Avenue public library to consult an oracle whose specialty was metaphor. And I believed in the magic of the oracle because, the baseball shelf being empty, there was no evidence to the contrary. And though it was soothing to have my sense of historical change reassured, I felt a personal loss. How dare they throw away John R. Tunis! What impatience and what desire drove them to it? And what happens to a culture in which even the public library throws out the past?

I drove from the library to the grammar school I attended as a child. And I combed the neighborhood for historical indices. The last horse trough in Rochester, opposite the Hickey Freeman clothing factory, was gone. Hickey Freeman itself, whose paychecks once dominated the economy of the neighborhood, was now just a division of a division of some corporate conglomerate. The Seneca Dairy was gone. (In times of despair, my father always wanted to send me there, with the punch line, "You could get a job turning sweet cream into sour cream at the Seneca Dairy.") The shack at the Avenue D playground had been replaced by a respectable two-story brick building.

In the postwar era, I had played in the Avenue D playground in a way that it is no longer possible to play. Time, in the corporate era, has been rationalized. Only irresponsible low-lifes and bums waste time; good people invest it. And it's not that the ground itself has changed much, but, where children used to play, they now exchange their time for a commodity called recreation. And so the sign that used to say playground now says "Avenue D Recreation Center."

Louie Sussman's, where we used to buy penny candies, was now Jose Vargas Spanish and American Groceries. The old soda shoppe was now Martinez Deli-Lunch. The railroad tracks that I walked home along during the wonderful season of the big bus strike, when teachers were not allowed to keep you after school, were intact. So was the Conkey Street Grill, and Englert's Live Bait Store. Conkey I understood, but why a "street" grill on Conkey Avenue? I felt the sadness of being worldly. I now knew that live bait was for fishing, and Englert's had none of the mystery it did in my early student days. The Double E Tavern, where courageous seventh graders skipped school to be pinboys at the six bowling lanes in the back, was derelict, but only recently so.

My alma mater, Number 8 School, was an ordinary red-brick building, just as unevocative now as it has always been and, clearly, the birthplace of no thrills.

The street names burned in my heart with the power of poetry. Tyler Street, Harris Street, Requa Street, they sent the same shivers up and down my spine as Elvis Presley's records once did. But everything else about the old neighborhood seemed orderly and predictable. Different cultures had taken over the old neighborhood, but long before that I had moved out. Isn't it better that the library should serve the people who go there than to be able to startle a collector of postwar remnants and memories? Of course it is. But wasn't any part of the culture that shaped my identity and determined my life worth saving? We know that baseball is intact, but what of the worlds that surround baseball and gave it its true substance as a cultural form? And what of the moral concepts that I am stuck with, no matter what is done to the world? And how does anybody know what's going on any more?

[154]

On Sunday afternoon, I wandered into the basement of my parents' house in the suburbs. And I began, carefully and cautiously, to look through the piles of junk everywhere.

The first things I found were my old baseball gloves. I am left-handed, which was rare in my neighborhood, and unique in my family, so I had to have my own baseball glove at an early age. Which is to say, I had reason enough behind my desire for a baseball glove to overcome my parents' fear of spoiling me.

My first glove was a four-fingered Nokona, Cal Abrams autograph model. I always suspected that my father got the glove wholesale, but years later I learned that Cal Abrams was not only left-handed, but Jewish as well. And this, undoubtedly, was the determining factor in my father's selection.

One evening, I left my Cal Abrams autograph model outside overnight. It rained for days and I forgot about playing baseball. And after some days in the rain, and some in the sun, I found it. Hard as a rock and shriveled out of shape, it was useless. I rubbed neatsfoot oil all over it, inside and out. I heated the glove when one consultant recommended that, and I cooled the glove when another suggested that. Nothing worked. The Cal Abrams autograph model remained the evidence both for my genuine need for a new baseball glove, and for my inability to handle the responsibility that went with it.

The dilemma took an entire season to resolve. I had to use an old right-handed cheapo Enos Slaughter model, which one of my cousins left at my house and never bothered to collect. Today that hated Enos Slaughter model is still in my parents' basement, probably not very far from where my cousin left it. Now it is a quaint relic, but I still hate that mitt. This mitt was so cheap that its five fingers weren't even tied together. It being a right-handed model, I had to wear it backward, which made it difficult to keep on my hand, no less catch baseballs.

The hard time was followed by a McGregor first-baseman's mitt, a Ted Kluszewski autograph model. It was a beauty, and now, sitting in the neatly piled junk, it still is. I don't understand why, but I soon got bored with the first-baseman's mitt and started saving for a new glove. Three years later, just before I stopped playing baseball, I bought, for sixteen dollars, the greatest glove I ever saw. It was a Rawlings VBM Snap-Action model. And it was autographed by the United States congressman who used to pitch for the St. Louis Cardinals, Vinegar Bend Mizell. I was never a pitcher, and I never liked Vinegar Bend, but that glove was so beautiful I didn't care whose name was on it. It was broken in perfectly, by me, and admired by players much older and much more talented than I. The tragedy was that it cost sixteen dollars, and the VBM came too late in life for me to use it for very long. Just before I went to college, I sold this glove for six dollars, an act I would find stupid and unforgivable in others. The fact that I did it myself seems both of these things and incomprehensible as well. The postwar era was not so near after all. And history shapes us in ways that we cannot even remember. And how did these baseball gloves survive the onslaughts of suburbanization, consumerization, and the destruction of roots and home?

It was a question easily answered, as I continued to snoop. Everywhere I turned, I seemed to come across my father's grade-school notebooks, my sister's grade-school notebooks, and my own notes from Number 8 School. Pictures cut out of the newspaper by my father when he was six years old, and pictures cut out by my sister and I when we were six. The weight of the family archives made me know that nothing had ever been thrown out, but was always mislaid. Somewhere in the haystack was a needle that sewed continuity.

This was the cultural junk of lifetimes discarded. And now, before the blinding effects of transition have faded, it was still possible to search through it and turn artifact into talisman. It was possible actually to examine these trinkets of rejected cultural forms. I couldn't resist trying to rediscover their magic, and take it with me as protector and guide through the marketing maze that cultural life has become.

By evening I was aggressively ransacking the basement, searching for my autographed pictures of Ted Williams and Robin Roberts. At the same time that I was cursing myself for having mislaid them in 1956, I began to remember that I was away at Boy Scout camp when my family moved to the suburbs, and they must have mislaid them. I was too embarrassed to ask, having remained silent these last nineteen years, and while I never found them, what I did find was always an encouragement to keep looking.

I found two autographed baseballs. One signed by Gene Green, and one signed by two famous old Red Wings, now both dead, who came to Rochester for an Old Timers' Game some time before I moved to the suburbs. Then I came across the Gene Green file.

Gene Green was a young outfielder of great strength, whom the Red Wings turned into a catcher. He played for the Red Wings for several years, and by 1956 he was a fine fielding catcher and an impressive power hitter. A natural ballplayer with everything it takes, he was snapped up by the Cardinals, and went on to have an undistinguished major-league career.

He was also, I now realized, very handsome. Gene Green was never one of my favorites; these were my sister's mementos. I never knew that my sister was interested in baseball, but what a cache this was! Gil Hodges, Pee Wee Reese, Jackie Robinson, and the rest of the Brooklyn Dodgers, informally posed in a photograph pasted onto the front of a loose-leaf notebook; Stan Musial smiled in close-up on the back. And inside, postcards from Florida and Cape Cod, and a wad of newspaper articles and photographs.

[157]

The wedding of Red Wing pitcher Eddie Ludwig, depicted in a photograph from the *Democrat and Chronicle*. Gene Green is best man, and the wedding couple is surrounded by Rochester Red Wings, including Gary Geiger, Joey Cunningham, and Cot Deal. And headlines:

GENE GREEN BLASTS
KEEP WINGS IN PENNANT PICTURE

GREEN'S HOLIDAY:
3 HOMERS, 7 HITS, 10 RBI'S

GREEN EARNED HIS WEEK'S PAY
COLLECTING 17 HITS, 4 HOMERS

There was a letter to the editor from Gladys Green, of Sanger, California, renewing her subscription to the Rochester papers and thanking them for their complete coverage of her son, Gene. And there were newspaper pictures. Gene Green arguing with the umpire. Gene Green smiling after getting the hit that won the game that took the Red Wings into the Junior World Series. Gene Green shaking hands with pitcher Gary Blaylock, after driving in three runs and winning the game. And a snapshot of my little cousin handing his autograph book and a pen to Gene Green.

There were also eight Rochester Red Wings official scorecard programs from the 1956 season, nearly all of them autographed by Gene Green. Where the score would be kept, Gene Green's name is entered in his correct batting position, and all the other spaces are either left blank or filled in with the titles of the top ten songs. Number one, "I Want You to Be My Girl," number two, "Why Do Fools Fall in Love?" number three, "Black Denim Trousers and Motorcycle Boots," and on down through "Hot Diggity" and "Jeepers Creepers."

Guy Mitchell's "Singin' the Blues," "Don't Be Cruel," by Elvis Presley, and even, "Out of Sight Out of Mind," by the Five Keys. My memory was definitely being stirred.

The hit parade on an old baseball scorecard. And if you add a piece of apple pie, a glass of cold milk, and a pile of baseball cards, you would have an evocative work of conceptual art.

Baseball cards. I had forgotten all about baseball cards. I know it must have meant something to have spent my childhood years carrying around pictures of my heroes. Their presence, even only as picture cards, must have offered some illusion of power or comfort, but I can't honestly say. In fact, I have no memory of collecting baseball cards. Which is not to say that I did not collect them, but only that events transpired which so destroyed the magic that attached to these cards that I can't even remember my relationship to them.

Of course, I remember the cards themselves. They were the same size as playing cards, and neatly fit into a deck, which in turn neatly fit into a back pocket. On the expensive side was a fancy color picture of a big-league baseball player, and on the back, information, cartoons, and statistics about the player. In the later years of my childhood, the pictures became more formal and more posed and there were fewer cartoons and more print on the back. The increased wealth and technical sophistication of the postwar era were creating professionalism, and baseball cards became a bigger deal. In earlier years, the cards were less classic and more expressive. The printing wasn't so good, the poses weren't so formal, and there was a sense of design to each card that even an eight-year-old fan couldn't fail to notice. One year, the names of the players were spelled out in letters of alternating colors. Often there was a small black-and-white inset, even more candid, showing the player sliding, leaping, or making a circus catch.

In the spring, flipping baseball cards was the most esteemed male activity in the schoolyards of Rochester. The fashion was to come to school with your collection in numerical order in one back pocket, and your doubles in the other. And, depending on how often you bought bubble gum, the bulge in your pocket would grow. The hope was that as the summer wore on, you would de-

crease the size of your double deck and increase the size
of your collection. It seemed quite logical, but it didn't
always work out. You always seemed to get stuck with
six or seven of Dick Schofield, shortstop, St. L. Cardinals,
and never a Mickey Mantle.

It is true that I know about baseball cards, but it
is also true that I preferred not to remember them.
Shortly before we moved to the suburbs, my father, who
earned his living as a printer, began work on a job for
the Topps Bubble Gum Company. The job was to print up
the baseball cards for the next year. On the one hand,
I was overjoyed, because I would have the entire series
for the first time in my life; on the other hand, this meant
that the magical baseball cards that came wrapped with
slabs of bubble gum were now part of that *stuff*—the
beer signs and eyeglass catalogues that my father's company usually printed.

One February night, when no child baseball fan on
the face of the earth was thinking about baseball cards,
my father brought home the proof sheets for me to look
at. There were two huge sheets, each containing several
hundred cards. I looked at every single picture. And I
realized that through all these years of collecting I had
been the victim, not of fate, chance, or luck, but of the
Topps Bubble Gum Company. There really were five
times as many Solly Hemus cards as there were Stan
Musials.

In fact, the more obscure the name, the more frequently the card appeared. All these years I had been
duped. Each spring, I had increased my consumption of
bubble gum to the borders of nausea, in the hope of
finally getting a complete collection. And now I saw that
my satisfaction was never the desire of the gum company.
They created the collector's desire in me, and they
frustrated it. Topps did not play fair. And at a tender
age, I knew it.

When the baseball cards were finally printed and cut,

my father brought home two complete sets. I didn't want them, but I saved them until spring. I feared that if I showed them to anyone, the gum company would find out and God knows what they would have done to my father and me. When baseball cards began to appear at school again, the coast was clear, and I gave one set each to my friend Irwin and my cousin, whose mouth hung open in appreciation. And I have not thought about baseball cards from that day to this; "KPAA," though, is another thing.

During World War II, when mothers worked in factories and adolescents, left to their own devices, made trouble, the benevolent Eastman Kodak Company attempted to remedy the situation by starting the Kodak Park Athletic Association, commonly known as KPAA. I knew its initials years before I knew what they stood for.

The Kodak Park Athletic Association was probably a lot of other things, too, but for me, it was the only official membership organization I took any joy in joining. My father had been fond of the Boy Scouts in his day, and so I was dutifully a tenderfoot Boy Scout for years. But I never enjoyed the great outdoors, as they knew it, or first aid, or being told what to do next by constantly supervising adults. I had enough of those circumstances at school. And Little League was no different. I couldn't play Little League because I had Hebrew School four nights a week, and then came the Sabbath. Though I hated Hebrew school bitterly, I never felt any sense of loss about missing Little League. I used to watch the occasional game on Friday afternoons, and Little League always seemed to be an extension of school into baseball. Little League baseball was always filled with sobbing strikeout victims, proud and dismayed overbearing parents, and dictatorial adult coaches. No one seemed to have any fun but the overgrown, overfast, twelve-year-old goons, who did the pitching and hit all the home runs.

But KPAA was different. It seemed to have no employees, and no notion of adult supervision, discipline, or even authority. When a fight broke out at a KPAA game, it was finished; in Little League, it would have been broken up.

KPAA used the facilities provided and maintained by Kodak. There were twenty or thirty fields scattered around the factories in clusters of four. Bats and balls and two umpires were provided for each game. There was a week of practice, after which you were handed a printed schedule of two games a week for the rest of the summer.

All other arrangements were left to be organized by the players themselves. Every spring, applications would begin to float around Number 8 School. So and so from Mrs. Mindel's sixth grade was trying to get up a KPAA team. A team was at least eleven players, but many people joined alone. So, however many players a sign-up team was short, they would be assigned from the pool.

Teams were arranged in leagues exactly paralleling professional baseball. Classes D to AAA, and the majors. I played on the Aces in the Atlantic League, and the Suns of the Southern League, and others.

Every player in the league was given a free T-shirt that had the name of his team and "KPAA" across the front. KPAA shirts were made out of some special thick cotton and they never wore out. In my neighborhood, like most of the neighborhoods I knew in Rochester, the most fashionable clothing item around was a KPAA shirt. And since they never wore out, you could always get one free from someone who had outgrown his. And, of course, if you won your league's pennant, you got a free camera and a chance to play under the lights at Kodak's own stadium.

After a disastrous year playing on my cousin's team, I played for my friend David Friedman and settled down to a few good seasons at first base, and then a season as the only left-handed catcher around. But my very first year, though I was pleased to have a brand-new KPAA shirt, was a disaster.

My very first game was the only one I remember playing in that season; I'm pretty certain that after it, I was permanently benched for the rest of the schedule. The field was so flat that it reminded me of Red Wing Stadium. It had chalk lines and white powdered bases. A mask for the catcher was provided. There were bleachers, and a few Kodak workers had drifted in and become spectators. This was the biggest-time baseball I had ever seen outside of Red Wing Stadium, and I was about to play there. I had always considered the empty lot on Nye Park the best diamond around, but this was unbelievable.

When I came to bat in the second inning, the effect of the whole business, as John R. Tunis might have predicted, went to my head. I hit the first pitch on the ground to the third baseman, but his throw was wide and I was safe at first. On the very first pitch to the next batter, I broke for second base. I was a slow runner, but the catcher threw the ball into the outfield and I was safe.

My cousin, the team captain, came tearing off the bench right up to second base and screamed at me for going without his signal. I calmly assured him that it was just a simple mistake, and that I would never again try to steal except at his command.

But I had just successfully stolen second base, and could not be intimidated. On the very next pitch I broke for third base, and would easily have made it except that, as I approached the bag, I recognized Harvey Hollander standing on the base. He was my cousin's next-door neighbor, our team's left fielder, and the batter who opened our inning with a double. And though I had completely forgotten about him, Harvey Hollander moved to third base as I beat out my infield error. And now, terrified by my ignorance, I remembered all about him.

"What are you doing here?" he yelled. "Get back to second base!" I tried to explain that it was too late for

[163]

that, but the ball suddenly arrived. Harvey was off, caught in a run-down, while I waited, anxious to take possession of third base, but not sure that it was ethical to make my move before I found out what happened to Harvey Hollander. To my horror, Harvey Hollander was heading back toward third base when, luckily, the over-anxious catcher threw the ball into the outfield. Harvey and I both scored.

I had single-handedly accounted for two runs and thought all would be forgiven. Harvey Hollander was torn between rage and disbelief. He could hardly speak. My cousin faced no such dilemma. He had accepted the responsibility for putting his relatives in the lineup. And one of the ingrates had responded to the gift of nepotism with mischievous disobedience. He believed what he had seen, and told me so in the unkindest way. I was removed from the game.

I didn't play the rest of the season, but this was not a case of peer-group tyranny, as later sociologists might identify it. KPAA was simply boys playing baseball. Simply young boys obsessed by baseball, and allowed by the culture to pursue that obsession without the help of the local Oldsmobile dealer, the mayor, or frustrated tactical geniuses who manipulated young boys only because the New York Yankees wouldn't hire them.

From the viewpoint of the times we live in, the adult neglect that characterized the KPAA seems a rare and special privilege, and it was. The Eastman Kodak Company put together a boys' baseball program on the cheap. And in so doing, they made that baseball devoid of any hustlers, voyeurs, or respectable hangers-on. KPAA was never reported in the newspapers and never discussed by adults. It was so simple, and so clean and so good. And it could never happen today.

My precious autographed pictures I never found. And while I will never know what they might have brought me, I had, as I ferreted through the basement, the distinct feeling that whatever the sentiments evoked through symbolism, they were arriving in advance of the locating.

What I had forgotten was that it was not just a matter of the game of baseball itself, or even the Cuban detente extension into foreign policy, but all the satellite worlds that surround baseball. Each satellite has its own part or orbit, and at each distance it defines a limit of obsession. These satellite worlds are part of baseball, in the sense that they serve it by maintaining the illusion that the limits of baseball are infinite. Baseball was not merely a game played by my friends in the lots and by professionals in Red Wing Stadium. It was a world that stretched to all of life, too vast and too complex to possibly comprehend in one lifetime. Playing baseball was one thing and watching was another, but taking up the slack between them was the overanxious desire to impose the framework of baseball on everything in life.

I was never able to conquer life through baseball. But I did become skilled in the art of metaphor, to a point where I could abstract baseball from the thinnest reality. Even out of the little game I played, bouncing a tennis ball against the back wall of our garage. I would spend the afternoon playing two major-league teams in a five-game series. I would try to mimic each batter's actual baseball style in the way that I threw the tennis ball against the garage wall. If I caught the rebound, it was an out; if it got past me, a hit. Power hitters boomed the tennis ball across the path and into the yard, bunters dropped it down into the flower garden. It wasn't really baseball, it was daydreaming. And it wasn't really daydreaming, it was metaphor. And it was a relationship to reality that has continued to shape my identity and determine my character.

The trick that made baseball games out of bouncing a tennis ball was keeping score. And correspondingly, the trick that makes baseball into history, culture, and learning is statistics. The record of an event has the power to re-create the event. Statistics is the key to

[165]

metaphor. And part of the childhood me, who considered statistics the sweetest of all metaphors, still exists today. There is nothing that can compare with the excitement of assigning a precise and accurate mathematical value to a central mystery of life. That mathematical value, which is, in one sense, absurd, seems just the opposite when applied to mystery in a particular way. All the tradition and care of computation. All the time-honored checks and verifications. Just the mental strain of long division gives credence to statistics.

Anyone who has ever spent an afternoon at long division knows that when the answer finally comes up, it feels like fact.

The truth is that statistics is really only an illusion set in motion by a traditional comparison of accountable events. Once this illusion suggests itself, as it always does, there is no alternative but to submerge yourself and, finally bolstered and reinforced by the precision of arithmetic, come to a concrete number which stands as fact and warms the heart against the cold wind of all that is unknowable about life. And so when we see that Tommy Burgess, Rochester, LF, is leading the league because he got hits 1.25 percent of the time more than his top competitor, we know that this is an impossible distinction to make, but we accept Tommy Burgess as the batting champion. That's the magic of numbers.

The baseball fan who cannot watch every game every night can know as much as if he did, just by learning the statistical codes and watching the box scores in the newspapers. Who did well today, who did poorly. Knowing this, you could actually feel the mood of the team. Not so much by mathematical computation as by statistical saturation, you could actually feel, emotionally, how things were with the team. The box scores provided access for statistical voyeurism. Through the box scores you could spy on the behavior of the players, and through metaphors of your own construction you could know the moods and personalities of the players and be smart about the game. Second-guessing was more than preparation for hindsight. It was the metaphoric link to that internal region of baseball where the mystery is created and understood. In my childhood, statistics had nothing to do with the concepts of samplings or population. It was nothing less than a matter of becoming one with that particular god who controlled destiny but who spent all his time arranging the outcome of baseball games. When I made my judgments, I knew that they were sound. I knew that I was qualified to manage the team. I called every judgment in the game, and I knew that if I didn't call them perfectly, at least I called them better than Cot Deal. And there have been very few situations in my life since baseball that have allowed me to see such crucial situations in such a concrete and decisive way.

The reason for this was that I had done my homework. While everybody else was guessing, I busied myself with long division. And while everyone else predicted by whim and desire, I proceeded through science alone.

In later years, my interest in politics led me to a very different sort of feeling about statistics. They are as accurate as any other system of poetry or beauty, when they are understood as such, but they are made by men from materials, and exist, finally, only in the eye of the beholder. And they are made for many reasons that have nothing to do with the pursuit of truth and knowledge.

The statistics tell us simply that fortune, chance, and quirks of fate are not random. Some people do, in fact, play better baseball than others. And though anything is possible, in the longer view, certain things are more likely to happen to some players than others.

All baseball players have their ups and downs, their slumps and streaks. All professional baseball players learned the fundamental procedures of baseball as children, and have practiced them to perfection. And yet, however perfect, these fundamental actions tend to produce successes and failures in long and complicated sequences. A player might have a bad game, a bad week, or a bad month. Or a bad season. He might snap back to superb performance, or he might never recover. Even a star might get into a slump and never return. Even the worst player can suddenly spring to excellence. In the newspapers, they call it maturity, or competitive spirit, or they call it a sore arm, or wildness, or off-timing, or bad attitude, but the origin and function of these changing and extended moods of actual performance are mysterious and much darker than anyone knows. These moods are very private, contained within playing-field personalities. Even for the players themselves, these secrets are inaccessible to consciousness. Players know of their own capabilities only by way of consequences. They are no closer to an understanding of the matter than the fans. They are forced to rely on the same inadequate statistics, because there is nothing else. That critical fraction of time and distance is beneath perception.

And in the midst of all this obsession with measurement, and the will to win, and the expression of personality, and the whims of chance are the myriad factors that link the little separate events of a baseball game to each other and to history. That is to say, baseball is what it is because of the attitude of its fans. Each fan must draw for himself the comprehensive patterns and the incalculable factors that emerge from games to form baseball history. Each fan does this differently, bound by the limits of personality. Perhaps it is a pleasant summer afternoon, whiled away drinking beer at the baseball game. Perhaps it is instruction in the good life, extracted from the behavior of the larger lives of heroes. And perhaps it will emerge as the archetype for all of life's experience. But whatever the form, the events and the statistics of baseball games will be remembered, and studied and discussed, and preserved in their retelling, because baseball, as well as being a game, is a way for people to say who they are, and where they have been, and what they may hope.

At Hebrew school, we used to play a game called Chinese baseball. This consisted of throwing a tennis ball against the back wall behind the Holy Ark. It would rebound into a cinder-topped parking lot of fielders. There were specific delineations for singles, doubles, and triples. Over the cliff was a home run, but there were those who were robbed by death-defying, climbing-down-the-cliff catches.

All base-running and scoring took place only within the minds of the players, but the image was absolutely complete. The reality of the situation was no more than throwing a tennis ball, but this time in company, and that made the experience as total as any big-league game. Despite the limitations, we all had our baseball personalities. The bunter, just trying to get on base, would use position and angle rather than strength, and try to get the ball to fall just over a jutting shed roof. The power hitters would take a long run and shoot for the cliff. All the tactics, strategy, and drama of real baseball, we had off that back wall.

Even as a young child, I knew, from my cousins, about Monopoly, Parcheesi, Clue, and The Great Game of Sorry, but my board game was All-Star Baseball. It was a simple affair. The board consisted of some glossy printing and two mounted spinners. The players consisted of round disks marked off in numbered sections. The numbers stood for various kinds of hits and outs. The game consisted of placing the disks over the spinners and awaiting fate's control of the spin.

It was a simple game, but still, the players were personalized. Each year, new disks were issued, based on last season's all-star team. Duke Snider had the largest angle of possibility for a home run, although my uncle's old set from the thirties was sometimes brought out by my cousin, and that had Babe Ruth, with a home run

[169]

angle even larger than Snider's. It was my understanding that the game was scientifically designed so that if you played an entire season of games, each cardboard disk would reproduce the exact performance of that player in that season. Even though I knew baseball wasn't like that, I trusted the statistics to intensify the metaphor. And besides, if you could have Duke Snider, Willie Mays, and Hank Aaron on the same team, you didn't like to ask too many questions.

I played with my cousins and always kept score. Since the action existed only as an abstraction, keeping score was all that the game actually was. I kept the score sheets in the bottom of my night table, until the drawer was so full it cracked. Then I threw them all out and began again. The summer we moved to the suburbs, where I didn't know anyone, I played a ninety-nine-game season of all-star games between the National and American League teams of the previous year. At the end of the season, I computed every imaginable statistic for every player. It was not quite science. Four hundred hitters were quite common, and the average number of runs per game was nearly twenty, more than double the number of runs produced in real baseball. As I look back and see the amount of energy and concentration that went into the cardboard disks and spinners, I am amazed by the way this game was able to pull me into total transcendence. At school, I was never very good at arithmetic. But I did all of the computation for all the various averages, and I was accurate. Arithmetic was a discipline, and something I was not good at, but baseball statistics were simply the logical extension of the need to know. They had to be done correctly, and besides, they were never a chore if you knew that at the end of the arithmetic you would have an up-to-the-minute batting average.

When I was about twelve, David Friedman, my old KPAA captain and my friend, sent away for a very expensive, fancy, mail-order game called APBA. What the initials stood for is something I never inquired about and never found out. I spent many days of my life playing that game, but, really, it came too late. I had moved to the suburbs and begun to dream of driving automobiles and chasing after fast women before ABPA ever had a chance to get its hooks into my imagination. Had the game come into my life when my dynasty of internal baseball was ascending, rather than collapsing, who knows how different my life might have been.

The game was very complicated, with many throws of different-size dice. There were different categories of pitchers, and the meaning of the roll of the dice varied accordingly. The batters were thrown with double-digit dice, allowing for the possibility of nearly every number between 11 and 66. A card for each batter translated the roll of the dice into that batter's performance, scientifically calculated on the basis of last year's actual performance. It was all very scientific and as manager you could duplicate the strategy decisions of real baseball. Yet the transformation from board game to mental baseball was never made for me by APBA as it was by All-Star Baseball. The trouble with the game was that it made you feel that you were always on the verge of mastering it, when it was clear that the game required at least a lifetime of devotion just to be comfortable with its mechanics. I kept waiting for the time when I would be able to jump up after throwing the dice and yell, "Eleven, home run, we win, yippie!" But that was a point I never reached. I seemed forever stuck at a primitive stage. The roll of the dice was always followed by "Eleven ... Let's see, right-handed pitcher, Class C ... No plus or minus, right? ... Okay ... Let's see, Roy Campanella ... eleven ... I think it was a home run, just let me check and make sure I looked in the right column."

What strikes me all these years later is not that APBA failed to consume me, but the extent to which it was given its chance. During that winter, my friend and I did manage to get through the entire National League season. That represents about six hundred games. And with the countless readings of all the cumbersome charts and tables, our commitment represents, by the standards of ordinary behavior, an overwhelming devotion to APBA baseball. Partly, this had to do with the scale of the game's price tag and our respectful desire to get our money's worth. But much more than this was the fact that we were not baseball novices. We knew the world of internal baseball, and we knew all kinds of other forms of transportation to get there. APBA was complicated, but nothing was more complex than real baseball, and so, with our difficulty, we came to believe that we were approaching a more complex, more exciting, and, therefore, a higher form of internal baseball.

Every religious sect baffles outsiders. As outsiders genuinely look for understanding through reasonable explanation, they are driven to accusations of hoax, hype, and fraud. When the believer comes in contact with his belief, some mysterious satisfaction is produced that no outsider can comprehend.

I played an entire National League season of APBA. The games took far longer than real baseball games, since with every pitch we were required to look through all the complicated charts that we had not yet completely mastered. But the time didn't make any difference. However awkward our approximation of APBA's metaphor, we were still playing baseball. Outside, the snow was two feet thick, and inside, we were playing big-time major-league baseball. So you had to look through some tricky charts. It was still baseball.

For the APBA score sheets, I devoted a second drawer of my night table. Time passed and the pile of score sheets rose, proving that even in Rochester, New York, there was one part of winter that could be transformed into summer, and thereby keep young boys who hated schoolwork transfixed and in a state of scholarship. The late innings were usually accompanied by the terror that I would be called home and the game would have to be postponed. At times like these I always thought my mother was lacking in compassion. She never quite believed that these board games had anything to do with baseball, which she didn't know much about—but she did know that baseball took place in a ballpark, and not on a card table.

My mother never understood the excitement of APBA, and she refused to take my word for it. At the time I thought this was a highly presumptuous stance, but now, sadly, I see her view far better than I do mine. I think of myself as faithful to baseball, but I was once devout. That sums up as a loss of faith. And while I cannot deny the loss, I can still remember the quality of that faith. There is a power in the possibilities of baseball, and for those truly obsessed, reality does not stand in the way.

During the time of my deepest involvement, my closest baseball compatriot was my friend Irwin. Although Irwin and I lived on the same street, he went to a different school. Ours was strictly a neighborhood relationship, with no overlaps or complications other than the fact that my mother hated him. For years, my mother would refer to Irwin in fondness only as the *minivil*, and in anger as that *minivil*. It was a Yiddish nickname that she refused to translate. But one day, in a moment of utter rage, she translated Irwin's nickname while describing him. A *minivil*, I learned, was a particular kind of mammal unknown outside of our family and characterized by its capacity for mischief. Which in those days was pretty dirty.

Despite my mother's feelings, Irwin and I kept our baseball file, which grew in our lives to a point where it was simply referred to as The File. I came across the green metal box that it was kept in, but I never found the entries. Like my autographed pictures, they are, no doubt, somewhere unknown, but safe.

When I was about ten years old, my father came into possession of an old, broken-down L. C. Smith typewriter, which he placed in the closet in my room. A short time later, Irwin and I checked *The Baseball Encyclopedia* out

of the Joseph Avenue public library, bought a pack of
index cards from Irwin's father's store, and began our
own Baseball Hall of Fame. To become a member, all a
player had to do was occur as a likely candidate in the
mind of either me or Irwin, and then have his statistics
looked up in *The Baseball Encyclopedia*. If the numbers
surpassed our minimum requirements of being really,
really good, we would drag out the old L. C. Smith, type
up the player's statistics, and place him in the green
metal box that housed the Hall of Fame.

It was a modest adventure, and it stretched out, off
and on, for years. Finally, one summer, a new edition of
The Baseball Encyclopedia arrived, and it got out of
hand. There were simply too many people that we had
never heard of who were as good or better, by their statistics, than our Hall of Fame's classiest members. And,
even though we had never heard of any of them, we had
to add those names in order to maintain our notion of
fair play, and to enhance the company of our favorites.
It got to a point where we were constantly behind on the
typing, and the typing consisted of the records of guys
we had never heard of, often guys who had died a hundred years ago, but who were, nevertheless, statistically
qualified to enter The File. At this point we quit.

When not attending The File, or APBA, or All-Star
Baseball, I spent the rainy days of those summers writing
away for autographed pictures of my favorites. And the
tangible fruits of that activity are the cache that I was
searching for. It was not that I needed to find the actual
pictures—what they represented was already firmly in
my mind—but I was caught in the paradox of all artifacts. When enrichment and understanding are derived
from an artifact, it becomes meaningless as an experience, because it has no more to tell you. But it becomes
even more valuable as an object, precisely because of the
depth of understanding it now holds. And so these autographed pictures were, on the one hand, twenty years

[174]

forgotten, and not a pressing need, but on the other hand, wouldn't it be wonderful to find them?

Most of my autograph collection consisted of recently promoted members of the Red Wings, now playing in the major leagues with the St. Louis Cardinals. No matter who you wrote to on the St. Louis Cardinals, the postcard reply was always the same. Half of the front of the postcard was a black-and-white portrait photograph of the player you wrote to. The other half contained one of two equally banal printed messages. Both began "Dear Fan," and went on to thank you for personal and team support, all in one sentence. And then "Sincerely yours," followed by a signature in genuine fountain-pen ink.

As each autographed picture arrived, and they were not all that easy to come by, I took them to my father for scrutiny. My father was a printer and he knew about these things. He would squint his eye right down close to the signature and study it. Then he would hand it back and compose himself, so as to give his decree with the proper emotion. My father was impressed and respectful when the signature was real, and contemptuous and disgusted when it was part of the printing. And thus I came to understand that only the cards with real signatures were valuable. The rest were just front-office promotional mailings, done by some hired hands and never even touched by my heroes.

And so, one day, I had the horror of finding out, on the day it arrived, that the large four-by-five glossy picture of the greatest living player in the National League was, Sincerely yours, Stan "the Man" Musial, with a rubber stamp. Rubber stamping was so cheap a process that it made my father laugh. It was a large glossy photograph, and it was worthless.

As the letter writing progressed, I developed a firm criterion: each letter would have to be different. I decided that you were more likely to get a picture if you buttered these guys up a little before you asked for it. And I was certain that they would be most impressed by how much you know about them. Since the largest part of my idle time was spent buttering up baseball players for myself, it was a task both easy and pleasant. So I would tell them in detail why I was their fan, and then ask them for the autographed picture.

My letter to Satchel Paige, who was pitching for the Miami Marlins at the time, was a personal breakthrough. I spent an entire morning deciding that "Dear Satchel" was too strict, and settled on "Hi Satch!" I followed with a brief, personal, and direct message to someone whose style I admired. As soon as I finished it, I felt it was a classic, but Satchel Paige, as I preferred to think, never received the letter.

As more autographs arrived, they began to mean less. By the time of my adolescence, when the generation of war babies, my generation, entered its crisis of the inability to comprehend feelings, the baseball autographs had become worthless, and were relegated to the junk in the basement.

And now, somewhere in that basement, is a box or an envelope with real signed autographs of all the former Red Wing greats. Wally Moon, Jackie Brandt, Billy Virdon. And Red Wings older than that. Rip Repulski, Ray Jablonski. And, of course, Ted Williams, signed in real ink, and two pictures of Robin Roberts, both in ink. The first Robin Roberts got lost, and after I had written for a replacement, I found it.

I can only be honest by admitting to the possibility, however remote, that I might have thrown out all of my baseball mementos myself. My friend Irwin and I grew a bit cynical and nasty in our last years of being pre-teens. As I recall the things we got up to, so crass an act of destruction does not seem beyond possibility. For example, one day Irwin and I stumbled onto the amazing Herb Score Fan Club enterprise. Quite innocently, as I remember it, but its very substance denies the possibility of innocence. To our eleven-year-old minds, it seemed to be the most airtight, foolproof confidence hustle that had ever been invented, and guaranteed to make us both rich before we reached the age of twelve.

Herb Score was the subject of the feature article in that month's issue of *Sport* magazine. And staring at us, as we concocted the idea, was a beautiful, full-color, eight-by-eleven-inch picture of Herb Score illustrating the article. Herb Score played in the American League, which I never followed. I didn't care what happened to him. Irwin followed the Cleveland Indians, Herb Score's team, but he had some personal grudge against him, so there were no problems of conscience.

Elsewhere in *Sport* magazine were listed the addresses and membership requirements of all new fan clubs started that month. And everybody read *Sport* magazine, a crucial part of our scheme.

Therefore, all we had to do was write in and announce that we were the Herb Score Fan Club. And we offered to send, free to each member, a full-color eight-by-eleven-inch picture of Herb Score. Dues, however, would be fifty cents, payable in advance.

It was not only that *Sport* magazine only cost a quarter. Irwin and I already had a copy each and we were quite prepared to tear out Herb Score's picture, even if it wasn't convertible to liquid assets. The barbershop at the corner not only agreed to part with the picture from their copy of the magazine, but even lent us the scissors to do it. And then, because we were deadly serious, and earnest, we scraped up a dollar and bought four more copies, to deal with the expected volume.

Sport magazine never printed our notice. No one ever wrote for their beautiful picture of Herb Score, or a fan club membership. How did the magazine know that we weren't legitimate? Then Herb Score got hit in the eye by a batted ball and never really recovered his brilliance or his status. We felt terrible that we had failed, and even worse that we had tried to build such easy fortune on so ill-fated a career. Irwin later confessed to me that he didn't really know what a confidence game

[177]

was. Clearly, I didn't know either, but I now knew what one wasn't.

I learned, at a very early age, how fascinating the role of spectator could be. I learned that what a spectator sees is nothing less than high drama and a continual attempt to humiliate the other team through the execution of noble behavior. Which it turns out is no humiliation at all.

What the spectator sees is heroism. In baseball, because of the very structure of the game, someone or other always rises to the occasion. And so, at a very young age, I had a broad exposure to the dynamics of heroism. I became its connoisseur, and a true spectator.

The spectator partakes of the lifelong fantasy of being snatched out of everyday life and suddenly put in charge of whatever it is. And then because of your careful, attentive attitude as a spectator, you handle things brilliantly, as if born to power. Against the realization of that fantasy, you continually prepare, and plan your policy and your strategy. But for the consequences of thought, being the spectator and being in charge feel the same.

Power is always preoccupied with maintaining itself, but the spectator, removed from all responsibility and consequence, has the luxury of being more perceptive. Having no power, the spectator sees the relationship of the elements at play, rather than a field in which to act. Having no responsibility, the spectator sees events as aesthetic, rather than consequential.

Mine was a generation of spectators. In fact, it was the first generation of the mass audience that power in the corporate era is built upon. As the postwar era began to unravel, my generation was determined to climb out of the grandstand and take over the game. But the critical number of volunteers did not come forward. Those who did were ambitious as well as brave. They enjoyed their

[178]

status and never accepted the necessity of playing to anything less than a capacity crowd.

Radicals wanted to be rock-and-roll stars, and their spectators, caught up in deeper and deeper levels of appreciating heroism, wanted to be radicals. A vanguard of radical spectators broke through and became performers, and the remaining audience was deeply moved, and swelled. The revolution was won. And then the lights came on and reminded everyone that theater might be life, but not necessarily.

Presently I would be embarrassed that I grew up in this kind of theater, and that I didn't know it was theater and not real life, but I was a baseball fan, and it was the postwar era. What other kind of radical could I have become? Given the available options, I was better and more interestingly prepared for the unseen cultural changes that were soon to follow than I had any right to be.

After all, what were the alternative forms of heroism, excluding baseball, available to my childhood world? I don't remember any. There was Joe Wilson, who took over his father's chemical company and turned it into the Xerox Corporation. He was a major local figure, and highly respected in my family, but I knew nothing about him except that he was very rich; and of all the people I already knew who were richer than myself, I knew he wasn't likely to be heroic. And there was the last Union Army Civil War veteran, James A. Hard. Every year, at the Memorial Day parade, he would ride past, in uniform, in the back of an ambulance, flat on his back, waving to the crowd. But he was over a hundred years old the first time I saw him, and none too impressive.

But there were better. There was Hy Navis, the mechanic, the plumber, the genius. Hy Navis looked and talked and smelled and acted funny. And he got drunk and fooled around with women. He was, in every way, a total washout in the Jewish community. But the man was a genius. He designed better washing machines than the washing-machine companies, but he had no education, no faith in himself, and absolutely no status in the community. And so he hustled around, doing odd jobs for a living. My father was baffled by his personality, but worshiped his intelligence, and so Hy Navis was often in our house, and I, taken along for an educational experience, was often in his.

In loftier times, Hy Navis had made money. And his partner, Jack Levine, had a glamorous past including a stint designing washing machines for Westinghouse. But now, both partners had their feet grounded in the reality of everyday life, where they traded honestly, under the misleading name of the Hi-Jack Electric Company. The Hi-Jack partnership could be persuaded to try and fix anything, but their staple was an unglamorous line of rebuilt washing-machine motors.

Could any of these people, by their activities in the world, touch the heart of an observant child? Could such a child even find out what adult life was like, not to mention heroic behavior? And for that matter, were there any local figures of sufficient exotica to even compare with baseball players? No, there was none.

But there was baseball. And the novels of John R. Tunis, and the glorious years of Red Wing championships.

Baseball was the catalyst, and it organized everything else to give me a training in the morality of heroic action far beyond my needs, or desires, or benefit. It was a training that held great pretension but, in the end, functioned only aesthetically. And though at various points in life I have cursed this ability, I have always known that it is special and important.

In godless times of bureaucratic religions, I was raised with a pantheon as complete as any, and this I owe to baseball. I know that it is a pity that I never learned that playing baseball is probably more important than watching it. But the need to know is a great joy, and I would rather have it than any life which doesn't.

There was a time, long ago, when history itself consisted of the tales of heroic deeds. Usually about warriors, these were tales of heroism, rather than gossip about heroes. These tales were yardsticks against which ordinary people could measure their own lives. These tales were repeated from time to time, and everyone was reminded of how enormous the human capacity for gesture can be.

Now history is about institutions, and processes, and forces. And our heroes are heroes just because they have emerged from anonymity into the public arena. Visibility is enough, nowadays. Whatever heroes do, and however they act, is okay, as long as a hero did it. And noble behavior is something we might almost forget. Something we would forget, but for the need. There is a desire to see that grand gesture is still possible. There is an inspirational longing in our cultural makeup that can only be fulfilled by witnessing noble behavior.

In my childhood, when it came time for Bible stories, Greek mythology, and Hollywood cowboy movies, I was already an avid baseball fan. I could identify the noble behavior, but the experience was no watershed. I had learned about it long ago. Heroic response in moral drama was what happened at the baseball stadium. I had seen it time and time again. Courage, strength, stamina, will, you name it. I had seen it all. Long before schoolbooks told me about the literature, I knew the world where emotions and character traits emerge from dramatic situations.

I was a baseball fan, but it wasn't just voyeurism. I was being educated. Nearly every summer evening, I saw human capability stretched to its limits by conflicting desire.

As I returned, evening after evening, I would have

one more lesson in the difficult attempt at right action, played out through the themes of courage and cowardice, psychological daring and collapse, the destruction of expectations and the triumph of will. And each lesson taught me what I might expect of myself and other human behavior. And it inspired me, in my own little Jewish boy's life, to be a little more grand, a little more stylish, and as noble as I could possibly be.

During the polarized, radicalized days of madness that ended the bloom of the late stages of the postwar era, I didn't need examples of noble behavior. I had dedicated myself to the revolution, and though my own particular duties to that revolution were never clear to me, whatever it was that I had to do, I did twenty-four hours a day.

There is nothing more noble than revolution; it was a glut of self-esteem. As a political activist, I often felt foolish, and always felt inadequate and ineffective. But I always knew that, even when I was plain stupid, I was part of the most noble cause that ever was. And I knew that however absurd or impossible the task at hand, and however inadequately or badly it was done, the work would always be noble. Because it was done for the revolution, because it was done for the grandest and most idealistic of all possible motives.

The radical community was not short of suitable images for hero worship. We preferred to think of ourselves as a community where the concept of socialist man alone was famous, but we, too, had been culturally incubated on Hollywood stories and the American cult of the individual. And no matter how radical our politics became, we were, more than any previous generation, susceptible to the notion of heroic behavior worthy of applause, and ever so slightly obsessed with the quantity and frequency of that applause.

We became, rather than a political organization, a gigantic expanding population of sympathizers, who by their very sympathy and understanding were unable even to recognize each other, no less get together and make politics. Even among ourselves, we came to accept as our leaders personalities we knew through the media. Even as our leaders, they entered our lives and our living room only by appearing on television.

Large numbers converted, and the conversion was instant. But what was created, in the end, was not a Woodstock Nation, but a shared loyalty to particular celebrities, and eventually, a specialty market for doing business in the corporate era.

The leaders, from Abbie Hoffman all the way up to Huey Newton, appeared on television and became celebrities. Television welcomed them with open arms. Radicals exude the glamor of antisocial public behavior. Revolutionaries got good ratings. And they were absolutely safe, since next season they would be, by definition, out of fashion.

The leaders themselves, in the process of becoming celebrities, confused fame with power. And in the confusion, they slipped out of politics and into pretending that they were already powerful. And this was the end of organization, and the end of real politics, and the end of that cause.

The time of that cause is over; the postwar era has ended. Its institutions crumbled, but rather than fall, they went up for grabs. And the corporations grabbed. The actual bodies of corporate business weren't that healthy any more, but the mentality that saw the values of corporate business enterprise as a guide to life seemed to weather the collapse better than most. People changed the way they thought and acted. The corporate mentality gained converts. Since the dust from that deal has begun to settle, we see those institutions, having had a coat of paint and some cosmetic aesthetic alterations, back in action. Perhaps not as strong as ever, but definitely no longer available for grabs.

Now the last shall be last, and the first shall be first, for just one more millennium. And I am back in the dominant American social flux. The individual, rugged or not, is trapped in these days of no alternative. And I too am the individual. The culture through which I learned to describe myself is gone, tied to the bygone era and its consciousness. My youthful dreams of community have been dashed. There is not, at the moment, any meaningful measure for my life, outside of myself. And for the foreseeable future, I must make up the criterion and measure it myself. I must judge myself.

First thing Monday morning, I trotted downtown to see George Sisler, Jr. He is now the president of the International League, a mature position in a successful career that has come some distance since the days of my childhood, when Sisler was the general manager of the Red Wings. George Beahon recommended him as my political source, since he had been in Cuba at the right time. Had I seen him two days earlier, I don't know what might have happened, but I had spent my weekend in reflection and basement archaeology and my perspective had changed significantly.

George Sisler, Jr., was exactly as I expected him to be. I was not. I came bouncing in wearing the brand-new overcoat that my mother had given me. When Mr. Sisler extended his hand for shaking, I filled it with a baseball signed by his late father, one of the great players of baseball's history, and by Estel Crabtree, who was considered the finest outfielder ever to play for the Red Wings. As he said good morning, I said, "Look at this! I brought you a present."

He looked at me, bewildered. Then he examined the ball quickly and started to hand it back to me. His arm halfway there, he changed his mind and put it down on the farthest corner of the desk. He pointed to a chair and wrinkled his forehead. I had not established intimacy.

I asked him what it was like to be the son of a Hall of Fame baseball superstar like George Sisler. The question was clearly a mistake. He answered it easily enough—

it was probably the most-asked question of his life. But in his answer I could see his impatience at being the son of a famous man. And through his praise of his father's diligence, fortitude, good looks, and graceful manner, I could feel George, Jr., telling me something else. Look, his eyes seemed to say, I am not a young man, I have two fully grown daughters, I am the president of the International League of Professional Baseball, and my dad has been dead for years, and still they come to ask about my father. Will my turn never come?

We began, as it were, on the wrong foot. I had stepped into the obvious famous-father trap. And in his reply, Sisler reeled off a string of clichés about the glories of family life. He saw me as the last and least interesting of his father's pilgrims, and I saw him as the professional family man, who, for the sake of decency, would not be prepared to reveal anything he knew about Havana.

But George Sisler had a story to tell, and after a while he moved into it. Yes, Rochester is a special kind of baseball town, but this is for a very particular reason. When Branch Rickey, in 1919, came up with his innovative idea of the farm system for the St. Louis Cardinals, the only team to copy it was the New York Yankees. The farm system was so successful that throughout the thirties and forties, the Cardinals and the Yankees each dominated their leagues. The other teams followed suit, but they were too late to catch up. Some of the glory of these two great dynasties rubbed off on their farm teams. Wherever the Cardinals and the Yankees operated teams, baseball took firm root as a principal point of local culture. The Yankees made baseball towns out of Sacramento, Kansas City, and Columbus. And the Cardinals did the same for Rochester, Houston, and other places. When the Cardinals left town and the team became a public corporation or, as they say in Rochester, "went community," the fledgling independent Red Wings established their link to the major leagues with the Baltimore Orioles. As soon as their agreement was signed, the emerging Orioles promptly turned into a dynasty of their own, and that glory rubbed off on the Rochester Red Wings. And so the Red Wings have remained contenders, and dominated the league, almost continuously for the last forty years. Not that they have always won, but they have almost always been good. As baseball teams go, the Red Wings have had an incredible history, and an incredible following and this was not by accident, by, chauvinism, or by ideals. It was strictly a matter of winning baseball.

The Red Wings have consistently drawn over 400,000 fans a season. In 1966, they produced a new profit of $161,472. This kind of success in minor-league baseball has been matched only by the Mexico City Reds and by the Hawaiian Islanders of Honolulu. But this wasn't always the case. Before the economic boom that followed World War II, minor-league baseball was doing quite nicely. It got a large chunk of money from radio-broadcast rights, and an even bigger chunk of money from its main product, the major-league baseball-playing prospect. Minor-league ticket sales never produced profit, but there was good money to be made by signing a youngster, turning him into a ballplayer, and selling him to a major-league team.

With the arrival of television, which brought major-league games into the living rooms of minor-league fans, radio stations were no longer particularly interested in paying large sums of money to broadcast minor-league games. Minor-league teams lost a large and vital chunk of their income and following, just at a time when the major leagues were experiencing a phenomenal rise through their television income and following. And with this newfound prosperity, the minor leagues were simply taken over by major-league teams and run at a loss, as a training program.

Rochester is one of the very few places left with a measure of independence, because it is in the rare situation of being able to make a little money at minor-league baseball. And that also has made Rochester a breeding ground for major-league baseball executives. Rochester is one of the few places in baseball, outside of the major leagues, where a businessman can learn the business of running a team profitably. Warren Giles, who rose to be president of the National League, started out at Rochester, and that's how Gabe Paul made it all the way to the top, where he remains today with the New York Yankees.

For some reason I asked Sisler about Cot Deal's resignation. This was a far more serious mistake than the ancestral autographed baseball. It was not that I was lied to, or that the story I got from George Beahon was contradicted, but he began his answer with, "I would never fire anybody, but . . ." He went on to tell me how Cot Deal was not fired, but switched jobs with Clyde King, who was then the pitching coach for Cincinnati, so actually Cot Deal got a chance to go up to the big leagues out of it.

Everything had been going so well in Rochester. And I wanted everybody to be plain, nice, honest, small-town folk. A homey view suited my purposes and, up until that moment, it was what I found. And suddenly, I realized that I was being handled by a small-town businessman to whom it had never occurred that I might know what I was talking about. It's not that I was offended, but I didn't want to ask him any more, because I knew he wouldn't tell me what he knew. Encounters with strangers always partake of long odds. I never expected George Sisler, Jr., to be a sure thing, and so I didn't feel bad that he wasn't. And no hard feelings for the long distance I had come, but it was time to be on my way.

Instead, though, I stayed, with my overcoat on, and we chatted about old ballplayers. How in the old days ballplayers were never booed, his father was never booed. Fans didn't do that until after the war, when both Joe DiMaggio and Mickey Mantle were booed. And we covered the now-familiar territory of the old Red Wings. Allie Clark was the old pro and Joey Cunningham was the overflowing youngster, yes sir. Gene Green was as strong as an ox. Harry Walker was smarter than his brother Dixie, and Cot Deal was a deeply, deeply religious man. And then we got off into the barbershop world of baseball clichés. I knew that this was the wrong thing to do, but I had given up on this meeting and was prepared to let it flow in whatever direction Mr. Sisler might care to take it. Meanwhile, George was telling me how some managers say they play by the book, but, well, in baseball there is no book, etc.

Fortunately, we were interrupted by a long-distance phone call from Pawtucket, Rhode Island, and some very important league business began to take place on the telephone.

The way the president of the International League picked up his own phone, and answered it, not with a message, but with the single word "Hello," the smallness of his office, and my failure to inspire him to poetry, combined to embarrass me. I went into the anteroom.

On the wall, there was a fuzzy photograph of the largest crowd ever to witness a minor-league game, 52,-000. It was the 1944 Junior World Series, in Baltimore. There was also a picture of the 1914 Providence team, International League champions. And a picture of the 1936 Buffalo Bisons championship team eating a banquet at Toots Shor's restaurant, in New York City. The players are all wearing suits, starched collars, and neckties, looking very adult indeed.

Sisler hung up the phone and looked at his watch. We were running out of time, but the phone rang again. He answered it, and this time I hid behind a copy of *The Sporting News* which was on his desk. The phone call proved lengthy, and I settled down to read a very interesting article about how Bill Veeck is getting back into baseball, and what he did in the past with the St. Louis Browns, the Cleveland Indians, and the Chicago White Sox. I began to remember how much I had loved *The Sporting News* as a boy, especially in the winter, when the Bible of Baseball was about the only baseball news there was. And I remembered how I combed through the garbage at Red Wing Stadium, collecting used ticket envelopes, each of which could be mailed away for a free specimen copy of *The Sporting News*. And there was *Baseball Digest*, patterned loosely after *Readers' Digest* in form, but a rather classy little magazine in content. And *Who's Who in Baseball*, always the last word in statistics. I had forgotten about that periodical part of the world of baseball I had known as a child.

Still engrossed in the paper, I happened to glance over the top and see George Sisler, Jr.'s, eyes staring into mine. The second phone call had ended and he was waiting for me.

What happened in Havana, I said sternly. Sisler folded his hands behind his head, leaned back, and smiled tautly at the ceiling.

"I was there when Verdi got shot, you know," he said. Of course, I knew—what did he think I was doing in his office? And he proceeded to tell me the story. Games started late in Havana, nine o'clock. And so, at midnight, when the celebration began, the baseball game was still going on. Sitting two boxes away from George Sisler was a soldier with a machine gun, shooting the thing into the air. And I guess one of these spent bullets nicked Frank. Nobody thought he was shot at the time; he didn't even fall down.

George Beahon thought that Verdi might have had a premonition and that's why he was wearing his steel helmet lining. Oh no, George Sisler insisted, it was nothing like that. The bullet barely frayed his hat. It tore only a few threads. Well, Frank was very excited and he really worked on that hat in the clubhouse. By the time the photographers arrived, he had a hole big enough to get his finger through, but it wasn't made by the bullet.

And, well, George happened to be in Havana for the last game, too. Yes, that blast, which was five miles away, was so loud it felt like it went off in the stadium. You see, Castro had all kinds of security at the ballpark by then, and all kinds of security in the hotels and restaurants, but if a gang of peasants wanted to tear something down, there was no one to stop them. George made it clear that he was blaming no peasants, and believed, in his expert opinion, that the explosion was set off by Batista supporters. The CIA? He didn't think so.

I didn't expect him to blame the CIA, but I had no access to hot spotlights and brass knuckles, and so while I might, in a Hollywood movie, have been able to get my truth out of him, I was stuck in the reality of small-time in Rochester, and decided to settle for polite conversation.

In order to save time, I went directly for broke, although a serious answer at this point was out of the question. What about the politics of disengagement with Cuba? Wasn't the State Department in contact with you people? Wasn't foreign policy considered? Wasn't there anything at all?

"I can't help you on that," he said and quickly went on to explain the history of the Havana franchise.

The other teams in the league thought it was too expensive to travel all the way to Havana, and so when the Sugar Kings entered the league, they had to guarantee all travel expenses south from Richmond. This ended when Miami entered the league, but it did make Havana feel like a second-class franchise, even though they had the largest stadium in the league. He ended by handing me a copy of the 1975 International League Annual White Book of facts and statistics, which he was sure would answer any further questions.

I asked him about the effect on baseball of detente with Cuba, and he answered that there were some good things about it and some bad. And then he stopped talking. I knew that if I pushed him, he wouldn't tell me anyhow, and so I thanked him, and with my new International League White Book under the arm of my fancy new overcoat, I left.

George Sisler, Jr.'s, office, the office of the International League, is located in an out-of-the-way place called the Times Square Building. It once housed the *Rochester Times-Union*, but today it houses only the dreams of real-estate fanciers who are impressed by big names. Not that it's a sleazy section, but what used to be the best part of town is splintered amongst the shopping centers of the suburbs, which is not the same concept at all. And somehow, in the translation, no comfortable spot was made in which to rest the International League. The corporate era has endorsed baseball, but only at its biggest. You better watch your step, Mr. Sisler. You may outlive your historical function sooner than you think.

Across the square from the Times Square Building is the Monroe County War Memorial, Rochester's largest hockey, basketball, ice capades, auto show, and concert hall arena. And as I attempted to think my way through my meeting with George Sisler, to see whether, in spite of how it had gone, it wasn't still possible to see if I had learned anything, I joined, in the most absent-minded way, the crowd of people flocking to the doors. It was eleven o'clock in the morning. The sign said "Rolling Thunder Review, featuring Bob Dylan and Bobby Newirth. Ticket office opens at 11:00."

For five days, Rochester had been saturated with Rolling Thunder advertising, but wonder of wonders, the last available ticket to the second show was handed to me. It was a lot of money, and it meant that I was committed to staying in Rochester for another night, but I seemed so lucky to get the ticket that it never occurred to me that I might not want it. Even as I bought the ticket, my mind was still preoccupied with baseball. George Beahon had told me that the team kept extensive scrapbooks in their offices at the stadium. I wanted to see them, and Red Wing Stadium was to be my first preconcert stop.

At the stadium, the general manager was out. The scrapbooks were, indeed, in the attic, but it would be impossible for me to look through them unless I was accompanied by the general manager. An attitude that I felt was necessary but not sufficient for a genuine archive, but since I wouldn't let them look through my scrapbooks, how could I disagree? Besides, George Beahon had said that Dick Sirens, the stadium's head groundskeeper for the last thirty-five years, had been around for longer than anyone, and knew more, too.

Dick Sirens is a keen baseball fan, and not a small-town businessman, but a gardener. And no gardener could be more straightforward than Dick Sirens. "They were all nice fellas . . . real nice fellas. I don't know how they were to anybody else, but to me, they were nice fellas." That was the beginning and end of our conversation. He was in the process of leveling out the infield, and if I needed him, he would be the one driving the tractor. And I suddenly felt that if I didn't learn anything else, at least I now knew the necessity of nuance. What would I need him for? What else was there to say?

There I was, all dressed up like a young success, sitting alone amidst the rakes and hoes and cases of empty beer bottles. My suit was already smudged, and as I looked around Siren's office all I saw were fishing rods, shotgun shells, and rubber hunting boots. The chair behind the desk was softened with a souvenir cushion from the Ryman Theater, postwar home of the Grand Old Opry. This was a pretty snazzy cushion for a baseball gardener, but it wasn't enough. For the first time in the history of my relationship to baseball, I began to think that this place was a bit too gentile for me. This guy must stay outside all day, and then go back out to fish and hunt. Even his office feels like it's outside. These were considerations I hadn't thought about since the days when I feared the United States Army.

Sirens had handed me a large cardboard carton that had started out a decade ago holding a case of whisky, but had since moved up to become the groundskeeper's storehouse for glossy photographs of old Red Wings. There was nothing to do but go through the pictures.

The photographs, as a whole, reminded me of almost everything that had happened to me since I entered the microfilm-reading room. There were hundreds and hundreds of photographs when, at this point, I would have preferred perhaps two dozen, at-the outside.

I began what seemed like a rerun of yesterday's memoir mayhem in the basement, but I couldn't have been more wrong. These photographs were treasures, every one, and clearly labeled as such. Nearly every picture struck an emotional bull's-eye in my childhood memories. There was Preacher Jack Fasholtz, who spent the off-season on church pulpits. And Lou Ortiz, and Wes Westrum, and Gene Oliver, and Luke Easter, and Chico Fernandez, and Vern Benson, and Charlie Kress. Everybody I had ever heard of, and some that I hadn't. And it was not merely the names and faces that evoked my memories. Some of these photographs were at least sociological artifacts, if not genuine works of art.

There was the nearsighted Ronny Plaza, squinting without his glasses as he posed at second base. And there he was again, smiling through his glasses. I put the two pictures together, and saw a particular expression of teen-age vanity that I have not seen in twenty years. And there was a close-up of Frank Verdi, his eyes staring deeply into mine, a face I could never forget. And there was Howie Nunn, the traveling journeyman relief pitcher, before he dyed his hair red. In fact, the real Howie Nunn looked like a timid schoolteacher, but I saw him only as the toughest of all double agents, and my most genuine link to the murky political underworld that sprang up in opposition to Fidel Castro. He could have been Lee Harvey Oswald, I thought, as I set his picture aside.

And here was Dixie Walker, the old manager who was rumored to be a bit flaky, whatever that meant. The picture caught him in the act of putting expensive leather suitcases into the trunk of his new convertible. Standing beside him are Sean, six, Susan, twelve, Mrs. Dixie holding Steven, one, and Mary Ann, fourteen. A small-town dignitary was gassed up and ready to leave for spring training. And a photographer had been dispatched to record this worthy event. Could any event be more foreign to the present? And the Dixie Walker family, frozen in smiling farewell, resembled something more like a Civil War photograph than anything from my own childhood.

And there is Billy Virdon, holding his two-year-old daughter. Next to him is Mrs. Virdon holding a gigantic box of Fanny Farmer candy. And there is Luke Easter, with Mrs. Easter and their three children. Each of the Easter children is wearing a button that says "Luke's Our Boy."

And there are the 1964 Rochester Red Wings lined up along the third-base line. I wanted desperately to steal this photograph, but it was too big to go in any of my pockets. If there ever was a historical mood caught in a work of art, this photograph was it. Approaching the lined-up Red Wings, from across the diamond, is a couple, so ill-matched as to nearly turn the photograph into a cartoon. Hand in hand they saunter across the field, a determined, angry man in a baseball uniform, taking big steps and looking down, and a syrupy, sweet stereotype of feminine beauty wearing only high-heeled shoes, a bathing costume, and a fur coat. He is the same Darrell Johnson who would take the Boston Red Sox into the World Series and, through television, into my life. In this photograph, Darrell Johnson is acting in his official capacity as manager of the Rochester Red Wings. She, his partner, is Johanna Coleman, the 1964 Monroe County Harvest Queen. And oh, how I want to steal that picture, even now.

Dick Sirens waved goodbye to me from the tractor. The Dylan ticket was not exactly burning a hole in my pocket, but now that I was finished with the Red Wings office, it was keeping me in Rochester. The general manager of the Red Wings still had not returned. And so I was left, at the outskirts of my old neighborhood, with time to kill.

The entrance to my old neighborhood, the Keeler Street Bridge, was now part of a superhighway. I sped across it, and in a matter of seconds the neighborhood I was born and raised in flashed past my window. The longest diagonal, from Red Wing Stadium to the bowling alley, I passed within the same minute. Was it that small a neighborhood, I wondered, as I made my cautious return through the back streets?

I went directly to Argonne Street to have a look at the house I was raised in. And my God, it was in much better shape than it ever was when we lived there. It had a brand-new coat of paint, gleaming windows, and landscaped shrubbery. Somehow, at a time when all the social indicators were pointing downward, this white working-class neighborhood had come up. I realized that the house I was raised in is now a classy house. The inaccuracy of memory and historical evidence being my favorite subject, I moved on to look at the rest of the neighborhood.

The neighborhood had changed, but the feelings seemed intact, though I would never have had the nerve to ring doorbells and find out. Smalline's Pharmacy is now the Adam and Eve "We Go to Your Head" Wig Shop, but the bus loop, at a time when real-estate values have forced bus drivers to go around the block, was still there. Most people don't even remember what a bus loop is any more, but my old neighborhood still has one.

John Gardens, the only urban farm I ever saw as a child—and I have not seen one since—was still going strong, selling flowers, onions, and tomato plants. Dr. Wronker's surgery is now a surveyor's office, but no wonder.

When Mrs. Kaiser, who was subsequently suspected of pro-German feelings, drove her station wagon into my Schwinn bicycle, the bike crumpled and I was thrown across the street. The fact that I was riding no-handed and standing up was noticed, but fortunately there wasn't time to discuss the fine points of fault, and I was rushed off to the healing hands of Dr. Wronker.

He examined me, smiled, and said that I was frightened but not injured. He could have said that I was a brave little boy but not injured, but he didn't. And he stuck to his hard rule—no injury, no lollipop. And with a bedside manner like that, a surveyor's office is all right with me.

I put on my car radio and fiddled for station WBBF. It was the station of my childhood when it was the home of the Big Three in R and B, and the Golden Triangle of Rhythm and Blues, the Scene for the Musical Teen, and so on. And now they were playing Bobby Darin's cover version of "Sweet Little Sixteen." Not Chuck Berry, but the white remake. And as musical background, it was perfect. This was not the history of rock and roll, this was the history of the white teen-age radio market, Rochester, New York, in the spring of the postwar era.

I went to the site of my old Hebrew school. It was now an empty lot with grass grown over it. You could see where the foundation of the building had been, but all that was left standing was a concrete stairway. The Hebrew school was gone, but its departure left behind a shadow of the feelings I had about the old place at that time: a stairway to nothing.

Not long ago, I was thinking about the tradition of Chinese baseball played against the back wall of the Holy Ark. Passed on from grade level to grade level, how long could it be carried on? And now the very wall is gone. And the minds that knew the rules and language have been scattered through the suburbs, and distracted, and with regard to Chinese baseball, they don't even know who they are.

I verged on sentimental memories of Talmudic training, but in the end my mind couldn't be serious about a vacant lot that geographically designated my old Hebrew school. Woe is not exactly the lot of the wayward, I thought. You did good not to pay attention in Hebrew school; why bother to come back?

When my sister and I attended this Hebrew school, she put a dead rat, which she had recently purchased for a quarter, in the drawer of the cantor's desk, and didn't tell anybody about it. When it came time for the cantor to reach into his desk for his own copies of the Five Books of Moses, he did. And by what followed, for all the class knew, it was Adolf Hitler himself in that drawer. The cantor screamed and ran to the coat room, where he locked himself in. And it was only long and gentle paternal coaxing from the vice-president of the Synagogue, Dr. Kravetz, that persuaded the cantor to come out some time later. This was the ugliest crime ever committed in Hebrew school, and it was famous as such. The faculty felt that they would not be able to walk tall in the classrooms until investigation and prosecution had closed the case.

My sister was never suspected, never questioned. For several years thereafter, she admitted nothing to anybody. The crime went unsolved.

I knew that when I started to see models for daring behavior wherever I looked, it was time to stop for a cup of coffee. What was leading me on this tour anyhow? Why couldn't I think about George Sisler, Jr., and why I had sent myself to him? I was prepared to view our meeting as a write-off, but I still wanted more insight into what I had had in mind when it seemed like a good idea to take George Beahon's recommendation and call Sisler up. Was he the wizard of some secret clan that I had noticed as a child in Red Wing Stadium, and repressed ever since because of the deeds they did? Was he the paternal pinnacle of the Rochester Red Wings' extended family, because his picture did appear, in every year's team picture, in its own box in the corner? Was there some secret signal that my childhood wanted to pass on? Was it the desire to link generations with appropriately autographed baseballs? Or was the whole thing just a bad idea?

I needed a place to stop and think, but it could not be any place. It had to be the Maplewood Diner. The most finicky tourists make the best tour guides, I thought, and I knew my territory. I knew that the Maplewood Diner was still in existence, because I had passed it in the spring, when I was on my way to the microfilm-reading room and, of course, couldn't stop. I arrived at the address, and what had been for all of my life a nearly genuine, nearly art nouveau, American diner. Now there was nothing but a blacktop parking lot. I asked around the neighborhood and was told that they had taken it away, which was clearly the case.

Undaunted, I drove straight to the North Park Bowling Lanes and ordered a bottle of local beer. I don't know why, but there is a joy to the perverse smells that often accompany childhood pleasures. I had heard my father's friend from New York praise a woman because she smelled like the men's room at the Roxy Theater. I didn't know the smell, and I didn't know the woman, and I didn't know what he was talking about. But the North Park Bowling Lanes has this smell, and as soon as I entered, I understood it. This is where I had come to bowl as a child, and that single smell of bowling-alley wax, dirty carpets, and human sweat was unchanged.

Today, something entirely different was going on. It was the Kodak Retirees' League. One hundred bowling lanes, packed with former Kodak workers, jumping and shouting, hollering and laughing and drinking. I have nothing to compare it to. These were old people having the kind of real good time that old people in the corporate era simply do not have. And there they were, with custom-drilled bowling balls, special gloves and wrist-bands, all wearing white bowling shoes, and carrying on. I had never seen old people acting like this before, I thought, and what is this really about?

Americans have always survived the critical social changes they are constantly undergoing by believing that knowledge and understanding can only come from personal experience. All else is unreliable and untrustworthy, and has probably changed already. In American life, you only know what you have done yourself.

And so, in raising their children, Americans don't pass along knowledge, but rather vocational skills. The knowledge they value most highly is personal, and cannot be passed along; whatever Americans teach, they teach how to do something—that is what knowledge is in this society.

At the same time that they are undergoing this process, American children are taught not to distinguish between work and play, in favor of play. Children are taught that the best and most appropriate behavior is play. And so play is remembered, throughout life, as the only authentic activity. Play is the archetypical activity. Because it sprang spontaneously, just from being a child, play is the purest experience and, therefore, the basis of knowledge.

All this being the case, the most appropriate setting for play, wherever it is, is in the midst of peers like the retired Kodak bowlers. And so children grow up with each other under the tyranny of keeping each other amused, rather than the traditional tyranny of authority. And all the while, they are trying and learning to have fun.

And so this is a society where the very essence of education is the pursuit of fun. And when it is found, that is what is called knowledge. We have come to live in a society where there is no honor higher than status, and status is determined by the ability to mistake the process of making money, for fun. Noble behavior, for the most part, no longer exists beyond its caricature, the successful ploy for attention. And so we live without courage, bravery, or determination. These have become aesthetic considerations, almost unknown as realities.

Honor and noble behavior are known. In fact, they are more widely known than ever, but only vicariously. This makes things not only easier, but more marketable.

As the postwar era progressed, and ordinary life began losing its public aspects, ordinary people responded to the loss by becoming more aware of games, and understanding that games as a metaphor for life can be successfully internalized merely by paying attention. Ordinary people learned to re-route their needs for glory, and they flocked to games.

By the time I was a child, the St. Louis Cardinal's glamor had rubbed off on the city of Rochester, and educated into a town of loyal Red Wing followers. It was possible to substitute baseball for life, and in a particular case like my own, difficult not to make this substitution. Baseball could conquer the dilemma of the inability to distinguish between work and play. Baseball could conquer the tyranny of the peer group, could resurrect imagination and allow you to wander through it. Baseball could erect a public presence while preserving privacy. The demands made on the children raised in the contradictions of the postwar era could be, and indeed were, resolved through baseball.

I arrived home from Boy Scout camp to see a "For Sale" sign on our house, and find out that on that very day, my family was moving to the suburbs. Shortly after I rested my knapsack, but before I had absorbed the shock of bewilderment, the Levine Brothers arrived. They were the professional movers my father hired to take our belongings to the suburbs.

The Levine Brothers were each classical archetypes of opposite forms. One brother was wiry, quiet, self-contained, and responsible. He drove the truck. The other was muscular, handsome, drove a convertible, and arrived late. They carried the sofa and chair up in the air, or out away from their bodies, so as not to stain them with sweat. They packed all of our possessions into a truck that seemed about half the required volume. My father and I were both in awe of their strength and style and talked of nothing else during the move. Least of all the neighborhood, and why we were leaving. We were going upward, to our suburban dreams, but the notion of community would never again touch our lives with the same legitimacy it held in the past.

We had dreamed the dreams of the postwar era. And we believed that we would be better off without all that we were leaving, and improved by all that we were going to.

My mother had three sisters, all of whom lived, with their husbands and children, on our street. We lived there for over a decade, in and out of each other's houses, lives, and good graces. When the living rooms got painted dark green, however, my father realized that the proximity and intimacy were driving him crazy. Shortly thereafter, we moved to the suburbs.

My father had decided to paint our living room the rather odd, but very stylish, color of dark green. My father always took a certain pride in being slightly unusual and so, despite the cries of horror and the insulting evaluations of his taste and sanity, he painted the room dark green.

A coat of paint, unlike a difference of opinion, has a finality about it. And because of this finality, the family sense of conventional wisdom was cut adrift. If someone who had been looked up to for so long could act so inconsistently with his character as to paint the walls dark green, what good was character judgment? To find so deep a flaw in the smartest brother-in-law after all this time was a serious crisis indeed.

Within a few weeks, it was decided that the rule of law was more important than justice, that the preservation of known truth was more important than discovery, and that the continuity between past and future was more important than a pastel living room.

And so my mother's sisters resolved the crisis by deciding to follow suit. A reasonable living room, they

[201]

announced, as if no one had ever thought of it before, could not be enclosed by anything other than dark green walls. My uncles dutifully responded with their paint-brushes, and within no time, our street had four houses with dark-green living rooms.

For his labor, and his taste, my father was made to feel typical and ordinary, where he wanted to appear special and unusual. And in more ways than this, our culture and our neighborhood conspired to move us to the suburbs. It was a reaction to the environment. The path of least resistance was to move up the social ladder and out.

The understanding was that as you moved to the house of your aspirations, so your old house was passed on, fulfilling a similar dream for someone farther back in the queue. We moved to the suburbs from our working-class neighborhood, leaving behind a house that we were now too good for, but a house that we knew represented luxury beyond imagination to the more humble dreams of someone who had just emerged from the slums.

The assumption was that we would all continue to move ever upward. And that process would never stop. Even when everyone lived like royalty, there would al-ways be new gadgets and appliances.

And this belief existed as a real dream, and a real goal, in the postwar era. How could you live in that time and not dream its dreams? And how could you live that life without believing its dreams? In this way, those who could afford it moved to the suburbs.

And now, after all these years, I am back at the North Park Lanes, watching senior citizens carrying on the way teen-agers used to. Now our old house, from which my family's dreams were launched, is classier than the dream house we exchanged it for.

And though the forms were everywhere the same, the contents had reversed. Now it was the FBI and the CIA being baited in Congress, and it was communist

Cubans being courted in spring training; now it was no longer my detente, not because it was impossible, but because television and the State Department wanted it for their own. It was time to move on. Who cared about a couple of lousy scrapbooks in the Red Wings' attic at this point? I had to leave town.

When people found out that the earth revolves around the sun, and, in fact, that the sun does not rise and set as it seems to do if you look at it out the window, they were first shocked, then distressed, and finally suspicious. When people found out that the very basis of their concepts of truth and knowledge were delusions and errors, they began to suspect everything but what they knew through their own personal experience. This suspicion led to the development of an industrial technology based on manufacture, and the accumulation of wealth, two of the only certainties left. And in the process of focusing all concentration and activity on manufacturing and producing, humans backed themselves into a social organization more incomprehensible than the mysteries of nature that drove them to it in the first place.

And we have come too far down the roads of industry and technology to turn back. Human beings still relate to each other, but the notion of a world common to us all has already been lost. And so we are made to live in the sad opacity of exclusively private lives. And life, against our instincts, has come to center around nothing but itself.

I too must live in this mass society and come to terms with all my ambition for history and philosophy being limited by the exterior surfaces of my own little life. Which is not easy. It doesn't seem like the same knowledge when it arises from the frustration of personal affairs.

We have lost our sense of tradition, and with that we are in danger of forgetting the past. If we do this, we are depriving ourselves of the only possibility for depth in human experience. Memory and depth are the same thing.

What we are in danger of losing is not merely an embellishment, but a whole aspect of life. We are in danger of losing the possibility of knowing who we are. We are in danger of losing all sense of identity. And to the extent that we still exist collectively, we are in danger of losing our culture.

Culture is, by definition, something permanent. It gets used and abused, but it remains. Entertainment, on the other hand, is a straight commodity that gets manufactured, sold, and consumed, after which it no longer exists.

The function of culture is to explain life, its possibilities, its actualities, and its hopes. The function of entertainment is simply to while away idle time. Culture speaks to genuine leisure—that time when we are free from the cares of the life process—but entertainment speaks only to the vacancy left over in the adjustment of life's cycles to the demands of industry.

And now it is the corporate era, and the demands of industry on life's cycle are greater than ever before, and more disturbing. We are past the point of using our spare time for either self-perfection or increased social status. We are the epitome of the consumer society; we spend all our spare time in consumption. We have become a society which feeds on an entertainment that, in turn, feeds on our culture. And it is getting used up. A consumer society destroys all that it encounters. Even culture.

Our vital energy is no longer spent in renewing life through labor, but in consuming. And consumers cannot take care of the things in the world. By their very attitude, they destroy things when they use them. Culture used to mean to take care of. If it still does, the inheritors of the corporate mentality are entering a very difficult and dangerous time.

I had taken the incident in Havana to home and back, and no more needed to be said. In some profound way, I had returned to Rochester for the last time. Even if I came back again, it would be different. My dreams of roots and home would never again float with quite the same buoyancy. My memory would never again be asked to confuse reconciliation with salvation.

I had learned that truth is a political reality, verifiable only to the extent of the number and power of the people who believed in it. Before the postwar era, when people lived in real communities and knew each other, and observed and gossipped about what they saw, historical truths and even character judgments had their political aspects. Life was lived in public. The creation of knowledge was a shared responsibility. Judgments, when not communal, were at least shared. And when not shared, at least identifiable as a quantity of consensus.

Nowadays, the notion of community exists only as an abstraction in anthropological studies and idealistic visions. Now we watch television instead of the behavior of our friends and neighbors. Now we make new friends easily, because we are no longer quite so interested in their behavior, or threatened by their closeness. Nothing is easier than moving on in a culture where we now all live as wanderers, at least socially, whether we wander or not.

How you would act if there were no rules for human behavior has increasingly become the only rule. And in that vacuum, balanced between the postwar-era breakdown and whatever comes next, we find that there is a greater truth than we are used to, and that is entirely personal. And that truth is revealed in the questions you ask, and the way you act, and the things you do.

And now my work is done. A statement that was true, but which, I suddenly realized, was also the contents of George Eastman's famous suicide note, and hence the punch line of countless local sick jokes that have floated around Rochester for the last forty years. And though

I always consider it a break through inhibition to be un-self-consciously corny, I knew that it was time to leave Rochester.

In fact, I would have already been gone at this point, were it not for the ticket in my pocket to the Rolling Thunder Review, starring Bob Dylan, which was about to take its place on an agenda that no ordinary baseball town could provide. I had been to the well of baseball memories, and returned to fall in, and now, as farewell and bon voyage, I was handed a cup of youthful revolution, postwar-era vintage.

To see Dylan perform, while still being steeped in Rochester, might be the test of everything I had learned. To see an old hero presented in a new time might reveal the essence of both. Because I had been so recently and so deeply immersed, and because I could see Dylan that very evening, the potential for the understanding of historical characteristics seemed limitless.

Rochester moves to its own unique chronology. The slow but relentless movement of the glacial tip of past excitement had finally come to Rochester. Now that the heart of the glacier was dead, and its structure melted, it was time for Bob Dylan to appear in town.

For the first time in a decade, I was wearing a suit with a white shirt and a tie. I didn't want to be mistaken for what I was, or what I was not. I parked my car and headed toward the War Memorial.

I had never been a Dylan die-hard, really. I accepted him as the poet of my generation, but it was never a passionate acceptance. I knew that he was suitable for deification, and I thought of him with admiration and awe, but I could not worship him. Of course, cultural heroes have their effect, personal preferences notwithstanding. As Dylan's cryptic albums became prototype models for the press releases from the fugitive Weatherman underground (who had named themselves from a Dylan lyric), I was taken through brief periods of Dylanological study that were, in certain circles, openly reputed to be as important as Engels and Lenin.

And I came, eventually, to hear an important political statement in the way that Bob Dylan sang. For me, as for most of my generation, it was, unlike ordinary rhetoric, music to my ears. It was the call not for revolt, but for defiance, even in the easiest of circumstances. Dylan always seemed to feel so proud and happy in denying the legitimacy of authority. And when we listened to him, we felt it too. And now, one space removed in the time frame, when none of it retained any cultural substance, and all of it was being purveyed as a high-class show-business commodity, this same poet was about to appear at the Rochester War Memorial.

Against all my identity preferences, I felt that I was about to undergo if not a religious conversion, then at least a significant cultural event. Bob Dylan was the poet of a generation which, it turned out, did not produce poets. He was the poet of a generation that did not recognize the function, or even the existence, of poetry. And somehow circumstances cut through these prohibitions and made him the one and only poet. And this was a very special role to play in a culture nearly devoid of high-class roles. At a time when the Joe DiMaggios are making television commercials, and old football players are running the government, what could be classier than being Bob Dylan?

There was a wait in the lobby. I looked around and saw that I was surrounded by children. This was peer-dominated America, after all, and I was standing in line with the wrong generation. Looking for a place to hide, I pulled out my ticket, turned it over, and began reading the fine print on the back.

The bearer agrees, as a condition of the purchase of this ticket, not to film or photograph or tape record this concert, or any portion thereof, and relinquishes the rights to his own face appearing in any movie, or segment

[207]

thereof, which rights for have been heretofore licensed to the Portland Street Company, of such and such . . .

And just as I was about three-quarters of the way through the paragraph, and its significance had begun to appear, a man grabbed it out of my hand, tore it, and handed me back the wrong half. I begged to have the other half back, at least until I had finished reading it, but the ticket-tearer said no.

Although I hadn't finished reading my ticket, I knew the sense of the paragraph on the back. It was a thematic outline for the concert, couched in the legend of symbolic message.

The message was that a postwar dream had ended, and in its image there was built a commodity of a status commensurate with the size of its buying market. In the postwar era, there were never any public messages written in a literary style so ornately legal. Bobby Dylan, the postwar icon, would not have been capable of singing behind such a message. Postwar dreams are finished now, the ticket said; the bearer is entitled only to a corporate-era commodity. And Bob Dylan, whatever his mental essence, however he might feel about his life, is the central figure in a particular business enterprise that has come all the way from alienated poems of anarchy to worrying about every petty detail of possible financial gain, right down to the last homemade cassette recording or snapshot. This was corporate-style business, extending the territory right to the brink of memory, in terms of what was for sale.

Long before the concert began, I saw Bob Dylan in the role his music scorned. It was now a decade later, and as something continues to happen in the corporate era, it is Bob Dylan that can't know what it is.

I had, on the back of my overpriced ticket, wherever it was, the rhyme of the new era. It spoke of the poet's gradual acceptance of soft living. It spoke of idle dreams that were now felt needs. Limousines at the curb, gadgets around the house, astronomical telephone and airplane bills, and a certain style of high living that comes with the acceptance of a career as a corporate commodity. And much more importantly, the message on the back of my ticket spoke to a corrupt inflexibility in the social structure which separates the poet from his poetry, at the expense of each. Even the particular poet, whose life and work represented a specific, heroic struggle to resist the temptations of corporate seduction, could not unite with his poetry and became powerful.

And now this poet, whose creative ego and public image came out of his joy in resisting the earlier manifestations of the corporate mentality, was, even against his own will, even against his activity in the music business, and even against his public presence to the contrary, a commodity. And all this was the work of history, not of human passions.

The illusion that I had purchased the last available ticket was revealed as no illusion. Just when I was hoping for luck, I found that there was still some justice. I had the last seat in the last row. In a just world, precisely the ticket that would be sold last.

Eventually the lights went off and the curtain opened. Spotlights were trained on the stage, where, about a quarter of a mile down the road from where I was sitting, submicroscopic insects began to move along the surface of the stage, and music filled the air. I extended my thumb in a straight line up from my knee and found that I could, with the top half of my thumb, cover the singer in the spotlight at least three times over. The distance was so great that not only couldn't I recognize the performers, I couldn't tell who was performing and who was hanging around.

The music stopped and a voice came over the loudspeaker: "My name is Bobby Newirth, and welcome to our intimate coffee-house tour." Laughter broke out among the first few hundred rows, but it was no joke back in my section.

"We're pleased to be here in the War Memorial. The

band is called Guam, and you'll be hearing from them later in the evening."

A band called Guam, clearly a reference to the name of the auditorium. If this is a War Memorial, then we are the Battle of Guam. Clearly a hostile remark aimed at the retentive quality of Rochester folkways. And yet, perhaps something much more profound was going on. The Monroe County War Memorial was the first and only grand monument of the postwar era to be built in Rochester. And now, to commemorate the passing of the era, if not of its monuments, a pageant would be created. And this concert would be a true war memorial. A naval epic, but, for a change, battling a sea of adoring admirers instead of salt water.

On such a night, my imagination was more easily carried away by the circumstances than it was by the music. Not that the music wasn't special, but the circumstances seemed to hold historical significance.

And then Bob Dylan appeared. He was wearing the same gray hat with a feather that he had worn in all his recent photographs and in the newspaper advertisements for this concert. That's how I recognized him. And, I began to realize, that was why he wore the hat. This was not the postwar era; corporate promoters knew about the people in the cheap seats, knew that they couldn't see, and knew that they would only come back if they could believe that they had seen. And so now I could say that I had seen Dylan, since I had, in the preceding month, unconsciously accepted the gray, feathered hat as the media symbol it was designed to be. And now I could identify the hat and know that I was seeing Dylan.

The music was moving, and not to be dismissed. The band called Guam was composed, almost entirely, of living legends, and it encompassed most of the academy of blue-chip folk artists that the corporate era now marketed as rock stars.

When the lights came on at intermission, I looked

around the War Memorial. Joan Baez had announced that the grape and lettuce boycotts were on again, and had been cheered. Then she dedicated a song to the United Farm Workers, and again she was cheered. And I was looking to see what such a vast and sympathetic audience for Dylan, Joan Baez, Joni Mitchell, and the United Farm Workers was like. And all I saw were teen-agers. Ordinary, sensible teen-agers. Alienation had no home in this audience. And what I saw in these teen-agers was neither the reverence for Dylan that had pervaded my generation nor the irreverence of drug-taking and loitering that characterizes American rock concerts, but a different kind of energy entirely.

This was no cataclysmic cultural event. This was the joy of being allowed to stay out late on a Monday night. Everyone knew that somebody like Bob Dylan would never play Rochester, and if he did, it was automatically the luckiest night of the year, no matter what happened.

This was a politically sympathetic audience, but an audience that had no concept of political activity. The silence on the political left was not created by any lack of charm and beauty. The American television audience of the late postwar era was charmed by the left, and these teen-agers were the children who constituted it. And now they were grown up, and still charmed, but they remained apolitical.

A generation of radicals never created any models for how to be. It was a classic tragic flaw, growing from the very heart of the matter. That movement itself had grown out of a particular generation's adolescent inability to know how to be good in a society that was rooted in evil. That was the extent to which they became a community. That inability is what they shared. Bob Dylan, in fact, became their star precisely when he didn't know how to act like one.

Dylan's status grew from his particular ability to be part of his audience, and to sing their songs for them. And now, a generation and an era away, here was Bob

[211]

Dylan singing that way again, and more so than ever before. But his life had nothing to do with this audience of the chosen many who were allowed to stay out past midnight. This was an act. This was entertainment. This was show business at its most deluxe, but it was not culture.

I felt that there was something very special about this concert. But feelings at distances beyond a thousand yards are often unreliable, and so I decided to hang around and see, at relatively close range, who it was that had been singing.

There were about fifty people huddled into the space between the tour bus and the War Memorial. The side and back of the tour bus said "Phydeaux," and underneath it was a cartoon dog that bore the same relationship to the bus-famous greyhound as Guam did to the War Memorial. One by one the stars came out and, to polite applause, wended their way through the crowd and into the bus-famous Greyhound as Guam did to the War Memorial and climbed into the cab of a big semitruck, which was very good for his image. Except that he didn't drive it; a moment later, he climbed back down and boarded the bus.

The bus drove away and I noticed that standing next to me were Allen Ginsberg and Peter Orlovsky. Right next to me, in Rochester, New York. My high-school hero, not all that far away from my high school. In the same spot where I had dreamed of being a beatnik, there stood the King and Chief Rabbi of All Beatniks, and his boyfriend.

I turned to Peter Orlovsky and said, "Nobody recognizes you; it's a different generation." He said, "Yes," and walked away.

About ten minutes later, still standing there, I realized that nothing was about to happen, so I turned to Allen Ginsberg and said, "I'm sorry. I think you're the most important person here, and I'm sorry because nobody knows who you are or where all this came from."

He smiled and said, "I am nobody, who are you? Are you nobody, too?"

I wrinkled my forehead but kept my mouth shut. I suddenly realized that I shouldn't have said what I did.

Allen Ginsberg didn't wait for my reply, or couldn't. And so he coached me. "Not exactly an admiring bog, is it?" he said.

Isn't it enough that I recognized him, I thought? What is he doing?

Then Allen Ginsberg said, "I am nobody, who are you? Are you nobody, too? It's from a poem by Emily Dickinson. Don't you know it?"

I'm from a generation that didn't recognize the existence of poetry. "No," I said.

And then Allen Ginsberg said,

"I'm nobody! Who are you?

Are you nobody, too?

How dreary to be somebody!

How public, like a frog

To tell your name the livelong day

To an admiring bog!

"It's a poem, by Emily Dickinson," he said. I nodded, and we stood there silently for a while and then he left.

At about three in the morning, the temperature began to drop, and the crowd shrank, but I had no sense of waiting. In Rochester the hardest core of Dylan fans looked like a bunch of Kodak workers waiting for a bowling alley to open. But the night was cold and dark, and the fact that they were still here was itself an exaggerated devotion. And whoever they were, the mystery of why they were here was much more interesting than Bob Dylan.

Suddenly Dylan, in his gray hat, appeared. The crowd surged and Dylan ducked back inside the War Memorial. Then, noticing how small the crowd was, he turned back and sauntered toward us. There weren't enough to create a crush. And Dylan moved around, trading thank yous with his admirers. I looked into his eyes, up close, and all I saw was strength, and health, and youth. And nothing to do with me, or my life, and everything to do with the enthusiastic teen-agers who clapped as he boarded his camper.

And so the evening ended. The camper carrying Bob Dylan turned down the entrance ramp to the freeway and, followed by twenty-seven cars filled with teen-agers, sped off into the night. I knew that there was not one more drop of time to be wrung from this experience.

As if the Red Wings and my own memory were not enough, the muses handed me, in the person of Bob Dylan, a flashing neon sign of historical absolution. You do your best and you are judged accordingly, but it is always important to remember that there are larger forces at work. And though personal responsibility makes it possible to keep score, it is, if taken too seriously, an absurdity. I looked into the eyes of Bob Dylan, and I had already looked into my own, and I would never again tell anybody that they are responsible either for making their own historical substance or for lying in it.

PART

3

And now my identity has risen up through baseball and I am, at last, waking up every morning and seriously asking myself: Who am I? What is reality? And what may I hope?

And I must answer that I am living up in Westchester County and collecting unemployment insurance benefits from the State of New York. To the hard stares that accompany the question of what I do up there in Westchester, I must answer that I don't know what I *would* do up in Westchester; I am on the dole. My financial profile is blissfully static. And as the weeks pass, my work life is divided between baseball and an increasingly educated appreciation for the expansive availability of internal space. There is, inside my mind, space in which to breathe, and sweeter air than my nostrils have ever tasted.

The first principle of business and capitalism and accounting, and the whole structure that determines relationships among human beings, is called marginality. The principle of marginality is that you must, against all impulse, limit the closeness with which you examine things, and the finitude with which you divide them. You must, in order to act, make insufficient generalizations long before you are certain. This is because there is a natural tendency to look closer and closer, and to di-

vide into more and more precise categories. And those
people who get lost in the lower regions of fascinated
observation tend never to come back. Never make any
deals, never do business, never act.

And so the rule in this society is that when you, as
a specialist, are asked, point-blank, how many angels
dance on the head of a pin, you lie. Adherence to marginality is the professional thing to do. And this is a difficulty that has run throughout my life. I tend to look at
things too closely for too long. No category is too small
or insignificant for my attention. Which is, of course, a
great joy to anyone interested in the subtleties of life,
but it makes the peaceful satisfaction of conclusion impossible, and it makes moving on very difficult.

And so, as the 1975 baseball season wore on, and the
pennant race began in earnest, I was not surprised to find
myself sitting in my room in Westchester County, still
sifting through the remains of the upheavals that my
childhood caused in my memory. What was significant?
What was significance? And who was I to judge?

I approached my landlady, as a regular American
and the only sample available unless I was prepared to
leave the house, and I asked her, "Did you have a dial
telephone when you were a little kid?"

"As opposed to what?" she answered.

When I was eighteen years old and about to leave
for college, we were still part of the old Hillside exchange
of the Rochester Telephone Company. We were still having to wait endlessly for the operator to tell our number
to, and still having to hold a screaming vacuum cleaner
over the receiver to get a certain neighbor, or her mother,
off the party line. And during all this time, my landlady
had never heard of anything but a dial phone. She didn't
even know that it was advanced technology.

At the time, this seemed so significant. Even my relationship to the telephone revealed where I had come
from. But now I can look back at the extreme minutiae
of my consideration, and the significance attaches not

to where I came from, but to where I wound up. Because I am sitting here in Westchester County, of all places, and however much I would prefer to think of it as the trees and flowers and birds I see out of my window, I know that it is, in fact, a very rare and very extreme kind of place, and that it too must have its effect on who I am and how I think.

The place mats in the local diner say, "Welcome to Westchester County, New York. The richest and most beautiful county in the world." And at the bottom, "Beauty and enchantment go hand and hand in Westchester County." The telephone installer who came to my home on the day I moved to Westchester said they were all sons of bitches.

I live about fifty miles north of the center of New York City. For those who stay at home, this is country living, in the manner of the postwar era; for those who go out, Westchester is the conspicuous glory of corporate success at its most successful. There are continual traffic jams on the country lanes of Westchester, but every frustrated driver knows that he is part of a special, chosen elect, and lucky to be here.

At the end of World War II, Westchester County, despite its proximity to New York City, was primarily rural. As farmland it was ordinary, and as real estate it was unpromising. New York City and its life force were still desirable, and generally speaking, the farther from that life force you lived, the less desirable, less accessible, and less expensive it became. After the war, private lives prospered, public life began to disappear, and in the process the city itself came to be seen as dirty, dangerous, uncomfortable, and worse. The calculating, cautious, foresighted corporate mentality quietly raised a mortgage and built a highway. And then whoever could see the inevitability they were creating, and could raise the cash, abandoned the city at dusk to sleep in the clean, safe, and natural air of Westchester. In the early nineteen-fifties, Westchester County became the first rural place

[219]

in America to be both urbanized and consumed socially by country evil.

There is a phenomenon, in this time, which has crept out of the new consciousness and into the landscape. This phenomenon grows from urban natives feeling that it is the city itself which is driving them crazy. They leave the city, with the dream of escape, and bring that craziness with them when they arrive in the country. There it flourishes, destroying the existing native culture. This is country evil.

At the dawn of the corporate era, Westchester had already established itself as the final certification and resting place for connivers, hustlers, gangsters, pimps, and other hardasses of the money jungle of New York. Meanwhile, fate and the eternal search for paradox have placed me in Westchester, practicing the profession of being unemployed. And if there is one thing that is more disturbing to Westchester County than the mosquitoes on a hot summer night, it is the word "welfare" uttered at a social gathering.

I have always been reasonably well mannered, and so I am always careful to point out politely that unemployment and welfare are distinct from one another in spirit as well as bureaucratic structure. "What do you mean, unemployment? That's welfare," they say, as eyebrows lift and tongues gag around the room.

I must be very careful about what I say, and even more careful about what I allow myself to hear. Self-designated success stories believe that poverty is a disease, but not a chronic one. And, when I am not careful, these sergeants of big-city business fill me, the financial leper, with their advice on how I might follow in their footsteps. And how could I possibly begin to explain to them about baseball and memory and the search for meaning and whatever it is that I do up here? And why would I want to try? In these times, costumed as the hardest of all times, I have secured, at long last, a patron.

And I spend my days in a room in a grand Victorian mansion, while the state picks up the bills.

This mansion that I live in was built in 1875, and for all the years that it was situated in a real place with a real culture it was one of the largest and classiest houses in town. Its owners had the first motor car and, later, the first telephone, in town. But now the paint is peeling, and the plumbing leaks, and the tennis courts have been replaced by the superhighway exit, and history is more grand than the present. And now the guest rooms and the storerooms outnumber the living rooms, and this grand machine for Victorian living is inhabited by the landlord, the landlady, and me.

And we have become, in a basic but nevertheless strange interpretation of the notion, a family. We came from the same historical, socioeconomic, emotional, and cultural backgrounds, as they say. We have thoughts and feelings to exchange. And there being more than a requisite level of affection, we live together as if we had always done so, and always will.

They are the proprietors and I am the lodger, but that is a distinction easily forgotten in the course of everyday life. There are other distinctions between us, not so easily forgotten.

The landlady was a cheerleader, the valedictorian, and the most popular girl in her school. The landlord was the quarterback of the football team, an all-county basketball star, and a similar social success. As children, they did not know the meaning, or the feeling, or the anger of alienation. As adolescents, they learned that the world was a nice place, and that reality was only benign. As children they learned that applause was frequent and spontaneous, and that the problems of identity in the world were resolved easily and naturally. To be somebody, you had only to desire it. At the historical juncture of social relationships, where public identity became available only to the few, the landlord and the landlady were of that few. As I was discovering the internal pleasures that come to spectators, they were performing, and discovering the public pleasures of victory and applause. And that has made all the difference in the world, and left us, all these years later, political opposites. Not political enemies, because we have no issues, but at the level of instinct, political opposites.

The postwar era has collapsed for all of us, and life has never been the same since. But formative years are formative. And once formed, identity is not entirely plastic. And so the three of us have arrived at this Victorian mansion together, but with very different expectations.

I am the lodger, living in my room, and within my means, confident about the present and suspicious of the future. They are the owners, living in a mansion they cannot afford, in a style that is beyond their means. But living in a reality that is only kind and generous, and awaiting a future that holds even more abundance.

From these opposite directions, we live together, each of us playing out our own eccentric notions of what life is about and of who we are. Dwarfed by the mansion, and secluded in the woodlands of the suburbs, the river of life becomes a pond, and we are floating on a lily pad dreamed up as a buffer against the cruel realities of New York City. There is nothing out there restricting our play. This is how protected my life has become. This is the distance between my own life and the life of this society and the reason why, with a world that begins at my doorstep, all of my wanderlust has remained personal, and all of my expeditions internal.

I was a baseball fan as a boy, but I was many other things, too. And however much I would have desired to squeeze all those other things, somehow, into baseball, I didn't. I couldn't.

Baseball pulled at my interest and diverted my attention, Judaism, on the other hand, was my heritage, and left me no choice. By the time it was handed to me, my heritage had lost its social context. In isolation its gestures no longer looked authentic. Its rituals were enacted with a sigh and its traditions were passed on and accepted with slightly embarrassed resignation.

The intention of my religious training was to teach me who I was supposed to be. But times had changed, and the lessons had not. Who I was supposed to be didn't seem to fit into the suburban scheme, and the only lesson I learned was to question who I was.

We were religious, but as devoutly East European as Jewish. And this was who I was supposed to be. And so I devoutly waved a live chicken over my head on the appropriate holiday, and searched for bread crumbs with a candle, and fasted and overate, all on the appropriate day and for the appropriate reason.

We were Jews, and therefore not like anyone else. And the things we did were not like the things other people did. I tried to accept all of this. I even tried to accept that it was wrong to eat candy at the movies and hot dogs at the ballgame, and that these things were only offered for sale to self-indulgent goyim, who weren't as special as we. But all of this was going on in suburban Rochester, amidst the bustle and optimism of the postwar era. Community was never less stable, and heritage never less certain. The material world was being conquered. Material vengeance was being taken, and nothing that was not new seemed to make any sense. The notion that I was a member of a distinct and separate tribe just didn't feel true. It was a time when life in America was a competition for the accumulation of tangible trinkets. And everyone seemed to be winning. It was no time for spiritual matters, no time for religion.

Compounding the irreligious and iconoclastic economic climate was the other great body of dreams that my relatives brought from Eastern Europe to Rochester. They brought Judaism, but they also brought its opposite, its contradiction—assimilation.

To blend in and be invisible was valuable. To study newspapers and television and movies was smart. To

[223]

learn the American way of life was intelligent. And to become American was wise—your safety depended on it. It was the persecuted refugee's dream of belonging.

No one realized how easily this dream would be fulfilled. No one imagined how impossible it would be to resist. I became more American than I needed to be, and less Jewish. I became more baseball, and less religious. And so I looked to baseball to organize my cultural needs, and Judaism became no more than a dark, unrelenting, ever-present discipline.

When ordinary children were still asleep I had to wake up early, and before I went to school I would wind the holy leather straps around my arm and pray for hours, bending and swaying with the precise velocity required to show comprehension and devotion. I preferred to pray silently, since my Hebrew was not very good, and silent prayer would allow me to drift to more interesting thoughts while skipping large chunks of the morning service. But my father was ever vigilant, and forever explaining that God could hear even a whisper, but he could not hear silent prayer.

It is so uncomfortable to describe all of this that it is making me very nervous indeed. It was no coincidence that drove me to my childhood in my search for meaning, and no coincidence that led me to baseball rather than any other aspect of my childhood life. When I try to organize my emotional past, the forms of baseball memories seem so clear, and so pure, and so natural. When I try, out of a sense of fairness, to do the same thing for my Jewishness, it immediately becomes difficult and awkward and, eventually, I feel dishonest.

As soon as I decide that the truth of my religious upbringing was the extent and absurdity of its discipline, I can suddenly remember holy days when things went differently.

I can see my Uncle Hymie brazenly watching his new television set, and taking more delight in the shocking gesture of disobedience than in the content of the program, which happened to be a Tarzan movie. Neither electricity nor entertainment was permitted on holy days; watching television should have been an unthinkable sin. As Hymie watched Tarzan, the children worked off the tensions and frustrations of sitting still for the entire morning service by engaging in vengeful play. My grandmother sat in the corner praying fervently, but noticing Tarzan out of the corner of her eye.

And then, within an instant, the tiger leaped at Tarzan, my grandmother dropped her prayers and screamed, and a cousin, having just found the horse chestnut hidden beneath my grandmother's false teeth in the glass of water, yelled, "Hucklebucklebeanstalk!"

For eight hundred years, my relatives had been digging up potatoes in Poland and Russia, but they were now in America. After generations of learning that subsistence was difficult and the good life impossible, they were suddenly living in a world where prosperity, and even luxury, came so fast that it left everyone slightly punchy. It was the postwar era, and my relatives, like everyone else, had their needs and their desires and their expectations inflated too quickly. It left them off-center, satisfied, but slightly out of control.

I went away and never came home again. The pull of home and hearth exists for every human being, and I was no different. But I was American, and accustomed to American ways, and a necessary part of that assimilation was to misunderstand and mistrust where I had come from. Long before I left home, I knew, as all Americans know in their own special way, that I would never return.

It is possible that memory really does drift for its own reasons and that I am easily impressed by the exotica of my own childhood. For I know that I will never be able to comprehend the deep dark secrets of my family life, no less tell them. I will never be able to know what drove us to such grand gestures of combat and love, motivated by conflicting desires for power and self-sacrifice, and always, played out along lines of the most grandiose emotional gestures.

And yet, as incomprehensible as it was, and remains, this was the only America I knew. And so I lived in this little pocket of esoteric Americanism and esoteric Judaism, and it seemed like ordinary life. No kissing on the Sabbath; whistling calls the devil. Double-pitted fruit was good luck; a brown egg was bad luck. And on the holiest day of the year, when religious Jews go down to the banks of the nearest river and with a special prayer throw their sins in the water, I stood dutifully, at my grandmother's kitchen sink, where, in the comfort and convenience of home, we were able to cast our sins into the water coming from the cold-water tap, and to know that they would wash down the drain, travel through the sewage network, and wind up in the Genesee River, as God intended. And that too seemed ordinary.

We were members of the congregation of the Big Schul. In its day, it was not only the largest, but the most socially correct East European synagogue in Rochester. My grandfather had been one of the founding big shots of the place, and it was not uncommon for my father, when entering the building, to stop at the stone tablets and point to my grandfather's name, chiseled in Hebrew into the marble.

The building was a magnificent Byzantine mosque, with domes floating on little stained-glass windows. In the morning the domes floated on colored sunlight, and in the evening on ornate designs drawn in rows of light bulbs, which from our seat looked like neon signs, and very impressive. But the schul also had spittoons, and a phone booth that smelled of gambling and tobacco. And ever since the time I saw my uncle find a dollar seventy-five in the coin return, I used to hold my nose and enter the reeking phone booth and check the coin return. But magnificence is not hygiene, grandeur is not repair, and awe is not envy. And so the Big Schul was able to exist,

[226]

warped out of social and financial context by the postwar era, and remain glorious, broken down, anachronistic, and enthralling.

We always sat in the same seat; my grandfather had purchased it in perpetuity. Behind us sat the Schneiderman brothers. I would shake their hands when I was supposed to, but I knew them only by sight.

The Schneiderman boys were baseball fans. They were four times my age, and infinitely more powerful in both familial and religious politics. Even on the holiest days of the year, they were sources of up-to-the-minute baseball information. They were devout, and never left the service, but somehow they always knew how the important games were progressing.

Since the holiest days of the year always occurred during the heat of the pennant race, or during the World Series, it was important to keep within eavesdropping distance of the Schneiderman brothers, which I did. I survived the deadest hours of the all-day services by slipping into silent prayer and listening to baseball discussions behind me.

One night, vandals stripped the copper off the largest dome of the Big Schul's roof. From then on it leaked, and the reliability of the electrical system grew marginal, but there wasn't money for repair. And shortly behind was urban renewal. There were threats, and even one Mr. Feigelmann who promised, in public, to sit on the steps with a shotgun if any bulldozers dared come near the building. But Eisenhower was still president, and in those days the inevitability of government quashed all anger. The building was quietly torn down. No fuss was created outside the hearts of a handful of Rochester's least prosperous Jews.

The Big Schul was not seen as the victim of a society in transition. The synagogue, as an institution, had come to be seen only as an emotional pull away from the good life in the suburbs. The destruction of the Big Schul was felt only as the removal of an annoying and old-fashioned impediment. The Jewish community of Rochester was prospering and becoming suburban and American. And looking forward to more of the same. Jewish Rochester was being reduced to a financial quota in the fund drives for Israel. Now there was no guilt associated with forsaking the old religion for a mild adherence to the irreverent Americanness of Reformed Judaism. Now modern Jewry was the only game in town, and people felt relief where they would, in other days, have felt outrage.

Now I can interrupt myself and look out of my window and see past the highway and the railroad tracks and the hills and valleys, all the way to the bleakness of the future for American life. It is a time for other worlds. A time for apocalypse and tambourines; a time for Oriental cults and spiritual techniques sold wholesale and retail. Materialism is failing, and the smartest of success-oriented Americans are switching their ambitions to the spirit. And though I can see it all, I cannot join in. I have a heritage, and it has its own version of the bright white light, and it has no glow for me. I was raised on the fault line of the postwar era. As the historical forces heaved, I grew up. And in the resulting cultural and historical realignment, the notion of heritage lost its meaning.

While still in high school, I became a beatnik. I polished my old baseball shoes and sold them cheap, feeling only the thrill of getting money for something that has no value. Baseball wasn't cool, but I was. I wore sunglasses and sandals, wrote poetry and listened to jazz. I carried the *New York Times* under my arm whenever I could. I worshiped Gregory Corso, Allen Ginsberg, and Jack Kerouac. I dropped references to Neal Cassidy, the world's fastest tire changer, wherever I could. But within a short time, peer and authority pressures arrived and caused me to suffer a failure of nerve, and I abandoned the whole identity. With an ease and facility unencumbered by psychological consideration, I altered the way I looked, the way I acted, and the way I thought. As easily as I took up being a beatnik, I abandoned it.

Then I went off to college and became the young scholar. By then beaniks were pretentious midwestern farm boys, and I was the rarefied, overeducated elite, or at least training to be. I spent my time in the library, smelling and reading musty old books about economic history. Now it was tweed jackets and bow ties, and a Scandinavian briar pipe. During this time, I pored through the writings of Karl Marx without ever becoming radicalized. But a short time later, Lyndon Johnson and his Vietnam war began to arrive on campus, and the students began taking sides. And I began to notice that the smartest and most interesting and the best people I knew were calling Lyndon Johnson a murderer, and themselves communists. And shortly thereafter, I did too.

What I actually did as a radical is hard to discern. I was an earnest field hand to the revolution, and always did what I was told. And I went to endless meetings. But left to my own devices, I never ventured beyond the process of trying to decide what work had to be done. In the end, I tried to justify my indecision by thinking of myself as a theoretician. But there was a tension to my radicalism, and it was never resolved. It was the tension between being a revolutionary twenty-four hours a day, while at the same time never doing anything that seemed to be genuinely meaningful. It was the tension between feeling total outrage at the nature of the society I was living in, and having no strong feelings about how it could, or even should, be changed. It was the tension of an anger that would carry me just so far and then, in spite of all my romantic yearnings, no farther. I couldn't become a real revolutionary, nor could I forget the circumstances that drove other people to do it. I was too radical to be peaceful, and not radical enough to be violent. Politically, there was no such thing as this, and no place in which to be it.

And so the sources of my alienation were never identified, and no organization was ever built around it. And this was no wonder. Confounding my situation into paradox were my circumstances. At the same time that my social life was becoming increasingly radical, I was also climbing the ladder of success in the liberal bureaucratic fantasy of meaningful work. And eventually I arrived at a point where I woke up quite prepared to smash the state, and went off to work in the White House, in Washington, D.C., where I was a bright young statistician in the Bureau of the Budget.

That intolerable situation couldn't last long, and it didn't. Without psychology, and therefore without shame, I felt that it was a time for change, and a time to grow. What should have come out of a soul-searching articulation of personal moral values, instead, as things tended to in those days, came out of nothing more than restlessness. And so without hope or doubt, and without commitment or nerve, I leaped into the unknown.

The beauty of naïveté is that it allows you to get mixed up in all kinds of things that you would never have had the nerve to pursue if you knew better. And the problem with naïveté is that it can't happen twice. Once you know better, you can't pretend that you don't, unless you are very brave and somewhat crazy.

But, thankfully, I was still naïve. And so, with no more thought than the desire to get away from America, I left the country. Away from its prejudices, its greed, its Vietnamization, its rednecks, its cops, and its oil companies. Away from family and friends, and the life I was living, and on to rebirth.

I packed my suitcase with radical literature and Salvation Army clothes and left for England. On arrival in London, I presented myself as an American hippie. In those days, it seemed, no identity was so socially desired, or quite so international. I preached love and peace, and revolution by life style. I spent my days wandering around, not out of work, but consciously and actively withholding my labor from the capitalist means of production. Stop holding it up and it will fall down, I still thought. Victory through peace and love, I urged.

And then the time came when I lost my naïveté. I saw bayonets pointed at me in the streets of Paris, and the newsreels of America were showing tanks in the streets of all the big cities. And unlike the Heroic Vietnamese, the people in the streets of Chicago didn't look at all invincible. And the brothers and sisters of the new era who slept on my floor often stole things when they left. And the tactic of withholding my labor began to reveal life as no more than a continual tea party, increasingly in need of a more gracious host.

My dissatisfaction once again became political moralism. I fled back to America to do what I had decided I always wanted to do. That is, to become one with those holy and homely angels, the working class.

And so I went to work in a factory. But not just any factory. My need for paradox demanded that I carefully select the nature of the shit-work I would associate myself with. My work would be lowly, but it would make me, in its own way, charismatic. And I became a printer. In Hollywood movies, printers were the most radical of all tradesmen, and printing was the trade that most romantically touched the hearts of the poets. And printing was an art. A good printer was a craftsman, respected in all circles. Intellectual and manual, bourgeois and proletarian, a printer belonged to no social class, but was respected by all.

There were some deeper, darker mysteries than I knew attached to my plans for working-class identity, because I actually did become a printer. Printing is my father's trade, and there was something about the smell and activities of the shop that I could, from my earliest childhood memories, identify as work. Work was a place where there were ink and paper, and people rushing around complaining that they hated every minute of it. Unlike the white-collar jobs I had done, printing was work, and I recognized it the minute I saw it.

I entered the working class, sweeping up and emptying the trash, and learning to be a printer. The work was exhausting, and for the first time in my life, I got strong. It was very odd; I would look into the mirror and all I would see was muscles.

In the silk-screen printing shops, where I learned my trade, all the sit-down jobs were done by Caucasians, and, since the end of World War II, all the actual printing, where your hands got covered in ink, was done by black people. This made it possible for me to get jobs quite easily; it was a novelty to have a white printer. But it was impossible for me to fit in. And I wanted to fit into working-class life more than I wanted anything. The relief of being neither bourgeois nor revolutionary was something that I didn't want to give up.

I studied my craft; I worked at it with terrifying intensity. I was special at work, as an outsider. At a time when black and white America were most separate and mutually fearful, I worked all day long at the borders of the forbidden zone. I heard stories and observed rituals of a foreign culture never before witnessed by persons of my ilk. And I was special in my social life, as an insider. I chastised my friends for being soft and protected, and for being ignorant of the reality of real working people's lives. I told the left what a joke real working people thought they were. Now the guilts were reversed, and the political moralists had to answer to me. Each day I did, more than anyone else I knew, an honest day's work. And in the evenings, I had stories to tell them of a world they had never seen.

So successful was my taste of working-class life that my ambition was only for authenticity. So, as soon as I learned my craft, I headed to London, where the working class was white, and where immigrants have no past and no comprehensible class characteristics.

In the beginning, I approached printing with confidence. But I was temperamentally and intellectually unsuited to the world of technical consideration, and to a life of doing something over and over again in order to see how perfectly it can be done. Competence came very slowly to me, and excellence seemed impossible, but there wasn't much competition and I persevered.

I rose through the ranks, getting better and better jobs. I was ambitious, but more than protected from middle-class life by the English working-class standard of living. And five years later, I was finally at that place where I had, for so long, wanted to be. I was a good printer, and I was working class.

Everything was fine until I realized what I had. *Oi vey*, I then thought, I really am nothing more than a dumb printer. I have lost my sense of humor, I have lost my articulation. I don't get halfway through the newspaper. I haven't read a book in months. I am a dumb, boring printer. All I ever want to do any more is to get drunk , get laid, and listen to loud music. What on earth has happened to me? What about honor and values? What about morals? What about the search for the meaning of truth? I thought my deepest fear: I have interrupted my education. This has got to stop.

I was stronger and better looking as a printer than I have been since, and that was sad to lose. And there is a sane simplicity and uncomplicated immediacy to working-class life, and that was awful to lose. But I was powerless to resist my growing feelings that I was cut out for something larger than this. Which is to say that I really did become working class: part of working-class consciousness is to have middle-class aspirations.

Thereafter, I was out of the fire and into a confusion much hotter. And when the pieces from all the emotional, geographical, and psychological explosions finally came to rest, I found myself sitting in my room in Westchester County, staring out of the window at nature, watching the choo-choo commuter trains go back and forth.

The sun shines brighter in Westchester. It floods my room, making it impossible to watch a day game on television. But baseball is mainly a night sport nowadays, leaving my days that summer of 1975 free for dreaming and thinking and becoming more and more deeply immersed in Cuban baseball, baseball detente, detente baseball, the peripheral issues of being a child baseball fan, and the political and moral assessments revealed. And more. And ever more after that. And finally I began to realize that my appetite was undaunted and insatiable. The failures of my dream of finding a CIA play did not deter me. Neither did the crumbling of my notion of historical absolution. And though this strange appetite began to reveal an eccentric streak in my behavior, this gave me no concern. A different story was revealing itself, but as long as it sustained the intensity of my powers of focus, it was all right with me.

This was no ordinary summer. While millions of Americans faced poverty and unemployment, and longed for the bygone days of last year, ten times as many other Americans successfully pretended they were still in the lap of a postwar boom, and the riches would never end. And I, far removed from all this, spent my days thinking about the Havana Sugar Kings, the Rochester Red Wings, and the upcoming detente. And worrying about my relationship to all of them. In the evenings, tired and exhausted, and somewhat guilty about the oddness of the obsession I had created and chosen, I would watch the baseball games on television.

In the beginning it was a distraction. A mind as busy and troubled as mine had been all afternoon could not be seduced into recreation by ping-pong or reading novels. Movies failed to work, entirely. On the few occasions I tried, I found myself sitting in the cinema, aware of the darkness and wondering: Frank Verdi, where have you gone?

As I watched more and more baseball games on television, I began to know these modern players and understand their playing personalities. And then I got caught up in the drama and tension of the game. And I began to notice that the agonies and anxieties and hopes and fears that the game produces provided me with an inner peace that I could not find elsewhere. Now, beyond Havana Sugar Kings, and metaphors for political science, was baseball, in and of itself. Not childhood baseball, not baseball for detente, but actual baseball games.

The repeated watching of baseball games gradually reverses the metaphor and in the end makes baseball itself the only reality. And while that reality exists, no others compete. Until the game is over, until the last out, time stops. Baseball, I began to notice, and to articulate for the first time, is consuming. Because all your hopes and dreams and strengths and fears are taken up by the game itself, no external necessity can impinge.

I was back into baseball and getting more deeply involved. It was never that I needed to watch the ballgame, just that I enjoyed it. This is an exploration and relaxation, I thought to myself; this is not a habit.

Late in the summer, as the baseball season wound toward its finish, I left a friend's birthday party and went to a seedy bar to watch a crucial National League playoff game. It wasn't a very interesting game, but it did, neverless, make me realize that I had become a very different kind of person this summer. Now baseball with implication was fine, but not enough. Now baseball, all by itself, was necessary.

I took the precaution of assigning myself the task of watching the World Series on television as part of my research. I had become an ordinary baseball fan, but what began in the microfilm-reading room had continued into the present. This World Series would have implications for Cuba and detente. After all, Luis Tiant would be pitching for the American League champions, the Boston Red Sox. And Tiant, a Cuban as well as a star, had already been earmarked as a trial balloon for political detente. Earlier in the summer, when his parents were

flown from Havana to Boston, they had the dual assign-
ment of watching their son pitch and softening American
attitudes toward Cuba. Surely, I thought, as Boston prepared to battle Cincinnati, American foreign policy is not
going to let the World Series slip past as an unexpected
backdrop.

If it turned out to be thrilling, exciting, and wonderful baseball, that would be the icing on the good fortune
that brought me this job. Even so, I resolved, however
willingly and enthusiastically, that I would glue myself
to the television set for the duration of the World Series
with a sense of employment.

Although I hoped for exciting baseball, for the personal consequences of history and for my role in this obscure area of international politics, I feared the worst. I
had spent all summer forging a metaphoric iron, and now
that it was time to heat it, I realized that I had never
worked out a corresponding metaphor for "strike." What
I feared was that history would make that iron hot, now
that I knew it was too whimsical to be useful at any
temperature. And these fears were no sooner dreamed up
than they were fulfilled. Two days before the opening
game of the World Series, the newspapers ran a photograph of Hirohito of Japan being introduced to Mickey
Mouse at his home in Disneyland. Mickey Mouse, about
six inches taller than Hirohito, gazed over the top of the
emperor's head. Hirohito, from the expression on his face,
might have mistaken Mickey Mouse for a potential assas-
sin at point-blank range. The text under the photograph
explains that Snow White, the Seven Dwarfs, and Goofy
all took part in the welcome.

Now, if there is one thing I learned from the experience of my Cuban baseball obsession season, it is that
surreal political events come in clusters. And though I
had no idea of the form it would take, I knew that something was coming. And sure enough, the very next day,
the day before the World Series, as I was reading through
the newspaper, I came across a sentence that caused my

heart to stop, briefly, and then accelerate wildly immediately thereafter.

Had it been a front-page headline, my heartbeat might never have been the same. But it wasn't. It was Earl Wilson's gossip column, "It Happened Last Night," and it said,

> Cuba and the U.S. will resume relations through a baseball game between the two countries next spring, predicted Roone Arledge of ABC Sports at a National Conference of Christians and Jews. . . .

My mind reacted to this statement by reeling in several directions. My first reaction was: look, this was a rather private theme that I helped dream up while visiting Rochester in an agitated state. It is not fair for the State Department to revoke our social-science-fiction visions for their reality so promptly. Of course, one little news item does not establish authenticity, but it does demonstrate the difference between the way I act and the way a political organization acts.

"I'm diligent, but I'm a dreamer," I thought. And this leaves me no caricature but crackpot.

My second reaction was: and what, what in the name of all that is serious and earnest, is it doing in Earl Wilson's column? Earl Wilson, in his time, was a foreman on the dream machine that the Hollywood studios built to produce economic loyalties to movie stars from their paying fans. In its heyday, Earl Wilson's column was the New York City outlet for a little world of make-believe, but it had outlived its purpose. Hollywood still produced films, but it was no longer able to manufacture dreams. Times had changed, and the authentic Hollywood style of Earl Wilson's column only made it seem tired, cheap, and dated. And *this* is where my dreams of joining the historical vigilantes and bringing political retribution in the service of moral right appears in print. Between Sidney Poitier's reminiscence about his days as a short-order cook and an item about some film rights just purchased by Cary Grant, there is the first announcement, by what is still the most powerful government in the world, that it intends to proceed toward *rapproachement* with its former enemy through baseball.

And so it was on pins and needles that I sat watching the World Series. In the center of the action was Luis Tiant, Boston star and a walking campaign for everything that was both good and Cuban. His body revealed absolutely no potential. Slightly toothless and seedy, he looked a bit old to be playing a boy's game, but at every moment he just happened to be in the right place, doing the right thing. His pitching brilliance eventually fell apart, but that didn't matter. The American public was taking its first serious political consideration of these Cuban baseball fellas, and the particular pitcher in question was very appealing indeed.

The announcers kept hitting the theme of detente with Cuba. Curt Gowdy, of NBC television, would drop little things like, "The Cubans just love baseball. Why, they must have fifty players of major-league caliber down there by now. . . ." And the cameras kept flashing to the Tiant family sitting in the stands. Luis Tiant, Sr., was not only a pitcher's father; he himself had played as a professional, pitching for the New York Cubans of the old Negro League. And while the Tiants smiled, the announcers would endlessly retell the story of the family reunion this summer. Trapped in Castro's Cuba, the Tiant family had not seen their son for a decade, but times were changing. And in the middle of it, Luis Tiant's wife waved a large wooden noisemaker made out of gears and slats. It was the kind of noisemaker they used to whirl around in the Big Schul when I was a child. On the feast of Purim, during the reading of the story of Esther, at each mention of the name of the villain, the children would all yell, and the adults would wave their wooden noisemakers.

As I watched the vehemence with which Mrs. Tiant's noisemaker whirled, I realized that this was no minor religious feast, but the noisemaking of the romantic ral-

lies of the earliest days of trade-union organizing. Luis
Tiant's wife united an East European Jewish rite to the
romantic union marches of the Industrial Revolution, and
to the World Series. Here was this great Cuban lady,
storming the knitting mills of Lancashire, denouncing the
Jew's villain, and rooting for her husband. And so beautifully was he pitching that the comparison seemed justified. Nearly.

I saw so much of the Tiant family on my TV screen
that I began to study their faces, and some things became
clear. Tiant's father was gaunt, and looked slightly foolish in his narrow-brimmed porkpie hat. But there was a
peace and dignity in his eyes. In contrast, his son, the
pitcher, looked overweight and old beyond his years. His
eyes drooped down and made him look like a Hollywood
pirate, weary from too many sword fights. His teeth were
crooked enough to make a hungry orthodontist salivate.
But the key to Luis Tiant's face is his mouth. A relaxed,
benign, and paternal mouth beneath a strong nose and
those pirate eyes. And surrounding that mouth is a mustache that I would have to call the most aggressive collection of facial hair that I have seen in a very long time.
Of course, it was the Cubans who taught America the
very concept of aggressive facial hair, but that was a long
time ago, in the days of the clean shave and the crew cut.
Nowadays, when every third businessman has a beard as
bushy as Fidel Castro's, it would seem impossible to make
a "facial demonstration," as they used to call it in the
courts. But Luis Tiant is, clearly, no ordinary person.

A few years ago Luis Tiant was washed up, and he
dropped out of the major leagues. He had so lost his stuff
that it appeared likely that even the minor leagues might
not hold him. And this was logical. He had played professional baseball for over a decade; he was in his thirties.
Baseball abilities tend to diminish when the strength and
optimism of youth are gone. It was time to pack up baseball and open a tavern with a picture of himself in uniform on the wall above the cash register. But instead,

Luis Tiant suddenly began pitching the best baseball of his life. And now he had just finished leading the Boston Red Sox into the World Series, and perhaps to the world championship. It was the classic comeback, immortalized as a concrete illustration of the rewards, in this world, for Calvinistic determination and perseverance. Luis Tiant's story was the embodiment of one of baseball's greatest dramas: how a failing arm turned a strong boy into a wise man who knows how to pitch better than ever. And Luis Tiant lived baseball's favorite story at a time when people had just stopped forgetting that these kinds of things can happen nowadays.

In a postgame interview, Tony Kubek, also of NBC, said to Luis Tiant, "Luie, we have a large Spanish-speaking audience for this World Series game, in our own country, in Puerto Rico, in Cuba, the Dominican Republic, and all over South America. Would you like to say something to them in Spanish?"

Then Tiant spoke in Spanish over the microphone. Kubek asked him to translate, and Tiant replied that he just thanked all his fans, especially those in Cuba, etc.

I turned off the television set, and as the picture faded, the reality of my circumstances reappeared. I would have to act. I was the world's expert on the political aspects of baseball detente, as well as the baseball aspects of political detente. And no one knew it, because I didn't think that there were even two of us working in this field. But now it was time to establish myself. I would strike, with refinement, somewhere under the rainbow.

I searched through my memory. This World Series was supposed to be earnest work, and all that I could see in my memory was Luis Tiant, the most Cuban of all Cubans, puffing away on a big Havana-Havana cigar, mowing down the opposition. He was the hero of the Sierra Maestra, surviving the suicidal battles of the revolution's earliest days through courage and conviction alone. Luis Tiant was the romantic revolutionary, shoulder to shoulder with Che Guevara and Camillo Torres. At first I rejoiced. A Cuban revolutionary pitching for the Boston Red Sox. Two idolatries in one, I thought. And then I realized the time-slip that my joy was based on. This was not the postwar era. This was network television. This was automatically a different Cuba, if network television was selling it.

The heroes of the Sierra Maestra would remain heroes, suitable for worship, but the deeds they did would have to be edited for television. Tony Kubek had already alluded to the television audience in Cuba, but for the last fifteen years Cuba had been sealed off. Ever since President Eisenhower suspended the sugar quota, Cuba was supposed to be stockaded and blockaded against everything American. How could they be watching our television?

Any smooth transition always begins by pretending that it has already happened. The lesson of the careful steps taken at the end of World War II to turn the French Resistance from a communist front into a club for old celebrities was not lost on network television. If I allowed it to happen, network television would re-educate me on the subject of Cuba, and forever after I would remember Cuban history as something like a movie made for television.

Except for the weekend games, the World Series was now played at night—something I couldn't reconcile with my childhood. But I eventually established a pattern of sleeping late, studying the sports pages and my own reflections in the afternoon, and watching the World Series in the evening. It worked well, but the series was interrupted for travel, and I was left with an empty evening and time, which I didn't want or need, to ponder. In the first two games, the baseball was good, superb in fact, but the other events drew into something less than a conclusion. Studying my notes left me with more wonder than understanding.

1. Ceremonial first pitch of the first game, thrown out by Secretary of the Treasury William Simon, whom

[241]

the announcer said was representing President Ford. The crowd booed Simon, and the announcer explained that New England had the highest oil prices in the country. Simon had been the official mouthpiece for the transparent campaign to make the world think it was running out of oil. It cheered me greatly to see a baseball crowd making the connection.

2. Ceremonial first pitch of the second game thrown out by Henry Kissinger, wearing his baseball hat and sitting next to his friend the commissioner of baseball. America's *Numero Uno* statesman had settled for holy matrimony, and was now attempting to fill the vacancy left in his public image with baseball. He threw the first pitch at the all-star game in mid-season, and now, resting up after doctoring Middle East politics, he was getting World Series exposure. His reception was mixed, but, to my annoyance, there were more cheers than boos. I prepared myself for seeing Kissinger snuggling up to Luis Tiant, but, thank God, it never happened, and probably won't for some time.

3. The television commercials are driving me crazy. I don't remember this from the televised World Series of my childhood. In the postwar era, the World Series was always brought to you by the Gillette Safety Razor Company of Boston. The theme song of the World Series was the Gillette theme song, "How Are You Fixed for Blades?" You could sneak up to any baseball fan, whistle it in his ear, and the first thing he would think of would be the World Series. "Gillette Blue Blades" was part of that special World Series feeling that I felt as a child, watching it on television.

And now all that was gone. All the television advertisements were regular seasonal stuff having nothing to do with baseball or the World Series: new cars, motor oils, antifreeze, beer, pills, and previews of upcoming television programs. As a child, I always had a sense of the Gillette Safety Razor Company literally bringing the World Series into my living room. But with the discon-

[242]

certing flow of modern television commercials, all I get is
a sense of being there half the time.

Interspersed with the voyeuristic scenes from everyday life, where ordinary people confessed the secrets of
their deepest loyalties to undifferentiated manufactured
products, was a showcase for the superstars of the American corporate system. The commercials always informed
you of your own needs, and only rarely mentioned the
products' names. The most snobbish of these prestige
commercials not only failed to solicit, they didn't even
mention what they were selling. Just hints: "The future
is here today . . . at Honeywell." And somehow, as I waited
through these commercials time and again, I couldn't help
seeing them as a cloak for something pathetic. They
emerged as the statements of those down on their luck,
looking for naïve partners in various games of chance
that have been widely exposed. Were they snobbish, or
were they just holding back, in these precarious times,
admitting to nothing but their name and rank?

I had to adjust to a brief moment between the last
word about motor oil and the first pitch of the inning.
There used to be a long wait between innings; now there
was just a flash. And as my mind lingered on the plot of
the last commercial, baseball resumed. The commercial's
setting had been a building site where a new house was
under construction. The owner of the house walked
through naked joists to the driveway, where he revealed
that he was able to meet the financial demands of the
mortgage by regularly changing the oil of his automobile.
No costly repair bills. The oil companies were passing up
their chance to sing the praise of oil in an attempt to
stimulate the sagging construction business.

The World Series was not like this when I was a boy.
Then, ceremonial first pitches were thrown out by sentimental baseball celebrities, and the World Series replaced
the regular television experience, rather than becoming
it. But more than this I had not learned. So I took advantage of the time between games. Political theory is the

necessary antecedent to a political position. Political theory cannot be formed by waiting, and there will be no baseball until evening. Research and study were necessary, I decided. Time to pay a visit to my local public library, I thought. And my day was planned.

I took down the weighty *Baseball Encyclopedia* from its shelf, sat down, and began leafing through it. Sort of wandering through it. It was all computerized and coded, more like a racing sheet than anything to do with baseball. And as I looked around and tried to acquaint myself with the format, the first evidence was discouraging. My old Havana Sugar Kings turned out to be slightly too international to suit. Elio Chacon is Venezualan, as are the Davalillo brothers. Nino Escalera is Puerto Rican. Ruben Amaro is from Mexico, and the Alou brothers are from the Dominican Republic. So, by midmorning, I decided that I would have to go through the entire encyclopedia and tabulate the Cubans, which I did.

And were there ever Cubans in the history of major-league baseball! From the times of my memory there were Carlos Paula; Rogelio Alvarez and his brother Ossie; Sandy Amoros, the Brooklyn hero; Joe Azcue, the bullpen catcher; Berto Cueto; Mike Cuellar, the Baltimore ace; there were Cubans everywhere. There was even a good-sized crop of native Cubans who played for the Havana Sugar Kings on their way to the top: Vincente Amor, Camilio Pascual, Orlando Pena, Julio Becquer, Jose Valdivielso, Tony Taylor, Chico Ruiz, Bert Campaneris. The recipient of the second bullet in the Frank Verdi incident in Havana, Leo "Chico" Cardenas, broke into the major leagues in 1960 and played around both leagues for several years. And Chico Carrasquel, Paul Casanova, Chico Fernandez, and Roman Mejias. All the names I had forgotten.

There must have been seventy-five Cubans to have played major-league baseball. What is more astounding than their number is the historical span that these Cubans cover. Rafael Almeida played for Cincinnati between 1911 and 1913. Merito Acosta played the outfield for Washington from 1913 to 1918. Angel Aragon played for the Yankees in 1914. Jose Acosta played for Chicago in 1922. And all through the thirties and forties, and really in every era, there were Cuban professionals playing baseball in America. This was no ordinary case of imperial export, I realized. And all of these big-leaguers coming from a tiny island of no more than a few million inhabitants, one-third of whom were black, at a time when only the lightest-skinned and straightest-haired Cubans were allowed to play in the leagues. Whatever its origin, baseball was also a Cuban game, and had been throughout this century.

Meanwhile, halfway through the World Series, in obscure corners of the sports pages, Cuban detente was meeting with difficulty. The Pan American games were getting under way in Mexico City. American athletes were being hissed and booed while Cubans were being cheered.

Americans are not used to being the underdogs. A series of incidents occurred which culminated on the night the U.S. rowing team made a giant slingshot out of surgical tubing and bombarded a dormitory of sleeping Cuban athletes with water balloons. The Cubans replied with rocks.

The riot was quelled, and the games finished in an uneasy truce, but the Americans had come through them, for all their bewilderment, as no better than slow-witted villains. Which was very encouraging to my expectations for the Cuban–U.S. baseball game, but very discouraging to the necessary precondition of detente.

The conspiratorial "they" were at it again, unleashing their schemes in all directions, when baseball alone was quite sufficient. They should have known better. And look: I am not so naïve as to believe that all this converging information was plotted in back rooms. It is a mentality, and those who hold it, whether they feel it or not, have been placed at the tip of certain historical forces so that they are now determining the nature of everyday reality. And I am sure that this mentality is only able to survive and flower where it is unidentifiable. That is, in personalities smothered in ambition, in the minds of those who are living their lives exclusively for private motives.

I know that I have a tendency to get carried away, but I do stop and remind myself of the power and extent of genuine social forces. And I am no more aware of anything than the kinds of forces shaping this new era. But, damn it, America has never let anything stand between its desires and their fulfillment. In America, waiting for something to happen is worse than having it happen badly. And these ambitious corporate schemers have never had to wait, and can't wait, and won't wait. I was halfway through this World Series, but already I knew that this detente would not be a sleigh ride.

Boston won the first game, Cincinnati won the next two. When baseball resumed, Luis Tiant was pitching again. I costumed myself in my Cuban detente framework, settled into television, and went to work.

By this time, the isolated camera covering the Tiant family in the stands had become a familiar fixture. They never sat in the expensive seats; they were always up with the people. It became quite common for an inning to close with the score written across the face of Luis Tiant, Sr., just before the parade of commercials began. The Tiant family was beginning to loosen up as it got comfortable with its media exposure. The old man in the funny hat who sat through the first games with twinkling eyes but tight lips was now laughing and waving and standing up. And as the power of Luis, Jr's., performance continued, the whole family was jumping up and carrying on, and beginning to have a good time.

Even though Tiant was no longer pitching so brilliantly, the announcers were still obsessed with him. But there was a subtle change. The Cuban stuff was being soft-pedaled. Perhaps this was a reaction to the problems with the foot races down in Mexico. Perhaps it was the first sign of a shift in policy. Or perhaps I had descended down the well of marginality to the depths of nit-picking. Either I was so close that I was blinded by the range, or I had become so attuned to Cuban detente that my pulse was synchronized with the State Department Cuba Desk. I was the Corsican twin of Cuban detente, feeling every subtle twitch in policy, even in my ignorance of its cause. This is what I longed to be all summer long, but achieving that identity still left me with certain obvious causes for concern. Perhaps I had drifted too far into abstraction. Perhaps my protective Westchester County lily pad had floated me off the surface of contact with the real world. Perhaps all the events I was recording were personal.

But the ongoing baseball never allowed me to come to any decisions. In the fourth game, Secretary of Commerce Rogers Morton became the third cabinet member to throw a ceremonial first pitch, and Boston evened the series at two games each. In the fifth game, Luis Tiant's star was put away, and Tony Perez, the Cincinnati first baseman and power hitter, emerged as The Other Cuban.

In the early games of the Series, Perez had gone hitless, and the announcers had been too busy to pay attention to the place of national origin of a hitless cleanup batter. Then Perez hit two home runs, back to back, to win the fifth game. Being the hero of the day, his circumstances became worthy of examination.

The papers began to notice not only that Perez was Cuban, but even that he came from a place called Camaguey. And that he was a big star in Cuba, just as he is in the United States. But no detente references were made. No one, it seemed, dared crowd Tiant just yet.

The action paused for a second travel day, and rather than take the long trip to the library, I decided to sit home and try to draw together the things I had already seen. My position had grown strange, and I felt it was necessary to either justify or change it.

My fears of the demonic archetype emerging as the defining characteristic of the clean-shaven team, I decided, were silly. This was not the postwar era. How you looked was no longer an expression of what you believed. Back then, Fidel Castro's beard meant something in America; now Luis Tiant's much more aggressive mustache didn't. In the cataclysmic days of the postwar era's demise, appearance and style were the only means of establishing identity. But the shrapnel from those explosions has long since settled, and appearance and style have returned to where they came from: entertainment.

"I am a conservative, I always wear a tie," said Sparky Anderson, the manager of the Cincinnati team. Not exactly the do-or-die commitment that half of that statement used to represent, but no less a statement, given the difference in historical context. Anderson is not a political simpleton, but rather a professional baseball executive, professionally merchandising his views. We are conservatives, he is saying, but all we do about it is play baseball. We stage games for the enjoyment of spectators. Our particular act has a certain military style and appeal, but there is no intent to offend. We just want to do business.

No offense intended, and therefore no offense taken. How clearly I saw this illustrated! Just before each game, the starting players of both teams are individually announced, and line up in order of batting position along the base lines. Most approaching players shake hands with those already on the field. For each game of the World Series, I watched in disbelief as the Cincinnati team went through its own particular variation of the team handshake. Rather than the firm handshake that shows respect for established order, if not the great republic itself, the Cincinnati players were locking thumbs in the old handshake that used to stand for membership in antisocial groups. Once, only radicals, black people, musicians, sharpies, and down-and-outs dared use this handshake. And here was the Cincinnati baseball team locking thumbs and rattling clenched fists, just for entertainment, and getting away with it.

In the postwar era, that handshake (not to mention the clenched fist) offended anyone who was even slightly squeamish about unwashed communists and hippie peace-creeps. The clenched fist was enough to turn a small crowd into a brawl, or to bring down the Olympic Games, or to announce a revolution. And now it was just a part of the gestural repertoire of the baseball team that fancied itself the most conservative.

So professionally was the message transmitted that, finally, even I understood. Baseball, for your entertainment. Identify with your favorite stereotypes, by all means, but remember that they are presented strictly for your amusement. This is the era of pure and detached business. This is the corporate era and we must all change, and baseball, like everything else still in business, is adjusting to more businesslike circumstances. Please be patient and remember that baseball is only trying to be merchandise in the largest possible market. Baseball is only trying to please.

And that is why all the players speak even sentences with well-projected voices, and fulfill the requisite baseball stereotypes. The character types of baseball players are not determined by coincidence; they are a central act in the great show of baseball.

And so Sparky Anderson, the Cincinnati manager, is the ideal Boy Scout troop leader. Firm, but at the same time fair, and truly the nicest guy on the block. And Darrell Johnson, the Boston manager, is the tight-lipped New England fisherman who never smiles, but never frowns. Who never speaks, except when he has to.

These are baseball personalities. Character types drawn from postwar life and preserved as show business. In an earlier day, these types were commonly encountered in ordinary life. Now, they exist only as characters in a costume drama. Genuine vintage Americana, suitable for framing.

I looked at Dave Concepcion and Cesar Geronimo playing baseball and I saw a style of public behavior that I have not seen since the postwar era. The easygoing Latins, gleefully pedaling their solid chrome bicycles across the harbor, secretly noticed and envied by everyone. Now they are respectable, in spite of their high jinks, because the threat implied in their style has no context. Now I saw Pete Rose as the obnoxious American tourist who hunched over home plate in checkered Bermuda shorts and looked back from the plate to the umpire, as if to ask how much of the local currency did he want for it. But this kind of tourist doesn't exist any more. Baseball, I began to realize, had survived, but its reference points had not.

The joy of baseball was a constant, but generations of fans differ in their conceptual metaphors. My baseball reflects a particular notion of noble behavior, and a particular triumph of morality, which seems archaic in modern baseball. My baseball has nothing to do with the big money, big-time merchandised glamor of modern baseball. But my historical notions fit nicely despite the intervening changes in American life.

Baseball is culture, and it is the nature of culture to be the most minimal and plastic vessel, which we not only fill, but which we shape to our own designs. All this time I have been watching baseball as if it were a map, and now it is suddenly a mirror. Very much a situation of being lost and found simultaneously, which, in addition to other things, is not very good for anyone's sense of direction.

If baseball is a mirror, then I am responsible for everything that I see in it. A responsibility I was eager to accept as I watched the World Series, but I was an adult now, and there were problems that my childhood didn't see. Baseball is a game that is played between men.

The better the baseball, the greater the likelihood that the players will be more than men: he-men. At the very top of the baseball pyramid, we find the most extreme obedience to masculine values. Baseball believes in the machismo claptrap that led America successively through world domination and internal self-destruction bordering on collapse. The mentality of never quitting, never losing, and never saying die was fine for the imperial phase of the cold war, but since then some fatal flaws have been exposed. The belief in the old one-two punch of military technology has never been quite the same since Vietnam. The rugged individualism of the self-made industrialist has never been quite so romantic since it destroyed the landscape and was seen, habitually, with its hand in the United States Treasury. And the self-sufficient small-town lawyer, ambitious and outspoken and unsuited to the ways of Washington, has never been quite so charming a national political leader since Watergate.

America has always admired its masculine values, but since the collapse of the postwar mentality, it has come to admire them less and less. Why didn't baseball notice this? Baseball is the closest thing America has to a pleasant game on a summer afternoon; why couldn't baseball see that winning is not all that matters? There was a bit too much of the craziness of machismo in baseball. That I was again drawn to it worried me more than that toughness itself.

With Cincinnati ahead three games to two, and travel completed, the World Series shifted back to Boston, and immediately it began to rain. It rained so hard during the night that the game was canceled first thing in the morning.

It was no baseball today and time to do my homework. I wasn't complaining. If this was work, then I was prepared to be a workhorse.

I began at what I thought was the beginning, just as I had done all summer. Facts at the beginning, and truth will surely, somehow, arrive at the end. And everywhere between, accompanying each discovery, a strong understanding of: if I had only known this, I would have seen the whole thing differently. And that was not only true, but also the sense of truth for which I was searching.

Cuba is a small island, but politically, it has always been one of the largest Latin American countries. It was discovered, along with other well-known places, by Christopher Columbus, in 1492. In its beginnings, as a Western country, it was governed by the people who bankrolled Columbus.

When compared with the exploits of the more Aryan Europeans, Spanish imperialism seems crude and basic. While the desire for Calvinistic salvation through keeping busy drove the North American imperial dream into turning over stones and planting vegetables so as to establish a new world, south of the border, the Spanish imperial dream was much easier. Why worry about the entrance to the kingdom of heaven, the conquistador reasoned, when we can pretend that it's already here?

For the Spaniards, unlike the colonists of North America, work was neither a virtue nor a vehicle for salvation. When the indigenous locals offered land to Cortez, he explained (according to W. H. Prescott's *History of the Conquest of Mexico*) that Spaniards "wanted gold, not to till the earth like a peasant." Like the upwardly mobile colonies that followed the original Puritans and spread across North America, Cuba, for its development, relied heavily on slavery. The population of Cuba has always been, and remains today, about one-third black.

Spanish slavery was different from English slavery, and within that difference lay a force large enough to change the direction of the history of baseball. North America has always been caught up in its Calvinist internal good-works race to the entrance of the kingdom of heaven. And therefore, North American slavery needed no less than theological justification. North American slaves were cursed by God, sons of Cain, or the offspring of the Garden of Eden serpent, and God knows what else; their punishment was legitimate, justified, and total. Cuban slaves, on the other hand, were merely the people who did the dirty work.

The Cuban slaves were treated just as badly, but this was only to satisfy the sadistic and authoritarian streak in their Spanish masters. Cuban slaves were abused for fun, and not in the name of God's work. Therefore, Cuban slaves were recognized by the church, could own and exchange property, and were understood by the courts to be human beings. Of course, these rights were abused—slavery is always what it's cracked up to be—but the notion that slaves were human did exist in Cuba and it did not exist in North America.

Meanwhile, baseball in its earliest days was the polite gentlemen's game, very badly played, but very classy for social circumstances. A select, obscure game, baseball was known only to the rich and idle. Then it changed. During the Civil War, some gentlemanly officers introduced baseball as a recreation for prisoners of war. It caught on. After the war, the released prisoners from both armies spread the game across the country. And without benefit of media, America acquired its national pastime.

In no time at all there were hundreds of teams and leagues. By the eighth decade of the nineteenth century, professional baseball had begun. An odd assortment of teams traveled around the country, playing exhibitions wherever they thought they might attract paying fans. Black players played on predominantly white teams, black teams played against white teams, and white players even played on teams that were largely black. The personalities with which baseball players conduct the game, unlike the personalities with which life is conducted, have nothing to do with race. So baseball, when it was new and young and not yet consolidated, did not

[253]

recognize skin color. But as its popularity grew, professional baseball teams began to show rising profits, and a different mentality seeped into the game.

The achievement of prosperity is always a relief to those who never expect it. But it is only a fleeting relief, immediately followed by a hunger for respectability that is every bit as terrifying to the hungry as their former poverty had been. Baseball prospered, and soon it was no different from anything else. By 1885, American professional baseball had purged itself of black players and begun its slow climb to respectability that did not culminate until the corporate era. For more than sixty years, baseball pretended that it had always been that way. The gossip of ungentlemanly behavior was only interesting to baseball after status had been achieved.

And so the color bar was eliminated, and Negro baseball, after it had disappeared, was apologized to, and sanctified as legitimate history. But this could only take place after baseball had arrived, secure and protected within the corporate mentality.

In Cuba, during this time, baseball was sweeping the land. There were nearly one hundred baseball clubs in Cuba before the end of the nineteenth century, and in the early eighteen-nineties, professional teams from the United States began to come to Cuba in the winter to play exhibition games. These exhibitions eventually became the Cuban League, and continued right up to Eisenhower's withdrawal of the sugar quota and embargo.

In many ways, the development of baseball in Cuba paralleled what was going on in the United States. There was, however, one great difference. In Cuba there were no distinctions made among baseball players on the basis of race, creed, or national origin, as they say. Which is not to say that Cuba was free from racial prejudice and its consequences, but only that, in Cuba, racism did not extend to baseball.

Cuba carried its unique baseball legacy through the first half of the twentieth century. For sixty-odd years, it was the mecca of black baseball, a place where black American baseball players dreamed of going. And where, in droves, they went. Cuba was the place where a black baseball player could make it. Where he could play with and against American big-leaguers, and often beat them. And consequently, Cuba assumed an importance much greater than any apparent reality. Cuba became the fantasy base for black American baseball. The example of Cuba meant that the problem was always whether integrated baseball would be allowed. The absurd racist pose of whether it was possible never appeared. Integrated baseball had been thriving in Cuba ever since there had been baseball.

In 1885, as white baseball purged its rosters, the first black professional baseball team in America opened for business. The players were from New Jersey, but they called themselves the Cuban Giants. Perhaps it was the desire for a larger gate through the pretense of exotica; perhaps it was no more than not wanting to be recognized as black Americans, given the difficulties that arose for that kind of troupe. Perhaps it was a dream, but they did call themselves Cubans.

In 1895, Bud Fowler, a black professional ballplayer, was able to lament his situation in political as well as racial terms. "My skin is against me. If I had not been quite so black, I might have caught on as a Spaniard, or something of that kind," Fowler said.

The history of most American black people is that they suffered severely for being black, and grew to despise their blackness and themselves for some time. Black baseball players were unusual among black people, in that they knew that the problem was not being black, but being American. For black baseball players, the misfortune was not being Cuban.

In the first half of the twentieth century, white and black baseball in the United States developed in opposite directions, with stringent guidelines for each route. White people could afford to pay more for baseball than black people could. White baseball flourished, and black baseball floundered. Black and white teams shared the same stadiums, but never on the same day, and never with the same financial success. During the winter, professional baseball players toured the American South, Cuba, Mexico, and wherever else they could get a game to supplement their earnings. Each winter, black and white American baseball players would get to know each other, and play against each other and scout each other, and intermingle in ways that were not permitted in ordinary American life.

While the financial fortunes of the two baseballs were as different as the color of the ink in their respective ledger books, the quality of the baseball they played was the same. Ty Cobb played winter baseball in Cuba on and off for years. His best season was 1910, when he finished third in the league in batting. Walter Johnson, the legendary pitcher, played in the same league that year, and though he pitched well, he didn't tear the league apart. And, according to the television announcers during this World Series, Luis Tiant, Sr., pitched against the great Carl Hubbell in Havana, and beat him. Judging from all of the observations and recollections made at the time, there was simply no distance between black and white baseball, the enormous financial gap notwithstanding.

Every once in a while, some black player would be seen to be so superior at baseball that he would be signed by a major-league team, and they would try to sneak him into the major leagues. If he were Cuban, and light-skinned enough, he would be allowed to play. The league would study the man's face and features and then decide. This is how the first seventy-five or eighty Cuban names got into *The Baseball Encyclopedia*.

The first Cuban to play American professional baseball was Vincent Nava, who played for Providence in 1882, but that was before the color bar. In 1911 Cal Griffith signed Alberto Marsans and Rafael Almedia for the Cincinnati Reds, and a few other Cubans for minor league teams. A Cuban correspondent began to follow the Reds that year.

To smooth the way, the Reds owner travelled to Cuba and had the local government prepare affidavits showing that only pure Caucasian blood flowed through their veins. The Cincinnati papers referred to Marsans and Almedia as, "two of the purest bars of Castille soap that ever floated to these shores."

In 1912, Griffith moved to Washington and signed two more Cubans there, Jacinto Calvo and Balmadero Acosta. A whole flood of Cuban players followed, all proclaimed to be of pure Spanish blood, with a drop of Indian, or negro, or mixed. But skin tones varied.

And every time the league admitted a Cuban who was a shade darker than was thought to be acceptable, a wave of hope spread through the hearts of black American baseball players. Perhaps this was the thin edge of the wedge, and they too would take their place in big-league baseball before they got too old. Their dream was denied, of course, until 1947, but that is another story.

Christobel Torrienti, a Cuban pitcher playing for the black American Giants, was signed by John J. McGraw of the New York Giants, but he never played for them. "He was light brown and he would have gone up to the major leagues, but he had real rough hair," his teammate Jelly Gardner said.

And back in 1917, a black American outfielder called John Donaldson was offered $10,000 to go to Cuba, change his name, and report to a club in the New York State League. Whether or not it would have been a successful test case is not known. Donaldson could not dream that dream, and refused the deal.

And so for the first half of the twentieth century, we have this sad story coloring baseball, and the only hope that the future might be better was coming out of Cuba. (The story, I should note, is preserved in Robert Peterson's *Only the Ball Was White*, Prentice-Hall, 1970.)

[257]

I do not mean to say that there were not other things going on at the same time. Politics and baseball were having their odd, occasional collisions, at the strangest times and in the strangest places.

In 1937 Rafael L. Trujillo, the absolute dictator of the Dominican Republic, decided, in a moment of egomania and foolishness, to call an election. An opposing candidate found the nerve to run against Trujillo and hit upon the novel idea of conducting his campaign solely through an exhibition baseball team bearing his name. The team toured the country, publicizing its candidate, and more than paying for itself.

The quaint little election that Trujillo called as a show of power backfired on him. Rumors spread that the opposition candidate's baseball team was unbeatable. There were suggestions that such a team should, perhaps, run the government. A game was proposed, and the Dominican citizenry considered wagering its government on the outcome of a baseball game. To the citizens of a dictatorship, government by a baseball game is naturally more attractive than the only existing alternative. Trujillo acted swiftly. A baseball team was far cheaper than a civil war, and perhaps the day might be saved. Trujillo paid $30,000 each to the finest black baseball players in the world to play one seven-game series for his team. When the big series finally took place, half of the audience wore army uniforms and carried drawn bayonets. But the Trujillo team, led by Satchel Paige and Cool Papa Bell, won the series, and the soldiers pretended that they were only there to enjoy the ballgame.

And in 1942, the American Communist party arranged a tryout with the Pittsburgh Pirates for Roy Campanella, who was then playing for the Pittsburgh Negro team. The party didn't have quite enough influence with the Pirates, who responded like Trotskyites, and nothing ever came of it. Years later, of course, Campanella went on to become a star for the Brooklyn Dodgers.

And lots more, but in the consciousness of black America, dreams of baseball were set in Cuba. Long after the original Cuban Giants, black teams continued to identify with Cuba. There were scores of imitation Cuban Giant clubs, and the Cuban X Giants, who were respectable enough to avoid a direct name infringement where no copyright proscriptions existed legally, and the Cuban All Stars, and the Cuban Stars, and every permutation possible combining Cuban, Star, and Giant, then multiplied by east and west.

These mythical Cubans had their hopes bolstered by the presence of authentic Cuban baseball teams. In 1906, the Havana All Stars and the Cuban Stars both arrived in America. These teams were racially mixed, but totally Cuban. And for the rest of the century, Cuban baseball players would continue to arrive, alone or in teams. Hundreds of Cubans played in the Negro leagues in America during the time that those leagues developed from carnival acts to a substantial force in the subculture of American baseball.

When the Brooklyn Dodgers finally broke the rules and signed Jackie Robinson in 1946, they had to take their spring training in Cuba. Baseball was ready for integration, but Florida wasn't. Diplomatic orchestration required Cuba. This meant little to white baseball fans, but to the subculture of baseball, the gesture contained symbolism as well as necessity. A reminder of how and where integrated baseball was done. And a guarantee that it could be smooth.

Jackie Robinson's season as the first black man to play in white organized baseball went, rather than smoothly, somewhat smoothly. He broke in with the Montreal Royals of my own International League, and played with them for an entire season before graduating to Brooklyn. Surprisingly enough, the fans accepted him in most places, but in Syracuse, New York, a scant sixty-five miles east of Rochester, they baited him mercilessly. In Rochester, the story is that on the first (or

[259]

possibly the second) time he came to bat, he got a hit and stole second base on the next pitch. The fans gave him an ovation.

Robinson hit .349 for Montreal, leading the league in batting. He also led the league in fielding percentage for second basemen, at .985. And he moved up to the Dodgers the next year.

When the Havana Sugar Kings joined the International League in 1953, with an essentially Cuban team, this seemed a novelty in my carefully naïve childhood. It was, in fact, a traditional event for baseball. Just as one would expect, a now integrated and prosperous American baseball welcomed Cuba with open arms. In so doing, baseball, quite coincidentally, joined hands with a broad range of other prosperous Americans and began to revive a centuries-old tradition of looking to Cuba as the center of pleasure in the New World.

As the twentieth century moved beyond Yalta and Potsdam and into the Geneva conventions of the cold war, the themes that emerged from the development of big-league baseball were continually increasing financial prosperity and, consequently, continually increasing professionalism and respectability. Whereas old baseball players often ended their days as drunks and winos, more recent stars began to find work as vice-presidents of local banks and purveyors of publicity for large corporations. And gradually the image of baseball players was remodeled. Gradually the irresponsible, mischievous, practical-joking, annoying little boy who never grew up was replaced by the brave, clean, and reverent professional athlete. This eminently more marketable stereotype was not only rich and famous, but an exemplary model of adult behavior, and an example from which to teach youngsters the rewards for virtuous living. Playing baseball was gaining respectability and losing pleasure.

The days were gone when rowdy, drunken baseball players suffered only hangover and dehydration. There were now valuable advertising contracts at stake, and an image that, if handled properly, might earn millions. A large yield for the sacrifice of a few restraining behavior patterns. But the decline of pleasure was greatly regretted.

And Havana had been viewed, for longer than any city in the New World, as a pleasure center. At the time that baseball was integrating and, in so doing, cutting the necessity of its ties with Cuba, Havana was reaching the pinnacle of its power to cast its spell on North Americans in search of pleasure.

Cuba, we will remember, was discovered by Columbus and settled by Spaniards, who went on record as wanting gold. And these particular Spanish gold-dreamers had made Havana their principal American port. What with gold on one side of the ocean and fulfillment on the other, Havana prospered. The harbor brought not only prosperity, but also sailors, settlers, foreign traders, and an extensive clique of low-life floaters who come to rest in those ports where the action is shadiest. And they settled in Havana and began a tradition that lasted for centuries. Havana became the home for fleecers and their prospective sheep. For three centuries, hustlers and their clients would cross paths in Havana as often as they could afford to. The whole thing lasted as long as it did because everyone who came to Havana to partake found, in some sense, the particular pleasure he was looking for. No one stopped to think that this was anything special, but over time he realized that it was, and Havana assumed a special place in the puritanical fantasies of American life. Only a country as puritanical as the United States could so revere its fantasies, and only in America could those fantasies be so outrageous that no link to reality could be found. And in these overblown fantasies, Havana meant pleasure.

Cuba was the origin of another special pleasure that Western civilization noted, admired, and prized. The Cubans could grow tobacco. All of the Western world craved tobacco, but no one could figure out how to grow

[261]

it. Tobacco was introduced in Virginia, and though the plants survived, the farmers couldn't figure out how to get it to taste right. They quickly stopped trying and concentrated on quantity.

In Cuba, tobacco was indigenous. Before the Spaniards arrived, the Indians had perfected its cultivation. They say that good tobacco is primarily a matter of soil and climate, but growing it perfectly requires more than special knowledge and the right conditions—it requires a special temperament, even a special kind of person, because it's too much trouble for anybody else.

So tobacco brought to Cuba a romantic admiration from the world's cigar smokers, and increased prosperity. Increased prosperity brought, as it always does, a new dimension to entrepreneurial ambition. This ambition led to the introduction of sugar. And sugar, because it must be processed within forty-eight hours of being cut, led to railroads, the fastest possible transportation. Sugar brought prosperity, and the railroads led to more sugar, and more prosperity, and then more ambition.

The United States of America couldn't help noticing that the Spanish were doing a nice little piece of business right in front of our noses. All this time, immigrants were flocking to Cuba from all over the world, but especially from the United States. What was to become the Bethlehem Steel Company opened for business in Cuba in 1885. The waterworks and electricity plants for Havana, both wholly owned by U.S. citizens, opened in 1894. And the last generation of wealthy Victorian tourists settled upon Havana as the fashionable place to go. Things were rather cozy, and steps were being taken to keep them that way.

As the nineteenth century drew to a close, a generation of Americans who had been raised on Civil War stories, and who had never in their lives had the chance to display a bravery and courage equal to the old veterans, reached maturity. They had waited longer than Americans can stand to wait. They wanted a war. With

[262]

patience already spent, the United States looked at the closest available candidate, saw that it was prosperous, thought that anything that went on there would eventually turn into pleasure, and invaded. The invasion was a mess, but successful, and so survives in American high-school textbooks as the Spanish-American War. From that point on, Cuba became Americanized to a point where the only real distinctions were linguistic, geographic, and racial.

Havana carried on, always special in its own particular way. And then it began to flourish in a way it had never done before. To be sure, it was a flowering built on graft, corruption, decadence, exploitation, and worse, but nevertheless, as fascinating a product as those elements could assemble.

In the boom years surrounding the Korean war, Havana was many things to many people, but most of all it was a place of pleasure. And most conspicuously, it was a place for the commercialization of sex, gambling, and drinking. There were twelve thousand prostitutes in Havana at this time, and blue films, as they were then called, were being shown in the back rooms of Chinese restaurants. There were glorious casinos, Hilton hotels, and famous places to get drunk. There was Sloppy Joe's, Manolo's, and La Floridita, where famous masculine archetypes like Errol Flynn and Ernest Hemingway hung out.

And beyond the liquor, sex, cigars, gambling, and delicious coffee that Cuba offered, there was the whole playground concept. Havana had its own American suburb called Vedado, and it was like nothing the folks in Indianapolis had ever seen. It was filled with big American hotels, nightclubs featuring big-name American acts, casinos, and mansions owned by gangsters and businessmen. It oozed with wealth.

Wealth is, for most wealthy people, the greatest of all pleasures. And the pleasurable playground of Cuba catered to wealth in all of its forms, both real and pre-

[263]

tend. In 1954, according to Hugh Thomas (whose *Cuba: The Pursuit of Freedom*, published in 1971, is the best source for such data), there were more Cadillacs registered in Havana than in any other city in the world. The classiest cemetery in Havana, at Colon, was indulging in vaults equipped with elevators, air conditioning, and telephones.

Cubans, though impoverished by the standards of the United States, prospered by the standards of Latin America. And Cuban prosperity was not only statistical but ideological. Thanks to Theodore Roosevelt and his Spanish-American War, Cuba was merged, economically, with the United States. The U.S. dollar and the Cuban peso were infinitely interchangeable. This was at a point in the cold-war era when Americans believed that foreigners would do anything to get their hands on American dollars. With a willing supply, the Cubans got their hands full, relatively speaking, and gained access to the American manufactured goods that had become great symbols of status throughout Latin America. Only Argentina and Uruguay had more telephones per capita than Cuba. Only Uruguay had more radios. Only Venezuela had more automobiles. And Cuba had 400,000 television sets, more than any other country in Latin America, and even more than Italy.

Now, some of the Cubans were annoyed by all this. Mostly because they were so poor, but some were upset because they weren't allowed to enter the playground, and this was, after all, their homeland. And some were annoyed just because they respected Cuban culture and resented its increasing Floridization. But none of this annoyance caused any concern. The gangsters administered the country, Batista grew soft and negligent, and the entire middle class, up to their necks in graft and fraud and gangsterism, grew increasingly cynical toward government whose capacity for corruption was greater than their own. But the tourists and fortune hunters kept flocking, and everyone was having so much fun that they couldn't imagine the native-born locals not enjoying it as much as they were.

The businessmen of America continued to hold their racier conventions in Havana, and American corporations continued to do business in Cuba. And Cubans consoled themselves by concentrating on the good things that had come from America, such as baseball. By the time Frank Verdi was shot, in the summer of 1959, the dollar amount of U.S. investment was greater in Cuba than anywhere else in Latin America, save oil-rich Venezuela. And on a per capita basis, U.S. investment in Cuba was three times greater than anywhere else in Latin America. As would be expected, North Americans seemed to be more popular in Havana than anywhere else in Latin America.

As a matter of fact, throughout the heyday of pleasure-palace Havana, the United States had only two arguments with the government of Sergeant Batista. The first occurred when a contestant on the American television program "The $64,000 Question" won the top prize by answering that Walter Reed had discovered the cure for yellow fever, when everyone knew that yellow fever was conquered by the Cuban doctor Carlos Finlay. The Batista government petitioned Eisenhower, but the protest fell on uninterested ears.

The second dispute was equally bizarre. It concerned a Hollywood film called *Santiago*. The film stars Alan Ladd, as Cash Adams, a dishonorably discharged Civil War veteran. Ladd starts out the film as a shady arms smuggler, and ends as the hero of the Cuban revolution. Cuban heroes are portrayed in minor parts along the way. Jose Marti, Cuba's greatest hero, is portrayed as a graceful cross between Xaviar Cugat and the Kentucky chicken king Colonel Sanders. His role in the revolution, according to the film, was to provide the carriages and the caviar. Antonio Maceo, another Cuban hero, is presented as an ideologically sound but unreformed drunk.

The film is awful, and watching it, I got the feeling

[265]

that you weren't supposed to be noticing the historical trappings. They seemed to be just straight lines to introduce the battles, but, in 1954, when the film came out, the Batista government protested.

Other than this, there were no complaints. The Cuban middle class was drowning in American consumer goods; the baseball team may have been up and down, but it did, in 1959, win the International League pennant, and the Junior World Series. And for America, there was a source of cheap sugar, and a repository for the most unusual dreams of pleasure that Americans, in the gaps between the hustle and bustle of work and business, could concoct.

This was the Havana that had produced the baseball team that I knew as a child, and this was the Havana that had produced Luis Tiant. It was the same Havana that André Breton, the acknowledged father of surrealism, described as too surreal to live in.

Back in Boston for the World Series, it continued to rain. Flood warnings were now up, and the sports pages were filled with the records achieved by rain. Morale fell so low that rain-soaked carpenters were hurried onto the ball field to build a podium, so that the baseball commissioner could inspect the field and the weather each morning without having to get his feet wet.

With American impatience beginning to focus on football, and the rain never flagging, it seemed that the World Series might never be finished, but if it was, two things would be certain. Luis Tiant would definitely pitch again, and I would be prepared for any unconsciously coded and transmitted secret message on the Cuba question. Already, I felt, I knew the history of the problem in ways that the State Department had not yet identified as part of the problem. And what with the way it was raining, I could get so far ahead that they would never catch up.

This, then, was the particular well of history that I peeked at, fell into, and floated deeper and deeper through as the rain continued. And then, one morning, the commissioner of baseball climbed his hastily carpentered podium and noticed that the sun was shining. It was time for baseball, and I was ready. Thoroughly fortified with scholarly preparation, I was anxious for baseball.

As if my studies had not overstimulated my attention to baseball to the point of distraction, there arrived in the mail, that very morning, a letter from Florida containing an odd newspaper clipping on the subject of baseball detente.

The clipping is a feature article about Cincinnati's (and Cuba's) Tony Perez, the World Series' most recent star. The article explains that Perez wasn't sure that his family in Cuba would get the news right away, but Buck Canel, who broadcast the World Series to Latin American countries for thirty-eight years and who now writes for a French news service, corrected Perez. "They don't publish American baseball results in Cuban newspapers any more, but people with super-antennae get the Miami TV and radio stations. They'll hear about it back there."

The article goes on to say that joining the celebration for the formerly hitless Perez was Roberto Maduro, who once owned the Havana Sugar Kings of the International League. Maduro, it seems, now works for the office of the commissioner of baseball. (And oh, how the historian would be pleased to inquire how recently they hired him, and how disappointed he would be to find that he had been working there for years on a part-time basis.)

"Perez, and Tiant, and Diego Segui, the Red Sox pitcher, and Mike Cuellar, the Baltimore pitcher, are all my old boys," said Maduro. "You might say they were the last of the capitalistic Cuban ballplayers." The article, from the *Miami Herald* of October 18, 1975, closes with two neat sentences that sum it all up without leaking too much of the plot:

[267]

Maduro's own capital, once estimated at ten million dollars, vanished when he fled Cuba, around 1960. "All I had left," Maduro said, "was a piece of paper saying that I once owned the Havana Sugar Kings. But this is a great World Series for Cuba, we are all very proud."

I laid the article aside, thinking to myself, aw c'mon, Bobby. You can't pull a fast one on me, not after all these years. And certainly not after my education in the microfilm reading room.

But Bobby Maduro was working for wages in the commissioner's office, and said, as all wage earners do, whatever he had to say. I did not attempt to judge the man while he was earning his living, but I did come to realize, on that World Series morning, that all these suspicious Cuban detente baseball media bulletins were being broadcast just for me.

I began to notice that throughout the rainy days, my behavior was not unlike my microfilm reading room experience in Rochester earlier that summer. Back then, I had only my dreams and my memories and my history. But now it was popping up all over the place, if not on the thoroughfares, then at least in the alleyways of the news of the day. And still, I thought, as I noticed my symptoms rising, nobody else is interested.

Once again, I was on top of it all. Alone. Which was fine with me, if people would only have given me a chance to explain, at least, what it was that I was on top of, or even better, how I came to be there. Of course, no one would listen to this. And all of the urgency and intensity that I had left in the microfilm reading room was back. I tried to counter this tendency by compressing a story that was growing longer and longer into shorter and shorter tellings. But this was to no avail, I realized, as I saw the bewilderment in my neighbor's eyes, and listened to myself telling my story faster than I could think. The charming madness that had organized my summer by shifting my gears, and then keeping itself under control, was in town for the concluding games of the World Series.

It wasn't really the same madness. The microfilm reading room experience blossomed in the wonder of discovery. That groundwork had come and gone. Despite my pretense of reluctance, and my transparent justification of just browsing, I had, in the course of the summer, given myself to baseball. I had learned a lot about other things. About my identity, about politics, about how history works, and about the nature of truth. But it was baseball that catalyzed all these various knowledges into relationships with each other. That I hadn't accepted this before the World Series was nothing more than the coy shyness of ritual delay. But that time, too, had now passed, and I was prepared, as I was for nothing else in life, for baseball.

And now I could remember Teddy Gold. In 1970, a young radical named Theodore Gold, who had been a leader of SDS at Columbia University, joined the Weathermen and went underground. A short time later, he was killed in the townhouse explosion in New York's Greenwich Village. He died attempting to execute the highly dangerous and extremely risky political act of calling for a civil war in order to see if the citizens will take you as seriously as the authorities. He died trying to make the bombs that would announce the revolution to a population that had to finish making their car payments before they could contemplate anything so drastic. But Ted Gold died for an ideal. And however remote his dream might seem to other people in other times, his seriousness cannot be doubted. He risked, and sacrificed, his life for what he believed.

And what he believed in was the truth of his own alienation. That this society and its institutions and human relationships were so bankrupt, corrupt, disordered, and awful that it would be worth risking his life in order to set in motion the forces that would change them. The first step was to destroy the illusions and the myths that hold up the institutions, and then perhaps even the odd bit of federal real estate or corporate headquarters.

And because he was known to be thoughtful, and intelligent, and serious, and because he gave his life, we also know that Ted Gold thought about these things. And thought about these things to a point where he was driven to become a bomber.

And in the end, Ted Gold was the Weatherman, the bomber, part of the fringe dismissed as lunatic by regular America. A very marginal member of society, indeed. Of all the kinds of people that this society produces, none had less stake in things as they are than Ted Gold. None was less committed to the preservation of traditions and institutions. None more desperate for change, and none more eager for total change. Ted Gold was not just willing to participate; he was willing to give his life.

And at the same time, Ted Gold was a fanatic follower of the New York and, later, the San Francisco Giants. He read the box scores every morning. And he was quoted as saying that he would have to wait until Willie Mays retired before he could become a true communist.

Now, the radical understanding of the function of professional baseball is: circus. Its effect was to divert the people from their natural inclination to think about their lot, and to keep them from getting restless. It was an opiate. It gave people room in which to tolerate intolerable circumstances. For a good radical, it was a joy of childhood, but definitely not worthy of serious consideration for anyone seriously political.

And baseball was also hero worship, and the star system, and the worst kind of indulgence in the American cult of the rugged, unique, superior individualist. A good communist was not interested in baseball. And so Ted Gold, who was committed enough to sacrifice his life for the cause, could not think of himself as a good communist. He was not prepared to give up baseball.

And now, in the middle of the World Series, near the very last moments of the baseball season, I finally understand Ted Gold's position.

Alienation is emotional, but radicalization is an intellectual process. Proposition, conclusion, and then anger. The process of becoming a radical is not only creating but channeling anger. And as the propositions and anger increase, they begin to form a pattern. It changes the way that the world is perceived. It changes the criteria and rhetoric for self-criticism. And it changes the way that you live and the things that you want from life. The illusion is that the process is one of genuine rebirth, causing a new and different human being to emerge from the same consciousness. But the evidence is to the contrary.

The evidence is that there are depths beyond which an intellectual process cannot go. The evidence is that there are aspects of your own identity so strongly established that they cannot be penetrated by conviction, not to mention thought. There are things about our own identity that we cannot alter by decision. And baseball is one of those things.

The baseball fan does not decide, and in fact cannot decide, about baseball if it has seeped into the deepest sense of self. Because if baseball is there, that is who you are.

It is not that I realized I was declaring myself for baseball, but just that I got so totally and un-self-consciously into the baseball that I forgot all about the work. And it is not that I abandoned my job, but that the excitement of the baseball caused such disarray in my mind and my notes that categories dissolved. And I could feel every bone in my body vibrating to the beat of the detente. And then, "From across the water came Cuban Pete, He was doin' the boogie to the rhumba beat," came from my record player, and Hank Snow's voice synchronized all the other patterns. It's the rhumba boogie done the Rhumba-Cubanal style. It's Luis Tiant pitching. It's Fidel Castro being respected instead of patronized, imperialism revenged. It's a reminder of the passions that baseball produces, and a mutual forgiveness between my childhood and myself. And, of course, it is regulation baseball.

The baseball was superb, which should have been enough. And it was more than enough, but the evidence for my personally observed system had begun to go awry. The Tiant family had started to go Hollywood. In the last games of the Series, they entered into a comfort with their celebrity. They were now mugging for the camera in ways that suggested they might have had a few lessons during the rain.

And their son, Luis, now aiming for immortality and even higher tax brackets, began to mix the metaphors in my mind. Luis Tiant, as he pitched, began the recounting of the storming of the Moncada Barracks, the young revolution's bleakest hour and most severe defeat. The stage had been set for the triumphal march into Havana. Instead, Tiant fell apart and was chased out in the seventh inning.

The ceremonial first pitch of the seventh game was thrown out by Joey Tramontana, a crippled boy representing the Jimmy Fund. The announcer told us that the Jimmy Fund was an old Boston Braves charity for crippled children that was taken over by the Red Sox when the Braves left for Milwaukee. A communal health problem in a culture which has destroyed community, I thought. But what did that make of the politics of the ceremonial first pitch, and wasn't it ever so slightly perverse to be looking there?

The national anthem was sung by the Winged Victory Chorus of the U.S. Third Army Airborne Division. They wore green sequined tuxedos and destroyed Boston's image as a city of conservatories. They were also a mistaken context for organized baseball. Baseball has prospered and streamlined its image for the corporate era. What were they doing, singing in sequined tuxedos?

But the World Series ended, and with it the impos-

sible threads that I had felt obliged to pursue. And besides, I had relearned the joys of baseball and the
subtleties of Cuban detente it might contain. There have
been some hard knocks. Luis Tiant will be remembered as
a King, but the very nature of the Series did not allow
for the kind of solo heroism that political consideration
desired. National television exposure, as well as diplomatic recognition, would have to wait. Detente, in a
pretty successful trial balloon, was nevertheless set back
a few cosmic places in the grand order of things. But Luis
Tiant planted a metaphor in the consciousness of the
American television public that was certain to bear fruit,
one day. Just not today.

The media, as fickle as any superficial fan who
pays attention to the World Series and nothing else,
shifted their focus to the winning Cuban. A newspaper report of the last game highlights Tony Perez. The story
wanders off the game and tells how, fifteen years ago, a
teen-age ballplayer named Perez got discouraged and decided to return home to Cuba.

"Cuba had just fallen into the hands of Fidel Castro,
and he had suddenly banned Cubans who played in
America from going back, once they came home."

One sentence later, Perez was saying nice things
about baseball, and in return, he was certified a World
Series hero. Anyone who has studied the case will remember the president of the United States imposing an embargo, but no matter. My professional expert opinion on
the matter is that the baseball expert at the State Department's Cuba Desk had staked not only some political
judgment, but probably a lot of money, on Luis Tiant and
the Boston Red Sox. And though Tiant came through
beautifully, all the money behind Boston was lost. Hostility followed regret, and revenge was taken in the only
area available. Tony Perez's heroism would be used to
throw one last baseball insult at Fidel Castro. It was a
small-minded exercise in bitter face-saving. Too insignificant a matter to alter the movement of baseball detente.

Too futile a gesture, even, to mollify a bureaucrat's gambling losses.

The World Series was finally won by Cincinnati, the tie-breaking run being scored on a bloop single by Joe Morgan, with two out in the ninth inning of the seventh game. Which was typical. This was the most even match there ever was, and it produced the most exciting baseball anyone has ever seen. As World Series go, this was a jewel, and a classic, and, some said, the greatest ever.

For me, this World Series was baseball's final seduction. I found many things in the course of the baseball season. But the World Series' final note rang in the deepest part of myself that I found, and that was baseball.

As I look back to the images of amazing baseball, there are too many instances too memorable to be contained in any one event. I think of Luis Tiant, bending and twisting and studying centerfield in the middle of his windup; base-running with his face as much as his legs; playing both cat and mouse to Joe Morgan's famous lead off first base. And by contrast, in between Tiant's appearances, Reggie Cleveland throwing sixteen straight pitches to first base to hold Morgan, all of them, eventually, in vain.

And that glorious sixth game. Tiant's shellacking, Dwight Evans' catch, Bernie Carbo's second pinch-hit home run, and Carlton Fisk's game-winning hit, a home run worthy of announcing a candidacy upon. And too many more feats simply to catalogue. They were all part of the dramatic pattern, and therefore more spectacular than their story will ever sound. I have never seen a more interesting sequence of heroic activities organize themselves into a baseball game. Not to mention my new respect for the subtleties of Cuban detente.

And so, amidst tears and laughter, and songs of praise for motor oil, antifreeze, and beer, the cameras cut directly from the world champions' locker room to the Johnny Carson show, and the summer ended. Pete Rose, still covered in World Series sweat, had just finished saying, "I wish opening day was tomorrow." I did too.

Cauliflower, the gastronomic bane of my childhood, I now eat, and justify eating, when and because it is in season. Doing things in season is less complicated, more natural, and cheaper. Doing things in season approaches the simple life for which I yearn. And now, as I declare myself for baseball, the leaves have turned, and the citizens have forgotten the pleasures of summer in their preparation for what has become, in the corporate era, the most economically terrifying of all seasons, winter. And I am left exposed as that most common of all varieties of nut cake, the baseball fanatic. And this has become a special vulnerability at a time when the citizens have learned to anticipate, and busy themselves in preparation for the problems and discomforts of cold weather and the rise in price of petroleum products and heat.

In agricultural times, the panic that accompanies famine always rose at the end of summer, when the fruits of the previous harvest ran out. In the postwar era, that panic never came at all, and lots of people learned to believe that it never would. But history has passed those stages, and profit maximization as the organizing principle of society has gotten out of control. And ever since things got that way, the winters have been getting harder and harder.

For those of us who lived in the postwar era, these winters have constituted the lesson that we had never lived through economic and psychic winters before this one. And as each winter increases in severity, that realization is sustained.

And I, too, am preparing for winter. Hoarding is a traditional form, but useless in the corporate era. Now financial speculators rush in and plug the market gaps with arbitrage, as families used to plug them with the fruits of leftover victory gardens. In the coming era, no

[275]

one will be saved by the size of their stores. I turn instead to the most dangerous and risky preparation of them all, which had suddenly become cautious and reasonable, if only by default. The alternatives are obsolete.

And so, I sit and remember the World Series, and the glories of the baseball season, drawing from the instructive examples of noble behavior. In baseball, difficult circumstances produce heroism, the most noble behavior of all. The circumstances of winter will be difficult, and the paths through them will be heroic, and I, through my knowledge of baseball, will be better prepared.

It was autumn, 1957. In the dense underbrush of the Sierra Maestra, a small and weary band trudged along. They were tired and they were hungry. For months they had circled endlessly in this underbrush. Their numbers had been reduced by aerial bombing and internal dissension. They were at the end of their food, their strength, and possibly their courage.

Some time ago they took to the mountains as a small band of revolutionary guerrillas. Since then many had joined them, but many were killed. Recently, the government had received, through an informer, reports of their whereabouts, and the air force was strafing these very jungles daily.

Their numbers stood at eighteen and seemed certain to reduce even further. There were thoughts of giving up, but these were never spoken. It was too late to give up. These men knew that they must either make the revolution or die trying.

Suddenly, at the edge of the clearing, a youth, wearing a baseball glove and carrying a ball, emerged. He was frightened by the rebels' appearance. Their matted long hair and soiled combat fatigues surprised him. The men had not washed or shaved in a long time. They looked hungry.

The youth was instantly seized and brought to the

band's leader. He was frightened, but he knew that for the sake of his own honor, he must not show fear.

The rebel leader puffed on his cigar and looked into the eyes of the youth. It was a hard look. "What's your name, sonny?" he said.

"Luis Tiant, señor. Luis Tiant, Junior."

"The son of Luis Tiant, the great leftie?"

"Sí, señor.

"*Caramba.* Why, I myself saw him outpitch Carl Hubbell of the great New York Giants when I was as young as you are. Your father had great control. It is a pleasure to meet the son of so great a family, little Tiant."

The rebel leader paused, and the expression on his face changed. "But what are you doing here?"

"Well, my family is poor, but each autumn, we take our vacation ..."

"No," the rebel leader interrupted, waving his finger toward the ground, "what are you doing here, in the jungle?"

"Oh," said the youth. "I come to practice my pitching. You see, I want to be like my father, but he says baseball is a hard life. He does not want me to play baseball. So I sneak off into the jungle to practice, where he will not see me. You see, sir, I know that I will be a great pitcher someday. And my father will be proud of me. But right now, it is easier to practice secretly, and not anger my father."

The rebel leader withdrew to confer with two of his men.

"You see, Che, we cannot harm this boy. One day he will be a great pitcher, and bring great glory to our revolution. The boy goes free."

The Argentinian shrugged. "If it must be, Fidel, but I still don't like it."

Fidel put his arm around the boy and walked him to the edge of the clearing. "Well Luis, I hope you make the majors. I was a pitcher myself once. In 1940, when I was a student at the university in Havana, the Washington Senators sent their chief scout, Joe Cambria, to have a look at me. 'He'll never make it' was all he said, and nobody ever signed me.... Maybe it was all for the best. Some things are more important than baseball. But Luis, I understand how baseball can get into your blood. If it flows through your veins, it is your destiny. Do not betray it."

The rebel leader turned, hesitated, and turned back. "Just remember, the most important thing for a pitcher is his movement. You must never stop perfecting your movement. Throw as hard as you can, but always keep your motion smooth."

As the rebel disappeared into the greenery, Luis waved and shouted to him. "You will see. One day I will pitch in the World Series." It was early autumn, and like all baseball fans caught in the off-season, there was nothing to do but dream....

Autumn, 1962. It was the dead of night after a warm September evening. The bureaucrats of Washington lay sleeping in their suburbs. In a tiny room at the back of Kay's Delicatessen, the president's advisors met in absolute secrecy, struggling with notions of patriotism, diplomacy, and power. Russia must not be allowed to land its missiles in Cuba, but neither would nuclear holocaust be an acceptable solution.

The strange face in the room was that of a rising politician from upstate New York. At the moment, he was a baseball executive, but he had done other things and was gaining a reputation as a man who knew how to do things in Cuba. He was talking to McGeorge Bundy when, suddenly, the secretary of defense shouted across the room.

"Mac, did you tell Mr. Kay that this pastrami and Swiss was for me?"

"No, Bob. You know that the secretary of this meeting is a top priority."

"Well, tell him next time, goddamn it! Mr. Kay always gives *me* two pickles."

Dean Rusk sensed a problem. "Boys, boys calm yourselves. My man will be here soon, if you can just be patient."

"His man," McNamara giggled. "Rusk expects to save the free world on the arm of a relief pitcher who couldn't strike out the Senate softball team."

"I will have you know," Rusk shot back, "that he was offered a contract with the Cincinnati Reds, but declined on grounds of national security. He is definitely major-league material."

The door opened suddenly, and in rushed a red-headed man, sweating and panting. "Here's the language," he said, throwing his report on the table. "You were right, Mr. Rusk, the Russians have a secret radar station at Camaguey that they monitor by sputnik. All the details are in my report."

Then he noticed the new face in the room. "Why, Mr. Horton! What a surprise to see you here. I knew you recommended me for this job, but I didn't expect to see you on it, ha ha!"

Before the politician could reply, he was interrupted.

"Hey, pitcher, show us your stuff," Robert McNamara said, "if you got any."

Arthur Schlesinger, Jr., joined in. "Hey, pitcher, stop any late-inning counterrevolutions lately?" The men broke into sneers and laughter.

"I've got to be back in Havana by morning. My car is waiting," the red-headed man said.

"Yes, you'd best go quickly," Dean Rusk said. "I've arranged a hot corned beef on rye and a bottle of celery tonic to take away."

Next morning, the red-headed man awoke in Havana with all the appearances of never having left town. It wasn't always like this, he thought. There was a time when they appreciated me.

Years ago, he had come out of the visitor's bullpen in Red Wing Stadium to pitch in relief. As he glanced to first base, checking the runner, he stared straight into the eyes of a child sitting behind first base. The seriousness, the belief, and the awe in that child's eyes was something he would never forget.

That was all over now. At an army reserve meeting he had been approached, introduced to the president of the Rochester Red Wings, and asked to keep his eyes open in Havana. Then politics played tricks on his desires. Moments after the shooting of Frank Verdi, no one noticed the itinerant hurler in a Havana uniform sneak into the clubhouse and dial directly to Washington's most secret telephone. Since then, it was one thing after another.

He dyed his hair red, and warmed up for the first game of a double-header against the Rochester Red Wings, but he did not appear. As far as anyone knew, he had not been seen since. The team moved to Jersey City without him, and that was the end of his career.

Now he sat at the bar in Manolo's and wondered if he still had the stuff to pitch in the big leagues. It was autumn, and like all baseball fans caught in the off-season, there was nothing he could do but dream....

It was autumn, sometime in the future. There was pandemonium in the ballroom of the Marriott Motor Lodge in Mexico City. Seated at the head table were Fidel Castro and the president of the United States. They were preparing to videotape their joint announcement of the big exhibition game to take place in Havana in one year's time.

The statesmen embraced and posed for still photographs, while around them photographers pushed and shoved each other. The scene was unruly, but the statesmen smiled.

Seated to the right of the American president were

the commissioner of baseball and his assistant, Bobby Maduro, former owner of the Havana Sugar Kings. Seated next to Maduro was Luis Tiant, Jr., former pitcher for the Boston Red Sox, who had recently been named by the Cuban cigar industry as director of public relations for all of North America.

I was seated at the very end of the table, and couldn't help but notice that though Dr. Castro looked quite elegant in his immaculately trimmed beard and spiffy officer's uniform, there was a sadness about his eyes. Yes, these are better times, his eyes seemed to say, times to trade sugar and cigars for the technology we need. Times to resume playing that great game of baseball with our closest neighbor. But, oh, how I miss those early days of the revolution. How much more glorious was the youth of our victory than the sober contracts of consolidation. How much clearer the notions of moral right and revolutionary duty used to be. Why, there was a time when, if I had found myself in a room full of such long-winded, hypocritical, capitalist politicians, I would have blown raspberries on my forearm and spit in their faces. And now I must shake their hands, and do these deals, because it is best for baseball, and best for Cuba.

I saw all this in Castro's eyes, and just as I began to worry about why I was sitting there, Fidel suddenly stood up and broke into a big grin, as if to say, fuck this. And then, still grinning, he picked up his glass of water and emptied it into the face of United States Congressman Frank Horton. And with a quick obscene gesture to the cameras, he exited.

Cripes, I thought. It was autumn, and like all baseball fans caught in the off-season, there was nothing I could do but dream. . . .

What is wrong with the corporate era is that the romance is gone. The little spaces between the rational and the sensible are no longer available as a place to do business. The sober minds have already exploited accounting procedures and computers, to limit themselves to considerations which are reasonable. And this sober, industrious, ambitious, and above all heartless mentality decides what paths will be followed. Those activities which are profitable within the constraints of the tax structure and control of markets are engaged. All other activities are forbidden, unless they are done strictly for fun.

All those people who preferred to earn their living by pursuing some outrageous dream have been banished from the marketplace and sent to work in the factories. The marginal business enterprises, the kind that make your hair stand on end, have either been made sensible or are gone. And those people who did their business on the byways, and in the darkest caves of metaphor, are simply gone.

Of course I understand that the American way is capitalism, but it has always been so. And, of course, I understand that, given capitalism, all large, significant political activities will be organized as continually profitable businesses. I know it is not new to complain about who is in charge, but what is new is how in charge they are.

Corporations and businessmen of the corporate mentality have been in charge for centuries, but only during the postwar era did they pass the critical volume and begin to spread so deeply into all areas of our lives that our very personalities have changed. During that time we became so accustomed to so many of our affairs being conducted in the style and manner of the corporations that our identities were reformed to accommodate this phenomenon. The process moved so smoothly, and made us feel so prosperous, that we didn't notice it happening.

One morning, long before it was true, we awoke to find that our culture had been replaced. Gone were all the restaurants shaped like chickens and ships. Gone were the coffee shops shaped like doughnuts and the diners made out of old railroad cars and quonset huts. Gone

[282]

were the greengrocers, and fishmongers, and hardware stores, and haberdashers, and who knows what else, all replaced by brightly colored plastic-and-glass shacks, where the real estate, the building, the merchandise, and the people were all selected with the single criterion of profit. And so the vast majority of human life became useful solely to the extent that it fitted into the profit-maximization curves of the corporate mentality.

And so we eat fried chicken cooked in a batter which was designed by a businessman to maximize profits. It is delicious, but something is missing. It tastes okay, but it isn't quite chicken. Now that we are prosperous enough to have our meals cooked for us, we find that they are no longer quite meals, and no longer, in the old sense, cooked. And from sales, the substitute for meals is wonderful. But the social order is being destroyed. Public life has ended. Something as basic as the mere possession of a public identity has been removed from our social life. And the availability of hamburgers aside, we feel the loss.

The goods and services we exchange in order to live have lost their human characteristics. And so has the exchange. That special quality that the human mind and hand give to the things that they care about is gone from the marketplace, and survives only in gift shops and hobbies. Even the institution of the salesman has been replaced, for the most part, by advertising. The brush man doesn't ring your doorbell any more, he appears on television. And all the fly-by-nights, the hustlers, the crazy people, the dreamers—all those who lived by shaping their dreams into public enterprise—have been divested of their schemes and pensioned away to wages.

The visionaries whose visions fit within the capitalist framework operated at the margins of the business world, but what they brought to the life of the society was not marginal. It was, in fact, central. It was the only culture there was.

The corporations, having grown rich and powerful off technological inventions, turned their attention toward

[283]

new markets, and in so doing they came upon culture. They too had noticed both the disconcerting effects of industrialization on the old-time ways, and the new culture that had already begun. They saw that the market was huge. And so they made their move and they succeeded.

In the olden days, culture was a matter of ceremony. Then it became commerce. Now it is mass distribution. The country fair fell into disuse as an institution when community ceased as a collective notion. It was instantly revived as the carnival business because the desire to cavort in pagan rites remained widespread, and socially acceptable. Now we must cavort in supermarkets, and at rock concerts, and at a hundred other places where public fun is offered for sale.

Of course, culture did not disappear, but it did change. Storytelling survived the death of face-to-face community and became the book business; music survived and became the record business; and performance became something done inside places you paid to get into. And, of course, all this was genuine social change. And, like any social change, it seemed invisible at the time, and it was. Only perceptible from a very great distance, and even then seen only as a gentle drift. But as technology matured, and began to exhibit its baffling eccentricities, the role of culture began to change. To the surprise of the staid and sober rationalists, moving pictures were invented, and phonograph records, and radio and television. And before it was noticed, the imperceptible gentle drifts caused by the self-indulgent demands made upon technology had brought a major realignment. Or really, I should say, were part of a major realignment. Community had so broken down that excess emotions were greater than ever. People's quantitative cultural needs were increasing. And at the same time, food and shelter seemed so easily available that matching the increased desire for culture was an increased market capability.

And culture began to assume an importance in business commensurate with its importance in life. Teen-agers dissolved into hysteria when Frank Sinatra opened his mouth to sing. That phenomenon constituted circumstances for a market situation that was not exploited for twenty-five years, but these things take time.

All of history's conceivable compartments follow their own rhythms. The corporate process always owned radio and television just because it was such an expensive business to get into. The movie business happened so fast that it looked like Hollywood could never be brought to heel, but Hollywood produced no second generation of visionary entrepreneurs. The first generation of moguls died and was replaced by accountants—serious, sober, rational men. And within no time, the movies were sold to the people who make money, not movies, and so was nearly everything else. Big money arrived, and dreams of even bigger money blotted out competing visions. Big money arrived, and everyone who had some began taking himself very seriously indeed.

When the postwar era was beginning its last escalation, the Beatles and several other English rock-and-roll groups arrived in America. They were able to cause money to rush out of the pockets of people everywhere, and into a pile a hundred million dollars high. Out of nowhere, in an instant, there was a *whoosh* as bountiful as that of any oil well. Teen-age roughnecks stood on the stage and sang, and by that act alone they were able to create an organization capable of generating millions and millions of dollars. The rationalists of finance noticed. They already owned most of the music business, but they bought up the rest very shortly.

Culture moved from being its own special business to business as usual. And so we lost our ability to choose, and were left with a take-it-or-leave-it aesthetic. Culture became something we were given to taste, good enough only to make us return. And, by design, no better than that.

Baseball went from being a small-time operation to being big business, and kept its illusion intact. And just thinking of the political differences between different-sized business enterprises, it seems no mean feat that the illusion was sustained.

In 1957, Walter O'Malley moved the Dodgers out of Brooklyn and into Los Angeles. The Braves had previously failed in Boston, and moved to Milwaukee. The Browns had failed in St. Louis and moved to Baltimore. But this was different. The Dodgers were the most profitable franchise in baseball when they moved. They moved because they realized that a baseball team was no longer just a wild little business scheme that sold tickets and divided the take between the players. A baseball team was part of our national heritage, a cherished cultural form. Baseball had always been cherished, but with the growth of the corporate mentality, the screwballs and the dreamers who were still running baseball as a ticket-sales operation became infected, and began to view their property in a new way.

What they saw was an extremely valuable cultural artifact, something they had devoted their lives to creating and building. And for the first time, they saw the fruits of their entrepreneurial dream as a piece of property which, finally, could be assigned a dollars-and-cents value commensurate with its worth.

As a source of income from ticket sales, a professional baseball team was one thing. As a piece of culture, studied, discussed, loved, worried over, chronicled, historicized, it was something else again, and much more valuable. Prosperous cities all across the country would bid against each other for the privilege of having the baseball business done in their town. And the prices were in the millions, so important had baseball become to the cultural commerce of the society.

So the corporate mentality was legitimized in baseball. Walter O'Malley forsook the adoring fans in Brooklyn, and auctioned off the aura of his baseball team to the highest bidder. Running a baseball team had ceased to be merely a matter of making a profit. The goal now was to maximize profit. And so the game began to change. Not how to please the fans, as it used to be, but how to attract that specific number which will be most profitable. A subtle difference for some, but for others it meant the loss of baseball for want of a parking lot.

As the corporate mentality began to reveal its hand, the game changed. And so we must assume that the sexy colorful uniforms were introduced to generate higher net revenues than plain white and gray could. The mechanical reason for changing uniforms had to do with the introduction of color television, but this is an extension that represents the same change of priorities.

In the old days, the function of profit in baseball was to make baseball possible. And since more people will pay to watch a winning team than a losing team, it was thought that the size of the profit could not be extended beyond the team's ability to win games. Identifying profit with victory was part of the dream, and since technology offered no seductions, baseball entrepreneurs never looked beyond it. They never realized that if the game were played on green plastic instead of grass, it would automatically become more profitable, win or lose. They didn't know that green plastic was cheaper than gardening, did away with rainouts, and could be rented to the football team in the off-season.

Then, when grass refused to grow in the Houston Astrodome, technology developed its bait, and baseball bit. And so the players slip around a bit on the field. And the baseball diamond with its green fields and earth crescents, implanted in the visual memories of generations of Americans, began to be replaced by chalk lines on an enormous rug. And gone from the game is one more of the immeasurable, unpredictable sources of mystery, the bad hop. But the dollars-and-cents value of this effect has already been calculated and considered.

And with all of this you can still watch a baseball

game. It is the same game, and it maintains a continuity with its own history. The baseball statistics have not gone haywire, at a time when nearly all other statistical indicators have. The game has changed, it's true, but there is enough continuity left so that you can drop back fifteen years later and still know exactly what is going on. And that is, indeed, a rare characteristic for a feature of American life. Not many things survived the postwar era as successfully as baseball. The continuity of baseball may be an illusion, but the ability to produce illusion is all that tradition can ever mean in a society with a habit for change.

When I compare baseball with the alternative forms of culture that flowered in the postwar era, my fears are calmed by the contrasts I see. Baseball has survived remarkably well. When I think of what they did to the baking of apple pie, substituting corporate rationalism for Mom's intuition; when I think of what television has done to the notion of theater, and with such devastation that the schlock commercial products of old Hollywood seem, by comparison, classic masterpieces; when I think of all the minute details of my everyday life that have been organized against my satisfaction and in favor of corporate profits, I think that baseball has survived miraculously. It is still baseball. It has been commodified, but so has every other external factor of life. And when I think of the ways we wash, and eat, and sleep, and work, and play, I can see that baseball has come through this drastic change in the way we live, not unscathed, but intact.

And in the end, everyone who writes, or thinks, or talks about baseball comes to the same end of amazement at the bottomless depth of the game. There is always another point of view from which baseball can be described. There is always a fresh new vision. And ultimately, there is always another depth from which an even more profound analysis can be made.

And every fan who makes the commitment to baseball because it is small and private and internal quickly
finds out that what he has discovered is no more than a
segment of the never-ending totality. that baseball is.

The statistics and the memories are available and accessible. The shelves of the public library are stacked
with baseball books. The price paid by baseball fans for
excessive enthusiasm is to find that while baseball will
always remain small, private, and internal, it is also big,
public, and external. Baseball is not obscure, and baseball
fans are not eccentric. And all of the demystified mystery
and uncovered secrets that obsessive baseball fascination
produces are quite common. And as fans sink deeper and
deeper into the profundity of the game, they take with
them the knowledge that they are floating through an
internal and private depth that is, nevertheless, well traveled. With each batting average laboriously computed by
pencil-and-paper long division goes the knowledge that
millions of other fans are undertaking the same computation, and will derive from it the same private pleasure.
And each private insight, of measurement, of timeless-
ness, of personality, will eventually come to be seen as
common. However startling and extraordinary these insights remain, they will always belong less to the holder
and more to the mania of concern that surrounds baseball. And so the institution of baseball persists, spectators
and players alike drawn into a large and populous universe consisting only of private, internal dreams, hopes,
and aspirations. The insights that grow out of these hopes
and dreams are constantly discovered and rediscovered.
And to that private and internal self responding to these
discoveries, they remain forever personal.

Since anything can happen in a baseball game, those
who persist in figuring out baseball must, from time to
time, collapse their understanding and move on to a new
level of profundity, because baseball can't be figured out.
The world of baseball becomes a never-ending parade of

loyalties and schools of understanding, constantly in flux, eventually interchangeable, and always private and exclusive.

Eventually, this too must be admitted, and recognized as having always been so. And even I, with my history of a particularly odd relationship to baseball, fit into all this quite simply. And I know from the ease with which I slipped back in after fifteen years' absence that a place has always been waiting for me in baseball.

In order to have a happy ending, or even resolution, I must disregard my hostility to the corporate mentality. In spite of the nice things about it, this is something I cannot do. The postwar era was characterized by a reduction in the occurrence of public life. The corporate era, extending the same tendency, is characterized by the death of public life. And that is just awful.

And so we enter the era without joy. And we function in that era with an ever-escalating longing for joy, at a time and place which has destroyed its natural institutions for joy. The presence of a man on the moon was a startling technological achievement and should have been a cause for joy, but it came at a time when there was no available institution for conveying the thrill of the moon to an eager public. And so it was put on television, and so it flopped. And ever since, all the money has been put behind professional sports, and burdened these cultural forms with expectations they could never hope to live up to in a sustained way. At the moment, these professional sports continue to ride high, but what of the death of public life? How could anyone approve of the death of public life?

Baseball is intact, but it now exists on its own. In the days when public life was a part of all lives, baseball represented some pinnacle of human endeavor. Baseball was the ultimate example of subordinating chance to human determination through the perfection of manual dexterity. That pinnacle was built on a myriad of esoteric gestures of dexterity approaching magic. Baseball was the pinnacle, and everyone knew what that meant. Everyone learned their little party tricks, or, in failing, learned just how much determination and practice go into even the smallest demonstrations of dexterity.

And so citizens who had no hope or interest in mastering the techniques of sports amused each other with small feats. The cigarette rolled, as perfectly as was ever seen in a Hollywood cowboy movie, with one hand. The coin flipped between fingers by knuckles alone. The transference, across the mouth to the opposite corner, of cigarette and toothpick, done only with the tongue.

But now the pool halls and taverns are gone, and with them have gone the last vestiges of public life. And now the bar tricks are gone, and with them our appreciation of ordinary capabilities of physique. Now the bus stations and the airports are merely used for waiting. Now we watch baseball on television, and expect to see superhuman achievement as a matter of course. Public life is dead. We get to observe the human body in deliberate motion only on television. We don't judge the feats we see on television by our own standards; after all, the camera is pointed at them, not at us. And so we come to expect miracles when we turn on the television, and we no longer know how rare and difficult they are.

Even the firm handshake, that last ritual of institutionalized touching and showing of strength without hostility, is neither as automatic or indicative as it used to be. We live on in private, our lives supported by machines where they used to be supported by human relationships. Our lives dependent on manufactured products, when they used to be dependent on how we treated one another. And sealed off within that privacy is baseball. Healthy, thriving, and perfectly preserved by its suspension in the medium of television.

I have no grand resolution. And there is no Captain Midnight decoder ring to decipher this message. The lesson of my youth, learned by disproving the contrary, is that resolution is work for history, and not a personal

[291]

moral statement. Baseball has been pickled by the corporate mentality, but it has been preserved. I am a creature of the cold war, but so are we all. Historical eras are drawn in lines of extensive time warp. And wherever the past gets ahead of the future, it leaves a little pocket of the past. And I could, if I chose, live in those pockets for the rest of my life. It is, depending only on my point of view, the same baseball. There is no unifying conclusion. The contradiction, trapped on different sides of the time warp, cannot be dissolved. Baseball is big business. And the same baseball is a child's pleasure on a sunny afternoon, and an internal world of knowledge and speculation, theoretical studies and practical theories, and a body of pure thought that is as likely to enchant a serious adult as it is a merry child.

EPILOGUE

I have no sense of beginning and end, beyond knowing that what starts at the beginning of the baseball season ends with the World Series. But the week after the 1975 World Series, on October 27, *Sports Illustrated* printed a little notice saying that an announcement was expected shortly concerning a baseball game between a team of American major-leaguers and a Cuban all-star team, to take place in Havana. It went on to mention the Chinese ping-pong tournament and the Tiant family reunion, and ended with a scouting report of the top Cuban prospects. The game was billed as "an important prelude to opening trade and diplomatic relations." The current relationship between Cuban and American baseball was referred to as "a prohibition."

And with that, all my carefully wrought interweavings got snatched out of free fall and plugged into reality. Someone out there was playing baseball with my aspirations.

On November 22, Paul Porter choked on a piece of lobster in a restaurant. He collapsed, lingered for five days, and died. Paul Porter had been chairman of the Federal Communications Commission under Roosevelt, and head of the Office of Price Administration under Truman. He went on to become a partner in Arnold, Fortas, and Porter, which was, in the postwar era, among the most influential law firms in Washington. Paul Porter was also a rabid baseball fan.

He shared responsibility for a social plan that had evolved into indecency, and he was accessible because he loved baseball. Therefore, I decided, Paul Porter learned all the wrong lessons from baseball. As an archetype and as a person, he should be told. When he died, I felt I had lost my audience.

While Paul Porter lay dying, on November 24, *Sports Illustrated* struck another blow for reality against my weakened fantasies. The story was called "Cuba Sí, Baseball Sí." It began with the last game in Havana, the double-header between the Red wings and the Sugar Kings. It went on to say that the upcoming dentente game had nothing to do with the State Department, but in fact was put together by two young independent TV producers, Barry Jagoda and Richard Cohen. Then it went on to tell Jagoda's story.

While I was growing up with the Rochester Red Wings, a Jewish boy in Houston, Texas, was growing up in the same way with the Houston Buffaloes, another St. Louis farm team. As the first seeds of Cuban detente baseball were sown in my mind by the television documentary of American senators visiting Havana, so they were sown in Barry Jagoda.

And then our paths diverged. Barry Jagoda left his fancy job at CBS and made his way to Havana, in person. Then he went to see the commissioner of baseball. A few secret meetings later, the game was agreed upon. ABC Sports put up $165,000 for the television rights. The game was a reality. Now "only administration approval" was needed to make the game official.

The 1975 baseball season, stretched out by days and weeks, continued. Since the World Series, news of Cuban baseball was popping up on sports pages everywhere. The *Washington Post* mentioned Joe Cambria, once the chief Washington Senators scout in Cuba, who scouted and rejected a pitcher named Fidel Castro. Even the *Wall Street*

Journal ran an editorial against the game, called "Cuban Bunt." Sports readers and sportswriters all across the nation now had something stylish to say about Cuban detente, and this stretched on into January and the new year.

Meanwhile, back in the first week of December, I happened to notice an old newspaper lying on the sofa. It was dated December 1, and in it was an Associated Press story by George Gedda on Henry Kissinger's press conference. Kissinger condemned the presence of Cuban troops in Angola and said, "We will never permit detente to turn into a subterfuge for unilateral advantage." The headline was: KISSINGER CALLS OFF CUBA GAME.

On December 15, *Sports Illustrated* explained what had happened. President Ford was nervous about losing the Cuban vote in the Florida presidential primaries. And besides, Cuba had voted in favor of the anti-Zionist UN resolution, and Castro continued openly to support the Puerto Rican independence movement. And now there were Cuban troops in Angola, for Christ's sake, fighting against pro-American forces. The detente baseball project would have to be shelved. The baseball season had finally ended in a straightforward case of wait till next year.

I invested more time and thought in Cuban detente baseball than any ordinary person would dare, but what was I supposed to make of all this?

My own approach reveals a certain preference for the style of sitting and smoking cigarettes in warm dark rooms and a certain inability to relate to things that go on outside. But the Jagoda-Cohen approach reveals a tendency to reduce grand ideas to business deals.

I saw detente baseball as political, and given my lack of power, a fantasy. They saw baseball as a television program, ultimately profitable, and therefore worthy of creating. They acted, and through the miracle of modern media, I reacted. And I know that there is a certain legitimacy to things that happen in the world that the mass media see as the only reality, just because they

[297]

happen, but there are reasons to deny that legitimacy and reject that reality.

Look! reality is never as it appears. No one can accept this as a rule to live by and still get through the day, but each time we forget it, we get fooled. And it doesn't matter what brand of good faith was exercised by the commissioner of baseball, the Cuban Ministry of Sport, or Jagoda and Cohen. Whatever they appeared to be doing, something else—and something of greater significance—was going on. And the truth of that significance can only be grasped as personal knowledge.

Which is a very long journey to take, when it leads back to a present that seems no different from what I had left so long ago. And though this is certainly not the time or place to ask, there is a part of me that has been in turmoil all this time, and which still asks me, Why this baseball? Why not Greek tragedies and symphonies? Why not economics, history, and philosophy? And if it must be so esoteric, why not something closer to a master plot? Why get stuck in a metaphor that does not even hope to ring universal?

And now, finally, I can answer that question, because this baseball is now a part of me that I can see. And I can see that it runs deeper than other culture. Not traditional philosophy, and not traditional history, because in my identity, baseball runs deeper. Baseball is so deeply rooted that it is not subject to will. Baseball is the strongest, least vulnerable, and most confident piece of myself that I am in touch with. And so I am able to see all I see, and do all I do, through the metaphor of baseball. And no other framework could do this for me, because no other framework could ever allow me the same kind of access to myself.

And so it is by baseball that I am able to examine and express myself. And now this no longer seems odd or embarrassing to me. This is who I am.